Promises
Beyond
Memory

A CULTURAL POLITICS BOOK

Edited by Ryan Bishop, Eva Haifa Giraud, Douglas Kellner, and Mark Featherstone

Promises Beyond Memory

*Archives, Art, and the Afterlives
of Violence in Latin America*

VIKKI BELL

Duke University Press   *Durham and London*   2026

© 2026 DUKE UNIVERSITY PRESS. All rights reserved
Project Editor: Bird Williams
Designed by Courtney Leigh Richardson
Typeset in Warnock Pro by Westchester Publishing Services

Library of Congress Cataloging-in-Publication Data
Names: Bell, Vikki, [date] author
Title: Promises beyond memory : archives, art, and the afterlives of
violence in Latin America / Vikki Bell.
Other titles: Archives, art, and the afterlives of violence in
Latin America
Description: Durham and London : Duke University Press, 2026. |
"A cultural politics book." | Includes bibliographical references
and index.
Identifiers: LCCN 2025021681 (print)
LCCN 2025021682 (ebook)
ISBN 9781478032960 paperback
ISBN 9781478029502 hardcover
ISBN 9781478061717 ebook
Subjects: LCSH: Memory—Political aspects—South America |
Archives—Political aspects—South America | Political
violence—South America | Memory—Social aspects—South
America | State-sponsored terrorism—South America |
Arts—Political aspects—South America
Classification: LCC F2237 .B455 2026 (print) | LCC F2237 (ebook) |
DDC 980—dc23/eng/20251113
LC record available at https://lccn.loc.gov/2025021681
LC ebook record available at https://lccn.loc.gov/2025021682

Cover art: Erika Diettes, *Sudarios* (Shrouds). Installation at Museo
Iglesia de Santa Clara, Bogotá, 2011. Photograph by Erika Diettes.
Courtesy of the artist.

For Paul

Contents

Acknowledgments

This book has taken almost a decade to write, and I have accumulated many debts. I would like to acknowledge first of all the wonderful colleagues I have worked with in our different research team configurations; without them, this book would have been impossible. To Mario Di Paolantonio, Oriana Bernasconi, Cecilia Sosa, and Jaime Hernández García, thank you for all your insights and creativity. It is one of the joys of academia that research colleagues can become such treasured friends.

All of the interviewees in Argentina, Chile, and Colombia have my deep gratitude. In particular, the teams working at the archives—at FUNVISOL in Santiago, the Centro Nacional de Memoria Histórica in Bogotá, and Memoria Abierta in Buenos Aires—as well as several previous workers and those in related organizations were unfailingly generous with their time and often shared their expertise well beyond our initial request. Several further those interviewees shared their reflections, not least the many artists and museum workers we interviewed. Among the interviewees, I would like to mention some individuals. Orlando "Caliche" Valdés Barrientos, whose story I tell in chapter 2, was an inspirational figure, whose ability to find laughter where many would despair was extraordinary. Once met never forgotten, he passed away in 2019. Gonzalo Sánchez, former director of the Centro Nacional de Memoria Histórica, was generous with his time and encouragement. Erika Diettes I thank for the beauty of her work and the kindness of her friendship. In Argentina, the Memoria Abierta team have made themselves available to answer questions across many years, and I thank Gonzalo Conte in particular for granting me several repeat interviews. Alejandra Naftal, former director of the Museum of Memory at the Space of Memory and Human Rights, ex-ESMA in Buenos Aires, has allowed the research to profit from her knowledge and understanding. I miss having my talented friend the artist Graciela Sacco to visit in Argentina, and remember her here.

For invitations to speak and the ensuing conversations that enriched my thought I would like to thank Sanja Bahun, Caroline Bennett, Jordana Blejmar, Patricia Bossio, Sebastian Bustamante, Emilios Christodoulidis, Chris

Decker, Jenny Edkins, Clara Garavelli, Liliana Gómez-Popescu, Yasmin Gunaratnam, Margarita Palacios, Tom Hastings, Beatrice Ivey, Michal Kobialka, Michael Lazzara, Bryce Lease, Mihaela Mihai, Rui Miranda, Kaitlin Murphy, James Scorer, Peter Schneck, Bernard McGuirk, Galina Oustinova-Stjepanovic, Bryan Wagner, Lars Waldorf; Javier Figuero, former Argentine ambassador to the United Kingdom, and Alessandra Viggiano Marra, who invited me to speak at the embassy in London; Canning House and the Parliamentary Committee for the Prevention of Genocide, where I was honored to respond to Estela de Carlotto. The panelists and participants of several Latin American Studies Association, International Sociological Association, and Memory Studies Association conferences have helped clarify my thinking over several years now. In Chile, Colombia, and Argentina, I would like to thank all those who have hosted, encouraged, and helped the research, with special mention to Marcelo Brodsky, Luis Campos Medina, Claudia Feld, Rosario Fernández, Silvia Grinberg, Jefferson Jaramillo Marín, Elizabeth Lira, Marcela Penna Brüggemann, Hugo Rojas Corral, Marcela Ruiz, Alicia Salomone, María Paz Vergara, and Lieta Vivaldi.

At Goldsmiths, my intellectual home for over thirty years now, I thank my colleagues, past and present, for making our intellectually creative and politically committed space and for sustaining our conversations within and beyond it. Thanks in particular to Les Back, Svenja Bromberg, Sara Farris, Natalie Fenton, Mariam Motamedi Fraser, Monica Greco, Angela McRobbie, Nirmal Puwar, Marsha Rosengarten, Catherine Rottenberg, Ghalya Saadawi, Martin Savransky, Susan Schuppli, Eyal Weizman, and Yesim Yaprak Yildiz. A special mention to Michael Keith at this time. To my students, especially of the postgraduate Critical and Cultural Analysis program, as well as the many doctoral researchers across the department, for their attentive critical thought. While I served as Head of Department (2016–2019), I was supported at every step by the meticulous work and good humor of Claire Betts, Violet Fearon, and Chloe Nast.

The sabbatical term I spent at the University of California, Berkeley, was a chance to finalize the manuscript. Many thanks to Leti Volpp for hosting me at the Center for Race and Gender, University of California at Berkeley, and for her steadfast support and kindness. For their extraordinary generosity I thank Judith Butler, Wendy Brown, and Isaac Butler-Brown. I am grateful for the friendships of Susette Min, Jeff Fort, Richard Perry, and Peter and Natalia Nordström. Thanks too to Sam King, Tamara Joseph, Charlotte Pomery, Sophie Pomery, Emilios Christodoulidis, Wendy McMurdo, Paul Gilroy, and Vron Ware. I would also like to remember here my dear friend Catrin Oliver.

For permission to use images I thank Armindo Cardoso and SPAutores, Biblioteca Nacional de Chile, FUNVISOL and all the families who gave permission via FUNVISOL, Erika Diettes, Marcelo Montecino, Graciela Sacco, Erika Teichert, Rosalba de Jesús Usma Patiño, and Wojtek Ziemilski. The research that underpins some of the chapters was funded by the Economic and Social Research Council (ES/N007433/1) and the British Academy (SDP2\100242).

Thanks to the series editors and especially Ryan Bishop for his support throughout, to Courtney Berger and Laura Jaramillo at Duke University Press, as well as to two anonymous reviewers for their generous reflections and guidance.

Thank you to all my family, including my parents, Claire and David, my sisters Jo and Katie, Ella and Theo, and all the beautiful people who call me "auntie." My children Tom and Lottie, thank you for being so supportive and loving; it is a joy to see you approach life with such openness and creativity, pursuing your own projects, academic and artistic. And finally to Paul, for always remembering to celebrate what is most precious in life.

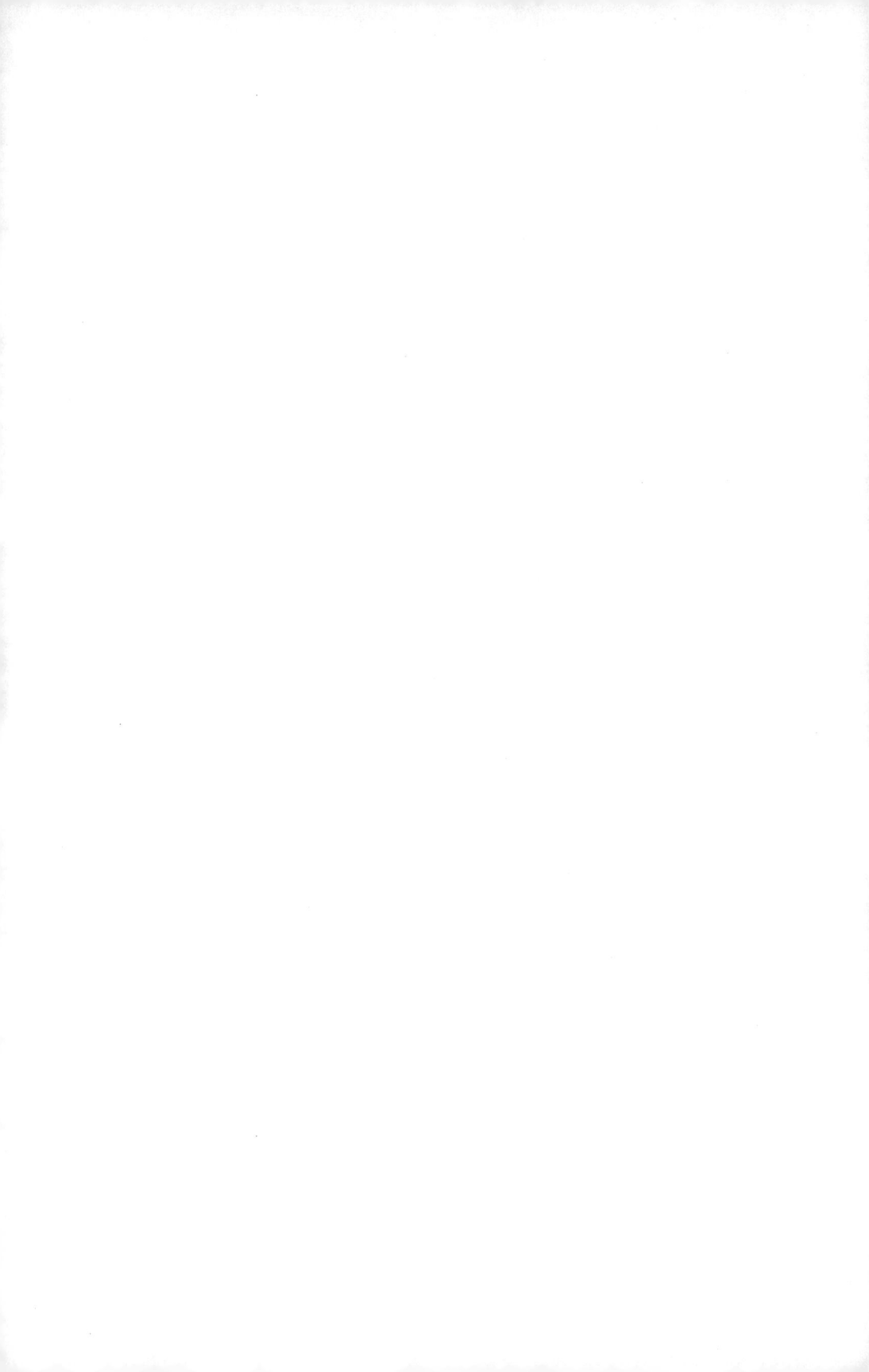

INTRODUCTION

Moving Stories: A Chance Encounter

Rummaging in the archive, researchers repeatedly consult items never intended for their eyes. Certainly, there can be the uncomfortable sensation that you are intruding into other people's intimacies, reading their documents and contemplating their photographs—especially with letters, of course, words explicitly for the addressee.[1] So it was for me one day in Santiago, Chile, at the archive of the Vicaría de la Solidaridad, an important organization that offered assistance to the victims and the families of the detained-disappeared during Pinochet's military dictatorship, when I came across a letter addressed to someone I know in the United Kingdom. Someone well known, that is: the film director Sally Potter. The case file I was consulting was that pertaining to a young woman disappeared by the regime in 1974, and the letter was from her father, reaching out as part of a campaign organized by the Vicaría to seek international support. It began:

Santiago, 30 May 1979

Dear Miss Potter,

In view of the laudable work that you and many others are doing to help the cause of the relatives of detenidos desaparecidos (detained-disappeared) in Chile, I write to you as a member of this group. It is very important for us to be able to count on wide international help to put pressure on the military government in Chile so that they might for once and for all account for the whereabouts of the thousands of people who have disappeared after being detained by the security forces. . . .

And it continues:

I am writing to you as the father of Carmen Bueno. My daughter Carmen was arrested by members of the DINA, the Pinochet regime's secret police, on 29th November 1974.

Señor Bueno continues to tell the harrowing story of his daughter's disappearance, and recounts the family's indefatigable efforts to uncover what had happened to her. I will return in detail to Carmen's story in chapter 2, but for now the point is that the letter in the archive, in addition to delivering its frisson of recognition, put me in an unusual position. I wondered what was the right thing to do with it. I was curious about whether Sally Potter had ever received it, and what she might recall. As it happened, she and I had recently been published together, where she had written precisely on the topic of letters, those exchanged between herself and John Berger, commenting that "distance is no impediment to closeness with John."[2] Encouraged by this sentiment, I responded to the letter not as simply a document in the archive, not only as a historical document with information of interest for my research, but as the letter that it still was. I undertook to send it on, just as if I had found an unposted envelope in the street and decided to carry it to the postbox, albeit in the form of a series of photographs that I sent via email. And I waited, with the hope that John Berger himself described as the excitement of a "little future" that accompanies posting off a letter or a parcel.[3]

Sally Potter wrote back to me. Of course, the story touched her: "This is heartbreaking," she wrote. The letter had never arrived in 1979, making me the tardy postal service that delivered it some forty years late. Had she received it, she assured me, she would have done anything and everything she could to help: "Solidarity is one of my favourite words." She ended her message beautifully: "Now, across the years, I feel deeply linked to Carmen and weep for her."[4]

The purpose of research in such archives—archives that comprise documentary evidence of widespread state violence, that is—is not usually to seek out individual messages to deliver to named recipients. Nor to make others weep. Rather, archives are usually interrogated beyond the initial purpose of the documents in order to understand more general historical patterns. An archive of state violence such as the archive of the Vicaría de la Solidaridad is an opportunity to understand historical features and practices such as how the systematic repression of Pinochet's Chile was organized following the coup on September 11, 1973: how the detainees were treated, how legal cases were brought and responded to, how resistance emerged and was sustained, and so on.[5] Such was the task undertaken by the team that has written the only extant book dedicated to this archive to date.[6] But arguably such research is also characterized by a desire to make connections, to consider those "missed appointments" with the past, and to bring these moving stories from the past into connection with the present, to make the past matter.[7] And if a sense of mourning accompanies and animates our research, it is because we too are moved by our encounters with the details of violence documented in the archive and are compelled to seek out new audiences for the stories found there. What researcher would not be affected by the precious personal stories of individuals subjected to incredible violence, the lists of names, the "ditto, ditto" of the archive, the mass of ultimately futile papers such as the habeas corpus filed and ignored, and of course the faces, the photographs?[8]

On the back of one of the portrait photographs held at the Vicaría's archive, another young woman—Jacqueline Drouilly Yurich—had written "this pretty smile of mine is only for my beloved Marcelito, 7 sept '70."[9] The loving inscription is betrayed by the context in which I came to see her smile, and hold that photograph. "What we mourn for the dead is the loss of their hopes," wrote Berger, on the very same page as he spoke of the anticipatory hope that accompanies the sending of a letter, of imagining its receipt.[10] Indeed. And in this atmosphere—of unimaginable violence, of mourning, of hopes lost—the research becomes a careful work of weaving that takes the stories that "belong to" others, but which touch and often inspire us, in order to lift them out of the archive and reconsider them. Not to fall into a collective melancholia, but for what they might collectively tell us, how they might offer a critical prism for an analysis beyond their time. Berger himself suggested as much, saying that we are charged with retelling the stories, of seeking out meaning, precisely because we are "beyond" that time and have the opportunity to offer a narration of them, to "grind the lens" through

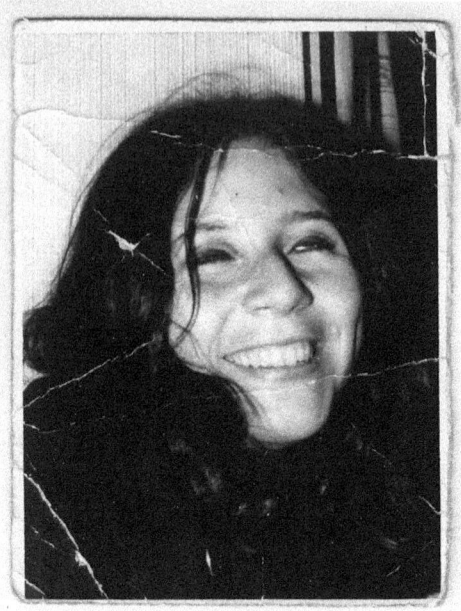
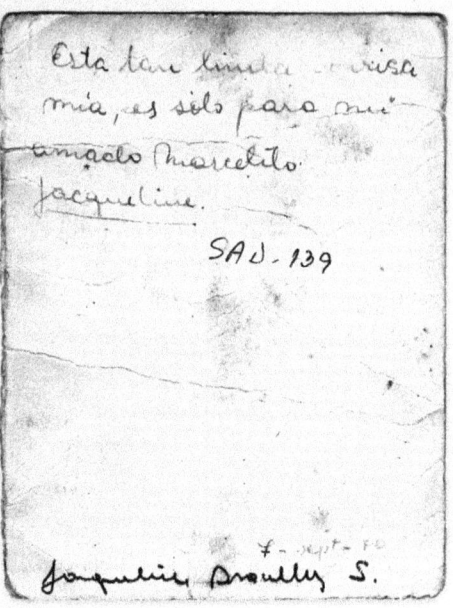

FIGURE I.1. Photograph of Jacqueline Drouilly Yurich and reverse. Source: FUNVISOL, with permission.

which they are seen. "Those who read or listen to our stories see everything as through a lens," he wrote, and "if we storytellers are Death's Secretaries, we are so because, in our brief mortal lives, we are grinders of these lenses."[11]

Such a task is fraught with important questions of responsibility, with ethical and political consequences. Writing about these stories and events involves making decisions at each stage, not least because our research process inevitably cuts into the past, shaping how it is re-turned and how it reappears in the world. If there is a responsibility to "take our turn," to be part of the intergenerational work that allows stories of past violence and, perhaps more so, of past *resistance*, their passage through time and space, it is also the case that, when we seek to fulfill a promise to remember, we assume a curatorial role vis-à-vis the past. In caring for it, we inevitably engage in fashioning it, editing and rearranging it like curators, conferring value on what we preserve and what we present. Our writing is marked by our own attentions and so too our inattentions, as it is by our contemporary political contexts and concerns. Likewise, it is marked by our aesthetic proclivities and judgments, as well as the technologies we have at our disposal. Indeed, since no promise to remember can truly hope to reconstruct the past without marking it in the process, "taking our turn" is never a perfect recirculation of past experiences and is not well understood as circular. Fritsch has offered the figure of the ellipsis that appears—and disappears—in Derrida's *Rogues*, understood as a mathematical figure, an oval cut from a cone (at an angle to its axis), as the better image.[12] The nonlinear and "bobbing rotation" of an elliptical wheel describes the turn we take better than a circular one, not just because we are likely to leave something out—as in the other sense of the word *ellipsis*, to omit something and so to fall short—but also because we are obliged to "take a turn" that in its re-turning risks veering off course.[13] Some of the most creative and influential recent writing on archives has argued that the inadequacies of the archive as a record of the past leaves no option but to embrace that veering, to engage in "critical fabulations," imaginative work that elaborates on fragments in order to begin to address—and so redress—the gaping absences in the records of violent pasts. Saidiya Hartman's point is not a methodological imperative that suggests that all archives must be approached through fabulation, however; rather, it is that in order to produce the prism for analysis, critical work must decide what route to take when faced with the lacunae and constraints of traditional archives, including allowing ourselves to pursue the risk of a speculative, creative dimension to the promise of memory.[14] Embracing, in other words, the responsibility of the role we assume as we move these stories, setting them in motion.

Promising Archives

This book arises from research I have conducted in Latin America over the last decade, where, as part of projects to consider the different forms and forums for the work of memory taking place in the aftermath of violence, I have spent time at several archives, with documents such as the files of Carmen Bueno (to which I turn in more detail in chapter 2) as well as interviewing the archivists and other workers who have set up these institutions. Arising as a mode of "answering" past violence, each of the archives exists and understands itself as an important pedagogical resource for educating present and future generations, but also as having critical force, standing guard against the reemergence of the conditions of erasure in which the materials were gathered. Each has been constituted and maintained in order to offer resources for explorations of several different kinds, for retellings of past atrocities, and for promoting deeper understanding. But this minimal description barely begins to convey the affective and the political investment in these archives, the collective outrage, the forms of solidarity, and the political hope they embody. They are first and foremost "archives of dissensus," to use Ann Laura Stoler's term, ones that have collected papers, testimonies, and other materials without attempting to explain the *arkhē*, the commencement of violence, nor to make commands over how its retelling should proceed.[15] They reject the power formations that establish archives as technologies of rule, seeking instead to build an archive that "invites dissension . . . allowing other defiant political visions, aesthetic possibilities and affective reflections."[16] These archives seek to arm the future—wisely, as it turns out—against those who will ignore or willfully rearrange the past.

These are archives that mean to invite new explorations of the past, promoting, as each of them does, an expansive use of their collected materials unconfined by the discipline of history. They are themselves infused with the potentiality of archival imagination, where the notion of returning is also a rereading, a restaging of the past that invites an attentive creativity that pushes at the boundaries of the very idea of the archive, inviting the breach.[17] Insofar as this is true, these archives are not only "answering" past violence but posing ongoing questions to both the present and the future. In this they are key examples of what some have recently started to call "transitional" or "justice" archives, but ones I will approach in an expansive sense of what that might mean.[18] Before I set out why and how I wish to situate the work of the archives in relation to other sites and modes of attending to the past—within an ecology of related endeavors—I will briefly introduce the three archives at the center of the research.

The FUNVISOL archive in Chile, where I found Señor Bueno's letter, was not conceived at the outset as an archival project at all, but results from the decision to preserve the papers of the Vicaría de la Solidaridad as records of a labor whose purpose was immediate and urgent: to help those targeted and affected when, following the coup of 1973, hundreds of people detained by the military failed to reappear. Established under the auspices of the Catholic Church to offer legal advice and representation, as well as financial and social support, to the relatives of the detained-disappeared and others affected by the detentions and violence, the Vicaría can be understood to have taken on the administrative and protective role that the state reneged on for those it targeted. Resisting the Chilean state's attempt to cast out these citizens, its workers offered their services precisely to insist that these people remained part of the citizenry.[19] When the organization closed in 1992, it had amassed more than 47,000 individual case files, and more than 80,000 documents. The preservation of these papers as the main holdings of the FUNVISOL archive conferred value upon them and established them as shared "social objects," and indeed the archive has become a valuable resource, consulted not least as a source for legal cases pertaining to the human rights abuses perpetrated.[20]

By its very existence, the archive confirms and seeks to extend the solidarity that was practiced by this remarkable organization in the past. While it is of course a reluctant archive that never wished to exist, it has been consulted repeatedly within trials of perpetrators by family members looking for information, and of course by academic researchers. To preserve these materials was a decision intended to offer the opportunity for such uses, to enable the legal, genealogical, scholarly, and creative rearticulations that arise from the work of those who consult it. So, although it is true that there is nothing inherently celebratory or "promising" about the archive as such, FUNVISOL shelters the documentation of past violence as a gift, a resource open to new explorations and new routes through its holdings.[21] Moreover, its maintenance insists upon the ongoing inclusion of those who have died, and their families and friends, within political discourse, providing as it does the conditions and materials to make that hope possible. However incomplete and incoherent an archive may be—with often frustratingly scattered contents, absences, or lack of authorial guidance—the gamble is that there are or will be those who seek out its holdings, enfolding those whose lives and experiences are captured there into the nation's understanding of its People. In this the archive is, as Arjun Appadurai has written, more like "an aspiration than a recollection."[22] He suggests, "We should see all documentation as intervention, and all archiving as a collective project. Rather than being a tomb of the trace, the archive is more frequently the product of the anticipation of collective memory."[23] A speculative endeavor itself, in other words, the FUNVISOL archive imagines a future in which its collection has an important continuing role to play. By exploring it and seeking to propose an analysis of what it could be said to shelter, my work means to respond to and affirm that hope.

The speculation entailed in the setting up of an archive has taken an ambitious scale in Colombia, where, as part of the stuttering attempts to bring about a cessation to the violence of its decades-long armed conflict, the government tasked the Centro Nacional de Memoria Histórica (CNMH) with the extraordinary work of creating an archive of archives, literally a gathering of all the archives that exist around the country. The aim, enshrined in law, was explicit that the gathering of such information would aid the nation toward the "clarification" it needed as to how and why the widespread and horrific armed conflict occurred. As I discuss in more detail in chapter 3, the CNMH archive was imagined as part of a transitional program that would gather all available knowledge from across the various territories of the country, digitalizing it to ensure its availability as widely as possible. The academic researchers at the head of the project, themselves well read in the philosophy of history and violence, including Walter Benjamin's writing on the philosophy of history, were deeply aware of the risks of such work, and of their responsibility in attempting to deliver on so ambitious an endeavor.[24] From across the country, they collected the accounts of those who had witnessed the atrocities, or their aftermaths, and materials that helped convey these accounts in various ways. Understanding that the archive's materials would be overwhelming and risk being the sky-high pile of debris on which Benjamin's angel of history fixed his gaze, the center also produced many reports on different incidents in the armed conflict, seeking to set out their understanding of them succinctly but within an analytic frame. Yet at the same time, they understood that their assignment was precisely not to "narrativize" the archive ahead of time. Instead, they sought to construct the "archive of archives" as a gift for the future, as a proposition to which future actors might respond, and indeed, which requires that response in order to breathe life "back" into the archival body. As such, the archive is a supreme example of Derrida's concept of *survivance*, explained in his last seminars as the possibility of living-dead machines: "*a dead thing that resuscitates each time* a breath of living reading [*sic*], each time the breath of the other or the other breath, each time *an intentionality intends it and makes it live again* by animating it."[25]

That the archive holds but does not really seek to enclose, that it is porous in that it exceeds its boundaries, calling out for and requiring the reader or user to fulfill its purpose, is also highly pertinent for the third archive chosen for the research, located in Argentina. The point is reflected in its very name: Memoria Abierta, "open memory." This archive was always conceived of as a resource that protected the knowledge built up by the groups that organized themselves to resist the violences perpetrated during the last dictatorship (1976–83). Understanding the importance of the information built up by those active in challenging the military state actions, a network of organizations—including the Abuelas de Plaza de Mayo, Madres de Plaza de Mayo Línea Fundadora, CELS, APDH, Familiares, and SERPAJ—established Memoria Abierta as an umbrella organization to coordinate and strengthen the links between them, motivated in large part by the concern that the democratic government of the time was turning its attentions to a notion of *reconciliation*, a term that in Argentina carries negative associations as it was understood as the state's euphemism for terminating the pursuit of justice or legal investigation of past atrocities.[26] These civil organizations fought strenuously against that course of action, and one of their responses was to seek to organize the documents held by each of their organizations, to pool their knowledge, as it were, and ensure their availability for widespread deployment whenever the need arose. The archive of Memoria Abierta is actually dispersed therefore among several organizations and buildings, all of which are searchable nevertheless through its single integrated catalogue. Alongside this coordinating work, at the heart of the archive, and what its key workers regard as their greatest achievement, is the audiovisual archive of witness and survivor statements. Set up at a time when Argentina's so-called amnesty laws made the prosecution of perpetrators seem unlikely, this ambitious project sought to interview all those willing to set down their stories. Its resulting collection of video testimonies is extensive and is now regarded as exemplary for similar projects, with the expertise of the team requested across the continent. This project explicitly prepared the archive for those seeking out testimonies, whether these would be in relation to the hoped-for trials—which finally arrived with the Kirchner government (2003–7) and has seen over a thousand people convicted of crimes against humanity—or in relation to other projects that might constitute their own forms of juris-writing through their distinct modes of informing public understanding and opinion.[27] Memoria Abierta is open in its very structure, therefore, being a network of organizations that formed in the context of the imposition of limitations on prosecutions, that furthermore and explicitly invites users to consult its holdings with an explicit hope that in doing so its contents will circulate in other contexts within and beyond Argentina. The porosity of the archive, then, an always relational calling beyond its own boundaries, is built into the structure and constitutes the promise of Memoria Abierta by design.

If the archive is by definition an attempt to "pre-occupy the future," as Jacques Derrida commented, an attempt to determine our future preoccupations ahead of time, these archives of dissensus are playing the same game.[28] Despite their distinctive conditions of emergence and contents, all share a heightened reflexivity about their role and purpose. They understand the critique of the archive that has repeatedly drawn attention to the omissions and constraints of archives, especially where the archive is the trace of the exercise of or encounter with hierarchical power, repeating its modes of registering and capture, classifying our worlds and simultaneously committing elisions and exclusions.[29] Insofar as a society's understanding of its past, and the future's understanding of our present, is at the mercy, in this sense, of the archive, these archives assert themselves onto the scene. "Which documents, which images, which stories do we want to send forward into the future?" they ask, as they select, organize, and maintain their contents, seeking to insist that these should be granted passage and have a chance to survive, to be perused, to be chosen for the future's attentions. As such, the archives that I have visited and studied embody an optimism and are structured around a promise, albeit one without guarantees. It is a promise *beyond memory*, moreover, since these archives' desire is not merely archival, as it were, not only a wish that the names, facts, and circumstances of violence are documented and remembered. They are also animated by past an-archival concerns and future an-archival moments, alive to the implications that the archive is not definitive nor over, so must remain open and attentive "to what exceeds it, to what is anarchival in the archive, to that moment or decision . . . when we affirm or promise a text for the future."[30] Moreover, if the archive is imbued with an optimism, it extends beyond the fact that the past is recorded, has been written down or otherwise inscribed, sheltering it and making it available to be recalled. It hopes too that the facts and stories held there might also be consequential, that they might reverberate, and move across the boundaries of the archive in order to act somehow, now and in the future. These are the political and ethical stakes, reflecting the importance attached to memory work that performs a work of care for the past in the name of a more complex reparation than the term *memory* is usually thought to imply. Certainly, this hope is intensely felt in societies such as Argentina's and Chile's, where the biopolitical caesuras so violently enacted by the last dictatorships still reverberate in civil society and political discourse, and in Colombia too, which is still attempting to fully emerge from the decades of armed conflict that produced such horrific scenes of violence, despite the strides made by the 2016 Peace Agreement.[31] In my analysis, I underscore the dynamics of preservation and desired intervention that accompany the selected archives, sites, and activities I have been privileged to study, exploring how they conduct their memory work in order to enter this wager on—and for—the future.

From "Archive Versus Repertoire" to Ecologies of Practices

In writing about the porosity of the archive I also wish to emphasize that the archive is of course only one modality of attempting to enact a promise of memory, to fulfill a sense of obligation to past lives lost to violence. As Diana Taylor put it some years ago in her influential *The Archive and the Repertoire*, the study of cultural memory in Latin America, and elsewhere, needs to reach beyond archives, to attend to what she termed the *repertoire*, the embodied practices that are as important in the transmission of knowledge.[32] It is worth recalling her argument that embodied memory practices have been delegitimized over written forms of documentation both theoretically and historically, meaning that nonverbal practices—she mentions indigenous forms of dance, ritual, and cooking—have not been considered forms of knowledge.[33] If colonial authority was routed in written forms of authority, the rift between the supposedly enduring (the archival) and the ephemeral (the repertoire) has continued to be articulated, shoring up the hierarchical relations of coloniality. Against this history, Taylor's central thesis was that both the archive and the repertoire should be understood as "important sources of information" in a "constant state of interaction," working "in tandem . . . [and] alongside other forms of transmission."[34] Our study of cultural memory must be expansive, she argued, and go beyond texts and archives to consider the roles, for example, of political protest as performance, of theater and of visual interventions. It is an argument that has become familiar and implicit not only in Taylor's own more recent work but across the now rich and expansive subdisciplines of performance and memory studies.[35] So do these axioms inform the approach I adopt in this work, not least in the sense that it became necessary for my research to leave the archive, as it were, to explore where the stories *from* the archives also appear and circulate beyond its perimeters. It is for this reason that I will wander not only through but away from the archives introduced above, setting them in relation and contrasting their modes of archiving the past, especially artistic practices such as those of Colombian contemporary artist Erika Diettes discussed in chapter 4. It goes without saying that institutionalized archives do not have a monopoly on feeling obliged to attend to the past, and engagements and reinscriptions of the past into the present are much broader than those we meet within the archival stacks. There is no archival "house arrest" that encloses traces of the past within explicitly archival institutions; the promise of memory is performed multiply and variously in what I understand as a much wider "ecology of practices," a phrase I borrow from the work of Isabelle Stengers, to whose thought I return below.[36]

While it may be tempting to regard the repertoire as the domain of anti-hegemonic resistance to the archive, this was never Taylor's view; the distinction will certainly deconstruct if interrogated, she noted, not least because the idea of the archive as unmediated and unchanging is "mythical."[37] As I have intimated in introducing the archives above, not only are these archives themselves modes of resistance, but also the work of selecting, classifying, and presenting the archival is a social process, contested and enacted as a mode of intervention that is itself embodied. Conversely, many embodied practices refer to and include "materials from the archive" that shape them without determining them absolutely, as with Taylor's example of the relationship between the text of a play and the performance of it.[38] There is no question, then, and as I also illustrate throughout this book, that the distinction between the archive and the repertoire exceeds any simple "text versus body" distinction. Many of the practices I consider in this book, similarly, have a relation to an existent archive, are themselves forms of archiving or constitute complex requests to be archived. And sometimes, even where their concern is ostensibly anarchival, even anti-archive, they remain nonetheless to be marked by a *concern* with the archive and with the future at which its promise of memory aims.

Beyond the archive, the scenes of my own research have been various—including the art gallery, the cinema, the memory museum, the law court, the ex–detention centers that have become sites of memory—as my concern has been how within these forums, people gather to establish or to (re)-consider their relation to the past. As my research has taken me between these different spaces, I have become intrigued by how the various types of forum and their respective modes of approach differ from each other. I ask, in other words: How is violence recalled or conjured up differently, how is it dramatized via distinct means, how is it approached, propositioned, and judged according to the specific constraints and prompts from the space in which it appears? This vocabulary and line of questioning anticipate my use of Stengers's arguments.

This is not the place to provide an extended exegesis of Stengers's thought, but a few thoughts might help attune the reader to some of the arguments to be found in what follows.[39] Given that the "work of memory" entails a plea for facts from the past to be returned, remembered, and passed on, its various activities are motivated by a desire that people will connect with that past and continue to be concerned with it. In order for any such "connection"—or *rapport*, a "relation that matters" as Stengers also puts it—and "concern" to be produced, moreover, requires some sort of forum or gathering in which an assembled company can be brought before those facts and convinced of their import.[40] Yet there can be no certainty that those gathered will in fact be concerned, or that they will be concerned in the manner that those arranging the forum imagined, that they will, in our case, pledge to remember or "learn from the past." If no rapport between the evidence brought from the past and the imaginations of those present arises, if no connection is achieved or if it goes awry in some sense, the promise of memory "fails." This is certainly the risk within art forums, in museums of memory or galleries exhibiting work by artists, where the promise of memory requests the attention of visitors who are under no obligation to be concerned with the presentation of past events. Since there are no guarantees of engagement, artists and curators deploy all manner of strategies to attract our attentions, to infect us with their concerns and purpose, to produce an encounter and to make us care, as they do, for the past.[41] Even transitional justice mechanisms like truth and reconciliation committees, or criminal trials, that gather people within quasi or actual legal forums, have to engage in what Stengers terms *dramatization*—laying out evidence, calling up precedent and performing acts of persuasion—in order to convince their audiences of the truths at stake. The "force" of law and the obligation of those present within a court to be concerned with the presentation of evidence from the past are insufficient. In order to connect audiences to events, to connect juries or judges to evidence, to connect evidence to rules, there must be a dramatization that employs the appropriate apparatus to achieve engagement and convince those present.[42]

As this implies, what is termed *evidence* is not self-evident precisely because it has to be set in motion, *moved* in order to move those who gather around it. "Evidence is what is used to persuade," writes Thomas Keenan of US legal trials, for it does not decide and "nor does it settle or conclude or determine"; rather, evidence is a *question.*[43] Indeed, the seemingly unmediated evidence that comes before a court—witnesses, photographs, bones—calls for a *staging*. In relation to art, as I will have occasion to repeat throughout this book, no artwork "speaks for itself," which is not at all the same as saying that the conclusions to which they may lead us are arbitrary. And to return to the archive, unless it can get *out* of itself, whether through technological innovation—such as digitalization—or through the attentions and creativity of intermediaries like researchers, artists, curators or lawyers, it will struggle to be a forum that can gather interest and persuade others to make its contents "matters of concern," to recall Latour's influential argument. "The critic is . . . the one who assembles . . . who offers the participants arenas in which to gather," he wrote.[44] Thus it has been important, for my purpose, to consider how the archives are consulted, deployed, and referenced elsewhere, as when academics—myself included—or lawyers consult the archives to research a case, or a curator uses an archival image within a museum exhibit. That these different spaces or forums each have their own specific arts of dramatization, their own apparatus promoting different modes of attention, different possibilities for persuasion as well as different constraints on what is admitted as relevant, means that both what and how one comes to be convinced—and the implications of that conviction—varies (which is not to argue that these truths are necessarily contradictory, nor even that they are isolated from one another). As mentioned, Stengers speaks of an "ecology of practices," and it is in this sense that I approach the spaces and forums where this research has taken place.[45] Through the chapters that follow, I consider their modes of problematization, their methods of animating those problems and their modes of paying attention to them in order to explore how these practices conduct their attempts to gather others, to persuade or provoke them (or merely to interest them). Attending to a diversity of practices, then, appreciating their divergences while allowing the shared resonances that exist between them to be heard, *Promises Beyond Memory* seeks to place the archival work that takes place within institutions that understand themselves as archival within these several related endeavors.

Outline of the Book

Academic work has its part to play in the ecology of practices that engage with the promise of memory, providing as it does another opportunity for stories from the past to circulate and be enfolded within conversations elsewhere, carrying these stories to new forums and new readers, aiding their survivance. Chapter 1 revolves around the question of which stories are proffered the chance to survive—or not. It takes the reader on a journey to return to those stories of past violence, opening with the trip I made to Chacabuco, an abandoned nitrate mining town in the Atacama desert, some 100 kilometers from the coastal town of Antofagasta, which was used by the Pinochet regime in 1973–74 to house an estimated 1,200 political prisoners. If the purpose of that trip was to search for stories, for how places hold stories, it became more about the complexities of how stories are articulated and passed on, how accounts of the past—along with the objects, photographs, even ghosts that may also be said to preserve stories—have to appear, be perceived, be invited, or made to speak. This is a precarious, contingent, and complex process. While multiple stories may exist potentially—and really— in a place-as-archive, they are crystalline, needing to be discovered and turned in the light to be revealed. Once these potential stories are actualized, furthermore, in order to stand a chance of surviving, they need witnesses of some sort, who must pay attention, be willing and able to receive and carry them elsewhere. All these requirements are complex and fraught, and also, as this chapter explores, interrupted and constrained. On that visit to Chacabuco, I was traveling with my research partner, Mario Di Paolantonio, with whom I shared the enormous privilege of meeting and interviewing—unexpectedly—two survivors of the detention center, who with much generosity and good humor, remembered their time there for us, passing the baton between themselves as they sought to give an account that could convey the horror as well as the extraordinary creativity and political camaraderie of imprisoned life. Simultaneously, they located their remembrance within the conditions of its telling, mindful as they were of the resonances of their story with other situations and peoples in past and in contemporary Chile, that is, with the former mine workers and the Mapuche and other indigenous peoples. Exercising caution over claims of ownership of the themes their stories raised, the care they took over setting down their stories for the record is punctuated by the sense of a future reception through which new entanglements might be ushered forth.

Returning to the FUNVISOL archive with which I began above, chapter 2 concerns the case of Carmen Bueno Cifuentes. The chapter is an extended exploration of how a single casefile that lives in the archive might be asked to tell the story of a disappearance. How might the documents and photographs held there speak of the forms of radical exposure to state power that she and her relatives experienced at that time? What does the sheer number of legal documents, which accrued as the family pursued every avenue to try to locate her, tell us? Can the typeface *talk*? What can a consideration of the photographs offer? Remembering Foucault's comment that the archive holds the details of ordinary people only because they were captured in the "flash of power," the chapter considers the documentation of Carmen Bueno's disappearance as indicative of a power struggle around the very idea of a People's democratic sovereignty.[46] Having experienced a modern existence in which the state shielded their lives, the detained-disappeared and their families were subject to the dictatorship's attack and distortion of their place and status in relation to the nation-state. If biopolitics had disciplined and invested the bodies of those who constituted the People as such, a military coup that hands power back to a dictator-sovereign also necessarily involved a scrabbling back of those forms of investiture. But this retraction—like the dissolution of the king's body in Eric Santner's provocative analysis of the transition to modern sovereignty—was never destined to be a neat achievement, precisely because just as becoming the People requires them to respond to those forms of investiture at the level of the flesh—at the level of their hopes, desires, and expectations for life—so too the removal of that positionality imposed a profoundly disorientating shock. My focus is on what insights gleaned from the archive might tell us about that symbolic investiture and its attempted removal, as Carmen's family refused to surrender their status as citizens, pursuing a battle about how the bodies of the disappeared were to be understood. A twist in this tale moves the consideration onto another form, and forum, of representing the People, as Carmen herself was an image-maker, involved in Chile Films, and her boyfriend, Jorge Müller, kidnapped at the same time as Carmen and also one of the *desaparecidos*, was the cameraman for the famous film that captured the events preceding the coup, *The Battle of Chile*.[47] Thus the chapter considers what cinema's potential is to continue the exploration of the contortions of attempting to be a citizen at that time in Chile's history.

As mentioned above, chapter 3 moves to Colombia where—drawing on interviews with members of the Centro Nacional de Memoria Histórica, conducted with the invaluable help of my research team on that project—I explore the methods by which the Center attempted to fulfill the task of creating an "archive of archives" of the violence that had (and has) caused decades of suffering. This remit, stipulated by law, and incorporated eventually into the 2016 Law, was vast and destined to be unwieldy. With extraordinary care and intelligence, the team—working under Gonzalo Sánchez, the first academic director—created a subtle methodology by which to reach out to communities across the country, to listen and help articulate the experiences of the people of Colombia. The chapter reflects upon the logic of this work and the archive at its heart, showing how in building this archive, from which so much was expected, the team had to address key difficult questions: How can an archive be created that could do justice to the complexity of the armed conflict while fulfilling the remit to provide clarification on how the country arrived at this situation? Which objects need to be included in an archive so that it can bespeak the experiences of those who have lived and those who continue to live through it? How could the archive be inclusive of those who did not believe they held an archive, maybe did not believe in archives?

The task was not without its challenges and controversies, especially as the leadership of the Center changed with the change of government and few of the original personnel remained. Interestingly for the perspective developed through this book, the Center was also then given the further task of developing the script and curatorial plans for a national museum of memory, now in the process of being built in Bogotá. The chapter discusses how the team responded to this proposition—with bemusement at first, then as an intellectual challenge to imagine how a museum might embody the promise of memory into the future. The chapter attends to the draft of a conceptual script for the museum that the team produced, attending to how it attempts to avoid the dangers of presenting a closed narrative or of "over-naming" the violence. Since the proposed museum is still in the process of being built, the chapter closes with a consideration of Colombia's only other purpose-built museum of memory, Medellín's Museo Casa de la Memoria.[48] Although this museum speaks only to its locale rather than the nation as a whole, it provides an interesting complementary discussion to the new museum, attempting as it does to create something akin to a collective account and a collective memory without foreclosing the complex and necessary continuing debates around memory in Colombia's context.

The questions of aesthetics and ethics within the museum, with which chapter 3 ends, is taken up in the following chapter, which considers the challenges in pursuing artistic response through a focus on one contemporary Colombian artist, Erika Diettes, as she seeks to respond to the devastating violence that her country has experienced. By reflecting with her on several different projects that she has completed and one that is still in process, it suggests that as Diettes attempts to do justice to the stories and the objects that are gifted to her in the course of her art-making, she must wrestle with the *force* of art, its potential promise but also its potential power to do harm. Through her series of installations—*Sudarios, Río Abajo, Relicarios,* and the *Oratorio for the Disappeared*—Diettes has sought to offer insights into the stories of the armed conflict without ever telling them as such; indeed, several of her works arise from working with the survivors but do not present the stories, preferring an approach which is often itself peculiarly archival, arranging images and objects created with materials given to her by relatives of the disappeared and murdered within installations that are beautiful but enigmatic. Chapter 4 draws on my interviews with Diettes over several years and demurs from overly optimistic arguments for the role of art, not least because images—especially photographic images—also risk gifting violence precisely the visibility that it wants. Such exposition is part of the monstrosity of violence, as Jean-Luc Nancy phrased it.[49] Moreover, as Nancy argued, images necessarily withdraw from the viewer and thus cannot be approached naively, not least because whatever attempt we might make to receive an image in its uniqueness, even the declarative "I am" of a photographic portrait, will ultimately be undermined by the references it cannot but simultaneously make to all other images, what Nancy calls the "colossal and labyrinthine phototheque."[50] Because making art after violence is a process of making decisions that must face and negotiate such dangers, Diettes exercises the utmost care. She has felt the need to tread carefully, to work sensitively with the survivors in long processes of preparation and creation before attempting to "give shape to the unimaginable," placing her artworks into public galleries and spaces where others are invited to engage and contemplate with them. The chapter traces her several thoughtful projects, ending with a discussion of the *Oratorio for the Disappeared*, a hillside installation she is currently constructing in the countryside outside Medellín, approached as an exploration of a positive project for what we came to call "tender forgetting," documentary but simultaneously anti-archival in its purpose.

Turning to Argentina, chapter 5 furthers these themes of the relations and distinctions between different forums and their modes of presentation, drawing explicitly on the thought of Isabelle Stengers to understand the modes of staging the past as forums that operate within an "ecology of practices." Based on interviews and observational research with key personnel—including archivists, artists, forensic anthropologists, lawyers, psychologists—the chapter considers the various sites and modes of conjuring up the violence of the last dictatorship. While each of the forums within this ecology addresses the violent past, what is presented and mobilized as evidence, what is dismissed as irrelevant, and what is "successfully" accepted are dependent upon the practices, constraints, and concerns of the forum. The circulation of truths about Argentina's dictatorship are consequently always situated forms of world-making and emerge variously from a range of sites and scenes of emergence, entering into an "ecology of practices." Within the resulting web of interconnections, the archive constituted through the work of Memoria Abierta occupies an interesting and important space, one that is clarified through the contrasts this chapter highlights; in the midst of this ecology, the archive plays its important but understated, facilitating role.

Chapter 6 focuses on the aesthetic interventions that have—gradually, over decades—taken place at the Espacio Memoria y Derechos Humanos, ex-ESMA since it became a site of memory in 2004. In the time that I have been researching there, the philosophy of what to do with the buildings has altered and the risk of images has been taken, so that a series of encounters have been staged for the visitor. With a focus on the Casino building itself, where over 5,000 prisoners were secretly imprisoned during the 1970s, the chapter considers the ways in which the images have intervened at the site, how they make propositions to the viewer, how they negotiate the concerns about their presence there. The chapter asks how these interventions seek to give form to what has been termed the "formlessness" of terror. It asks, moreover, how these operate in a mode that distinguishes the space from other spaces in which the horrors committed during the dictatorship period appear, including legal courts. It is striking that this most controversial and resonant of buildings now houses footage from the trials, projected onto the walls in the very spaces where the kidnapped were held in "kennels." How does the redeployment of legal forums within a site of memory alter the way in which the visitor is asked to participate, and to judge? How does this intervention differ from the often opaque contemporary photographic works that have also been shown as a temporary exhibition? And how to think about the contentious performance piece by Polish artist Wojtek Ziemilski, staged in 2019, that featured a film of an actor portraying a perpetrator in which he attempts to articulate an apology, continually breaking down and being unable to speak. Drawing on an interview conducted with Ziemilksi, the chapter considers how this piece raised the question of how the perpetrator (or *represor*) is scripted within contemporary memory works, how "impossible scenes" such as this are infrequently imagined but may be conjured up in the spaces of artistic intervention as the artist did here, deliberately drawing on the anachronisms his outsider status afforded him.

As a whole, *Promises Beyond Memory* explores moments and spaces where events from the past are reinscribed within the present through intentional acts, creative endeavor, and various modes of curation. It bears repeating that as the archival institutions studied here show, the promise to remember is not fulfilled merely by the act of collecting and preserving. If these archives enshrine an optimism that the future might dwell upon and learn from the past, they rely also upon a fundamental wager that their contents will be attended to, that the stories contained there, and any lessons that the architects of the archives believe they contain, will remain of interest and be heard into the future. Without being able to direct those future attentions, however, the archive must live with a profound uncertainty about how its collections relate to the fulfillment of its promise. How the spirit of the archive—the spirit that is, in which it was established, constructed, curated, and maintained—survives into the future, will rely upon those who respond to that wager, who cross its threshold, or otherwise feel its reverberations. Who will respond? Where will these stories travel to, and how will they be "turned" as they are presented? How will inscriptions of the past move beyond memory, beyond the facts of what happened, in order to prompt deeper reflection and provide a convincing analysis of the past? How will curatorial and artistic imaginations (both within and beyond the archive) facilitate or prompt reflections on the past? Will they be aligned with or challenge the archival impulse? Into which other spaces will these stories move and how will they be deployed there? Each of the chapters explores these questions in different ways. Throughout, *Promises Beyond Memory* seeks to avoid a simple celebration of archival projects, and to hold in question any simplistic notion that memory is a bulwark against the repetition of political violence. Its proposition is that memory requires active engagement, and more specifically, forms of dramatization that are necessary in order to ensure stories from the past a form of survivance. That passage "forward" will not be confined to one site, but there will be a myriad of sites and actors involved, with their own parameters, concerns, and approaches. Beyond the mere repetition of facts, these will certainly involve modes of engagement that also run the risk of failure, of missteps, and of controversy. Indeed, these risks inevitably accompany the retellings, restagings, and recirculations that are, as I have argued, not actually circular. To acknowledge them is important both ethically and politically, as an openness to a democratic future subtends an openness to new dramatizations of the past, to grant those in the future the opportunity for new debates about how the refracted past appears.

PART I

Chile

1

ENTWINED TELLINGS

Detention and Survival in Pinochet's Chile

So you were in Chacabuco? Did you spend the night there? The stars are amazing, so beautiful. . . . At night, you could walk by their light. —ORLANDO "CALICHE" VALDÉS BARRIENTOS

The time, and therefore the story, belongs to them. Yet the meaning of the story, what makes it worthy of being told, is what we can see and what inspires us because we are beyond its time. —JOHN BERGER, *And Our Faces, My Heart, Brief as Photos*

The Trip to Chacabuco
Signposts

We drove past the geoglyph—a large image formed by moving darker rocks to reveal lighter sands beneath or vice versa—on the hillside along the Pan-American Highway, twice. First time I missed it completely, concentrating as I was on the road ahead, somewhat anxious to be in the midst of the desert in a hire car with a troublesome gearbox and sharing the road with infrequent but huge lorries plowing up and down the motorway. I did see the road sign with a symbol of a camera on it. I didn't look up. There are very few turns on the road, but nevertheless we managed to take a wrong one, leaving the highway too early, which obliged us to come back on ourselves in a long-ish loop, back down the motorway and up again, taking us past the geo-glyph once more. This time we saw the figure, and although we did not stop, Mario snapped a quick photograph (fig. 1.1). Reading about it later, it seems these figures—often llamas or other zoomorphic figures, only occasionally human—probably date from AD 1000–1400; they could be signs of moun-tain worship, of solar alignment or offerings to Andean deities, although they may also have acted as signposts for safe routes for llama caravans trans-porting food and cloth. They are, in other words, "part signpost, part story telling."[1] This longer history of indigenous peoples and beasts marking out lines in the landscape to connect their worlds with others in the skies or on Earth, beautiful as it now sounds, was not in my sights that day. Instead, I was pursuing the threads of a more recent history of this desert, as we were en route to visit the ex–detention center at Chacabuco, where during 1973–74, hundreds of men were held prisoner in an old nitrate mine, political prison-ers of the Pinochet regime. There, we were under the impression, we would learn something of the ways places "hold" the stories. We were being drawn into the inhospitable landscape of Chile's northern deserts by an abandoned site precisely because we sensed the possibility that there we would find clues, "part signpost, part story telling."

On arrival, I stop the car a little before the entrance and we both jump out and start taking photographs. We cover our faces with lens and hardly speak; relieved to have found the place, we are also a little spooked. The site is huge and rows of single-story brick buildings extend into the distance, their backs to us, as it were, creating one long wall (fig. 1.2). A tall, thin chimney rises up from within some way off, and further still, there is a wooden water tower; a few signs of the industry that once took place here are apparent. There is the sense of profound desolation that haunts many industrial ruins, exacerbated here by the desert that extends beyond its perimeter in all directions. And the sun is beating down, unforgiving.

A little further down the track, there is, precisely, a signpost. It is old, its blue metal battered, but still clearly legible. It gives one of the histories of this site and some data: "Ex-Oficina Salitrera Chacabuco Construida en 1922–1924. Cant. Trabajadores 1.700. Poblacion 7.000 Habs Produccion Anual 180,000 t/m de Salitre . . . 1940 Cierra sus funciones como Oficina Salitrera 1971 Declarada como Monum. Historico."[2] As the signpost attests, the way in which Chacabuco was being inscribed into national memory in 1971 was seemingly motivated by a need to honor the efforts of the workers who lived

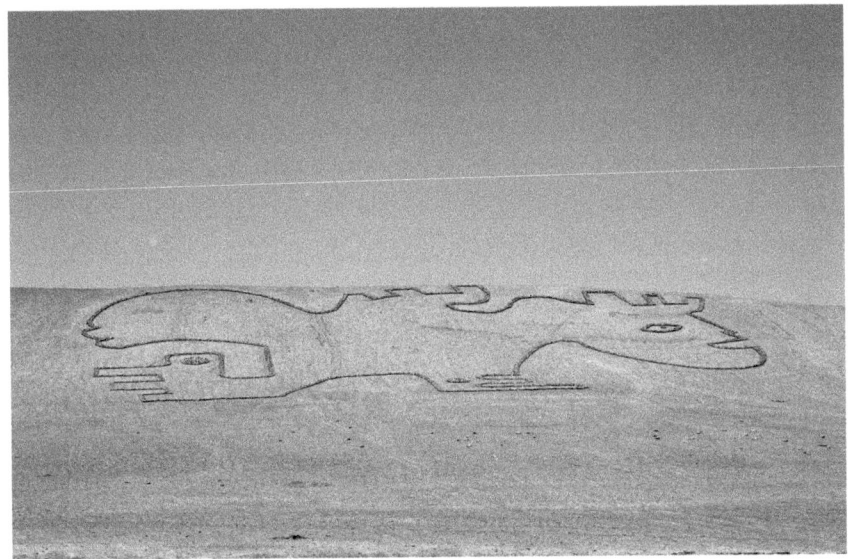

FIGURE 1.1. Geoglyph in the Atacama desert. Source: Mario Di Paolantonio.

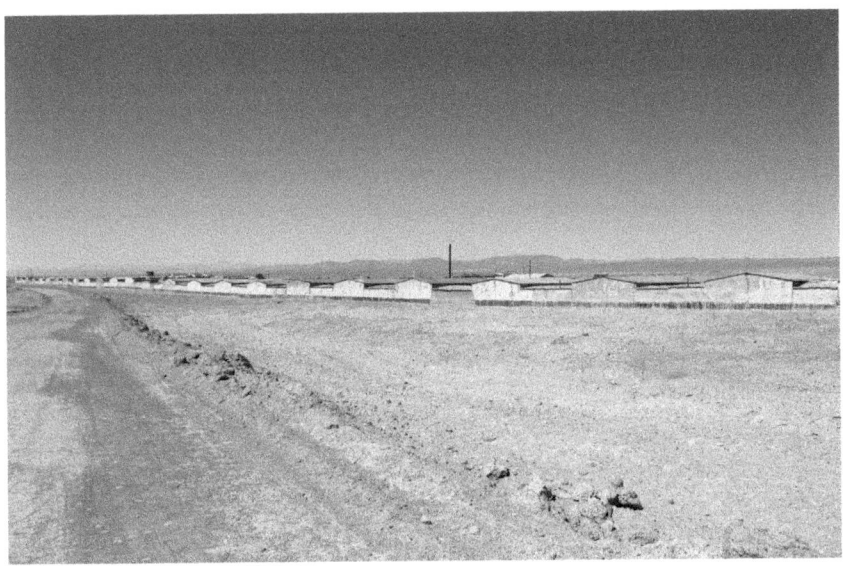

FIGURE 1.2. Chacabuco from the approach road. Source: Vikki Bell.

in these mining towns in harsh physical environments. Immediately we noted that the more recent history is absent from this first signpost. Unsigned.

I park by the entrance but someone—later we'll meet him and come to know his name, Walter Robertson—beckons us in, lifting the barrier and waving us on. We drive into what was once the central square of the Oficina, parking in the shadow of a large theater that has been partially refurbished, relatively recently painted white, and for that reason now looking somewhat out of kilter with its abandoned surroundings. Wandering away from the car, my attentions are still drawn through the lens of the camera, framing images, the sun creating bold stripes where the wooden struts of porches cast shadow on the buildings (fig. 1.3).

I am aware I am approaching this task aesthetically, maybe even defensively. Yet there is something about the slats and the shadows, that draws me, and draws from me, a memory-image.[3] I'm reminded of the work of Argentine artist Graciela Sacco, whose art frequently becomes a meditation on shadow, and who returns in particular to the use of a slatted fence or blinds, which, as I've argued elsewhere, is in large part because her work is also a prolonged meditation on the problem of discontinuity, and on how our ways of seeing and telling create ways of living with discontinuity.

For many years, Sacco's art has used the motif of fencing, slates or sticks, as in *Adelante,* from the series *Cuerpo a cuerpo* (1995) (fig. 1.4), in which by heliographic method she transfers the image of an unnamed uprising from a photograph onto wooden planks. She has commented herself that while sticks, fences, thrown objects participate in a riot and may themselves retain an impression of what has occurred, they tend to be forgotten in narratives of such events. Like my concern in this chapter, Sacco suggests that multiple potential tellings accrue to any event, reminding us that we need always to be attentive to how accounts, stories, rumors, eyewitness accounts, and indeed even sociological investigations circulate and come to repeat each other, refracting and jumping gaps, producing accounts that borrow and countersign each other, while other accounts fall "through the gaps," as it were. As do Sacco's pieces in this series, and as do shadows that both interrupt and sustain the image, so too ways of telling in academic work are distributed across many aspects of the research and are produced relationally. In other words, each production and presentation of the story attends to different aspects and accentuates the assemblage differently, not because we are negligent or subjective—although we are that—but because we are always producing and presenting the story *in relation* with various materials, (memory-)images, evidences, and accounts.

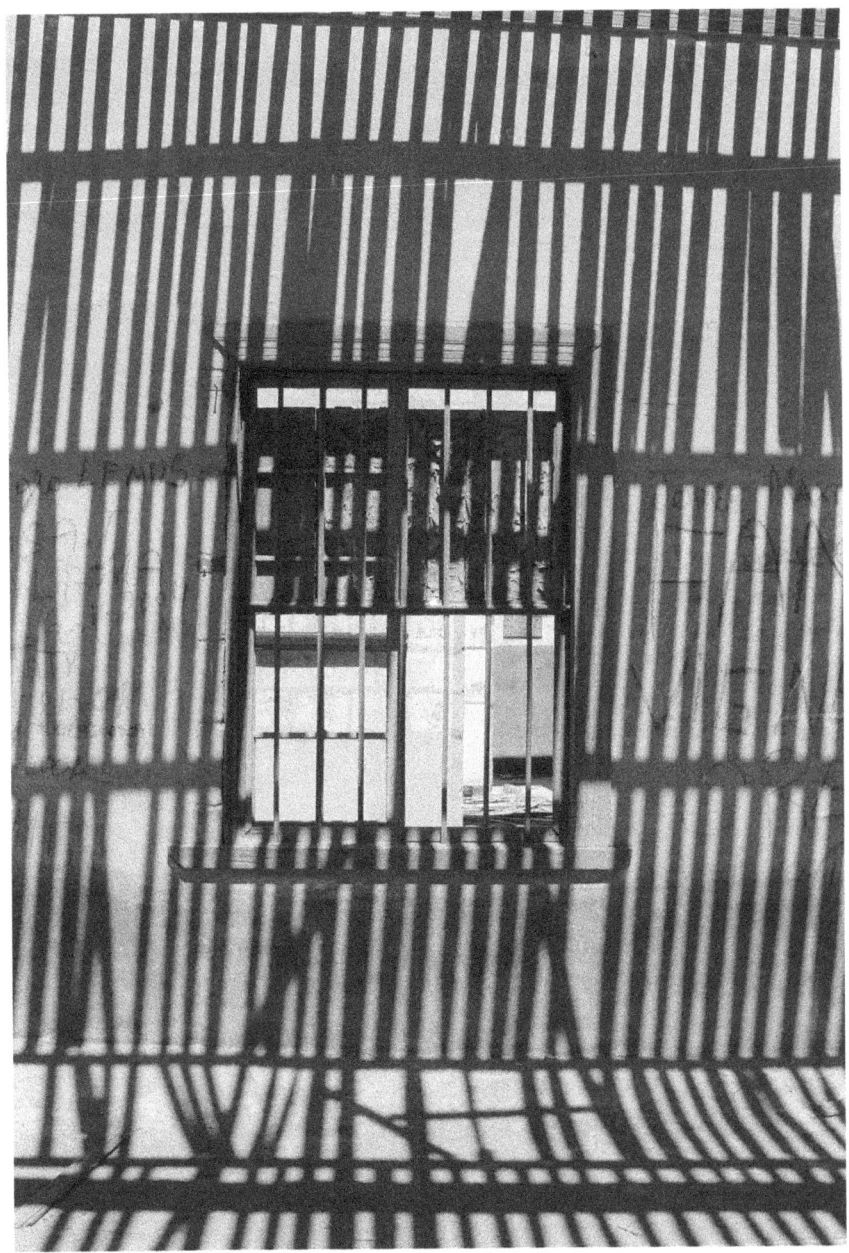

FIGURE 1.3. Chacabuco shadows. Source: Vikki Bell.

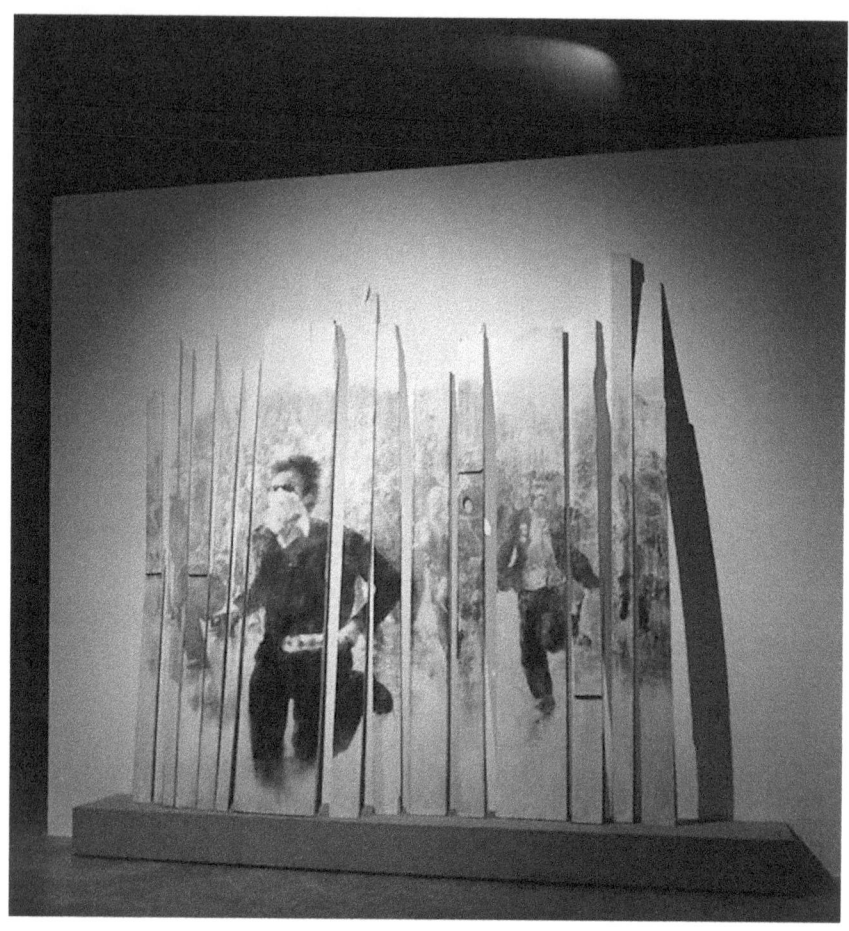

FIGURE 1.4. Graciela Sacco, *Adelante,* from the series *Cuerpo a cuerpo.* Heliography on found wood, 1995/2012. Source: The artist, with permission.

The story of Chacabuco as an *oficina,* a village complex built around and for the mine, is told inside the fairly large theater, which stands improbably in the central plaza of Chacabuco (fig. 1.5) and where in a room on the first floor, a small museum displays old photographs, objects, and information sheets about the village at the height of its production. But the museum is not functioning as such. Despite the smart facade of the building that makes the exterior imposing against the skeletal remains of the mine and the mostly crumbling buildings that sprawl away from its central square, these efforts of only a few years ago have been halted. There are no personnel here, no

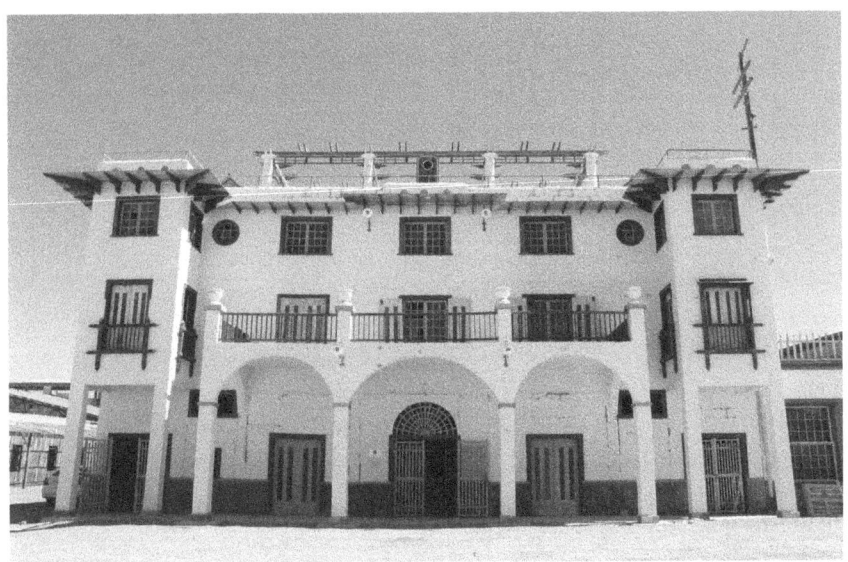

FIGURE 1.5. The theater in Chacabuco. Source: Vikki Bell.

one at all in fact, as we wander between the glass cabinets covered in dust with their contents dislodged, some having suffered damage. The project of memorialization that is announced by a plaque declaring that the building was declared an historical monument in 1971 has been halted; the plaque itself was affixed to the exterior in only 2010. (Unlike the external signpost, it does add the additional information that Chacabuco was used as a camp for political prisoners in 1973–74.) This relatively recent project clearly aimed at restoring the theater, included the restoration of the wooden bench seating, the repainting of the murals above the stage, and the hanging of the claret-red velvet stage curtains. But the painted scenes of green fertile landscapes and women dancing the cancan are in stark contrast to the air of neglect about the place. So much is broken, creaky, and tattered; it is becoming-ruin. The blustery wind that courses through the theater causes the curtains to billow, and catches a roofing sheet of corrugated iron somewhere backstage, which bangs intermittently like the stamp of an animal in pain.

Clearly these restorations were abortive attempts to preserve the history of the "white gold" period (between 1870 and 1929), when the nitrate mine was in full swing and the enormous sales of potassium nitrate—an excellent agricultural fertilizer widely imported into Europe and the key ingredient of explosives in high demand in World War I—brought wealth to the

English-owned company Lautaro Nitrate Company, to the nearby towns of Antofagasta and Iquique, and indeed the whole of Chile.[4] In the foyer there are several tall posters that reproduce old photographs of the mine, workers in long-sleeved shirts, sometimes overalls, and an assorted array of hats, posing with machinery during various stages of the process—drilling, exploding the caliche,[5] lifting it up on cranes, transporting it on lorries, crushing it—and of the commercial village of Chacabuco, with impressive shop fronts and modern motorcars of the era. We step out onto the stage. Someone has written on the wall backstage in felt tip pen: "How beautiful to remember the times of our parents and families. How we struggle to achieve lives like theirs. The mines of the pampas: Historical Monument. 2/11/05."

One of the glass cabinets in the abandoned museum collects objects from the period, including tins of condensed milk, beer bottles, clothes, a set of dominoes, details about the Chacabuco hospital, and several handbills from the theater itself, advertising plays and silent films that were shown there. Quotations from oral history interviews made in 2004 describe the dances with live jazz bands and orchestras, and the visit of the tenor Enrico Caruso, which drew crowds across the desert from other Oficina, filling the square in front of the theater. One image in particular catches my attention. "Masquerade at Coya Office," a photograph from 1913, shows a group of men in fancy dress standing in front of a banner held by a young boy: "Viva El Carnaval" (fig. 1.6). They are men of all shades, dressed as clowns, priests, conquistadors, some holding instruments (a guitar, bandolin, lute). They are posed, unsmiling—no doubt the photographer required them to hold such glum expressions so that they would not blur the image, but they look exhausted, and one suspects not from entertaining but from the grueling labor—and they stare out at us here as if to defy the accompanying text that would have us see them as an example of "men's strength, imagination, creativity and adaptability, both with regard to developing a new industry and to being able to survive the harsh environmental conditions inherent to the medium in which the mineral is produced (extreme thermal variations, great luminosity, intensive working hours etc.)."[6] The creation of cultural forms—forms of sociality created against the backdrop of such conditions—are described in the text accompanying the image as "heroic": "Men and women from all over the world participated in this heroic deed, shaping a culture of their own from which stems the 'Pampas Feeling' represented in innumerable works."[7] The photograph, in other words, both confirms and questions this narration of events, working as Adriana Cavarero has said of the photographs in Sebald's majestic novel *Austerlitz*, where the inclusion of

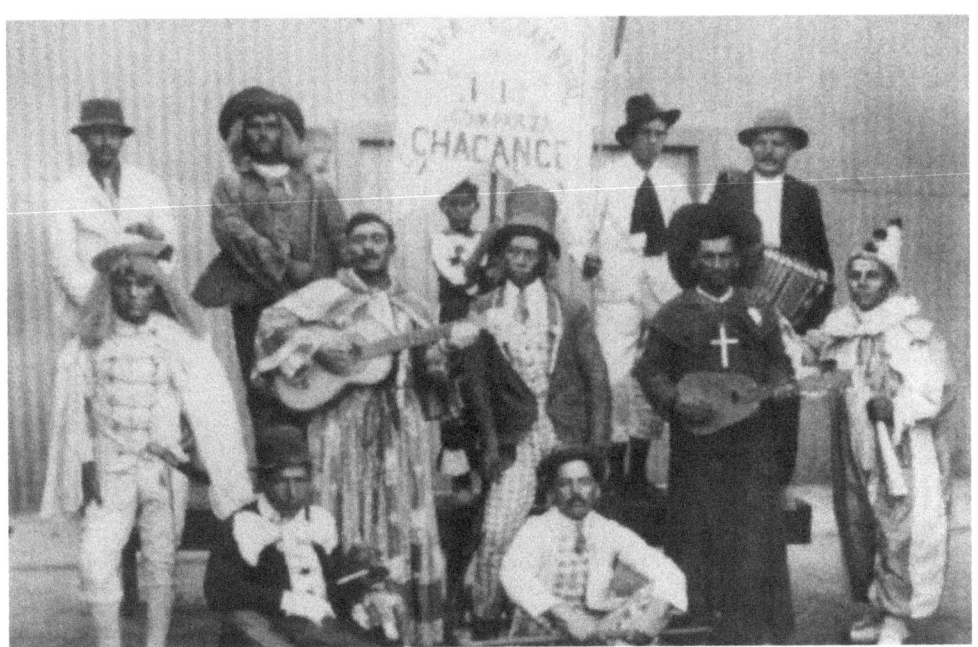

FIGURE 1.6. Masquerade participants at the Coya Office. A photograph from 1913 on display in Chacabuco. Source: Vikki Bell.

photographs provides "validation" for the "truth" of the story being narrated, while also "allowing an inquisitive gaze that questions the narratability of this very story."[8] While Sebald has argued that narratives rely on the passage of time, and fiction must move through time, there is a power of pictures to seemingly "stem the flow of time," interrupting, displacing, escaping. The workers were organized at their entertainment, but likewise, they gathered themselves to listen to the leaders who organized the unions in order to protest the conditions of their labor, their effective imprisonment in the oficinas *salitreras* from where they required permission to leave, where sanitation was lacking, where their payment took the form of vouchers that could only be exchanged in the town's shops.

The implications of this tension between the narratability of stories and that which halts or punctuates it takes on greater resonance still insofar as Mario and I are here in order to seek out the history that brought us here, across ocean and continents, that is to say, the more recent history that saw this place used as a detention camp during Pinochet's regime. In the theater building, this narrative is struggling to be heard, eclipsed by the heroic

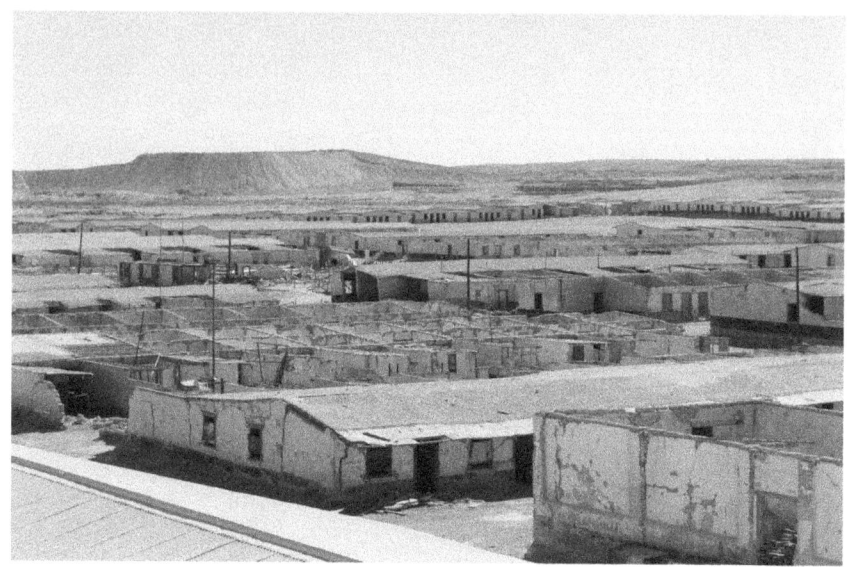

FIGURE 1.7. Chacabuco, view from the theater rooftop. Source: Vikki Bell.

narrative of the mine and workers. The museum's focus reaches back past the 1970s, through them, as it were, and trains the eye and imagination on the white gold. From the very top of the building, risking stepping out onto the unrestored roof that gives in places and scares me a little, I feel nevertheless that I am taking photographs of a detention center (fig. 1.7), haunted as I am by the images my research has formed in my imagination. So poised, I am "looking for signs."

Habla por sí mismo

I had not visited Chacabuco before, but I had entered through that same entrance gate imaginatively; I had seen Chacabuco full of political prisoners in 1974, had "met" them through the screen. The film *Yo He Sido, Yo Soy, Yo Seré* (Heynowski and Scheumann, 1974) is a remarkable document, breathtakingly bold in its undercover documentation of the prisoners held in Chacabuco.[9] The East German filmmakers used footage shot by Miguel Herberg,[10] who had gained permission to enter the camp from Pinochet himself, on the ruse that the film was going to show the world that the camps were not as terrible as they were portrayed. The permission was granted but stated explicitly that the film-makers were not to speak to the prisoners; however, by placing the letter together with other documentation granting the right to fly up to the north, and correctly betting on the authorities not to check the papers too closely, the guards were tricked into not only allowing the camera in, but also allowing the prisoners to be filmed. They were even able to conduct short interviews with them.

The interview with Allende's doctor, Danilo Bartulin Fodich, who was taken prisoner the day after the attack on La Moneda, is alone testament to the suffering caused by indefinite detention. The filmmaker's seemingly simple questions reveal its physical and psychological effects:

INTERVIEWER: How long do you think you'll be here?

FODICH: I don't know.

INTERVIEWER: What do you do in the camp?

FODICH: I'm in charge of medical care in the clinic we have here.

INTERVIEWER: Are there many patients?

FODICH: We treat a population of 850. More or less, we see between thirty and forty people daily.

INTERVIEWER: With serious illnesses?

FODICH: The most important are neurosis, psychological infirmities . . .

INTERVIEWER: How do these manifest?

FODICH: In insomnia, restlessness, trembling . . .

INTERVIEWER: What do you think has provoked these illnesses?

FODICH: The situation in which we detainees are held. And the uncertainty about our cases.[11]

Remarkably, even at this point in 1974, the film's approach is not simply to denounce the regime for its incarceration of these men and the lack of process. Or it was not *only* a denunciation of the cruelty and injustice of what was happening to these men and at that time. There was also a thesis argued through style, a multilayered approach to storytelling that posed the issue of time as a complex theme. *Yo He Sido* is quoted by the magnificent *Nostalgia de la Luz* (2010), but its approach was also clearly a direct influence and forerunner to Patricio Guzmán's later film, as both play with the same "crystalline images," as one analysis describes it.[12] Both films capture the sense in which, although time divides—as the actual present appears but passes, while virtual pasts are preserved but unactualized—at a certain point their distinction becomes "momentarily indiscernible."[13] Like the moment in jazz improvisation when several musical ideas may exist potentially, before just one of those is played, the desert holds many stories that can be told. To understand the Atacama landscape as archival is to hold it up like a crystal, turning it in the light to consider the lines of enquiry it holds in potentiality. Thus does *Yo He Sido* see the story of Chacabuco the nitrate mine and the exploitation of the workers, whose labor was relentlessly hard and barely recompensed, refracted through the contemporary conditions suffered by the political prisoners. These older stories of laborers "arise like stones from the quarry," the voice-over says, creating Neruda's "comrades of the spade." Even in this extreme moment, even considering the risk the filmmakers took to enter the camp in order to prove the prisoners' detention without due process, the film becomes a story entwined with that of the earlier exploitation of the laborers. The relation between the two films is prefigured then in *Yo He Sido* as it itself references "back" not only to the archive images of the workers, through shots showing the remains of the abandoned mine, but also through interviews the filmmakers sought out with an elderly man who had worked in the mine and another who had worked there when only a child. *Nostalgia de la Luz* is indebted to this older film, and thirty years later elaborated its theme, approaching the Atacama Desert as an archival landscape, turning its stories to create refractions, allowing resonances to arise between the women who search the desert for the bones of their disappeared relatives, the observatory where telescopes are trained on the stars, and the geological and human histories that lie beneath our feet.

Like the photograph of the workers who made carnivals during the time of the mine's operation, *Yo He Sido* shows the prisoners in Chacabuco engaged in creative pursuits, particularly woodwork, carving, and making. In an interview with the filmmakers, the military officer in charge of the detention camp, General Lagos, calls it "recreation" and implies this is a sign of humane treatment. But the prisoners describe it as a way to survive the boredom and pointlessness of each day. One artwork and one prisoner that the film returns to several times, and that act as something of a leitmotif through the film, is a sculpture by Orlando Valdés. It consists of the handle of a spade that he had found in the camp, which he placed in a wooden display box of some sort, and attached to it a metal tag with someone's name on it, another found object. The filmmakers ask him what the sculptural assemblage means. Valdés replies "it speaks for itself" (*habla por sí mismo*), perhaps an evasive response to a film crew coming into the camp, about whom the prisoners knew nothing, nor whether to trust them nor for whose viewing this film was being made.

This response points to the role of such creative works; while they blatantly fail to *speak* for themselves, they gather and give form and duration to concerns of present and past. Valdés's response was remarkable therefore for its unintentional mimicry of the filmmakers' own crystalline approach to the different stories about Chacabuco to be preserved and to be held together until such time that they might be told. For while the sculpture absolutely could not speak, it nevertheless "proposes," as Isabelle Stengers might put it, and was an explicit attempt to put things in relation, to create an assemblage that would provoke viewers—whether in the present or future—into thinking how multiple pasts leave their traces. His evasive nonresponse, moreover, suggests that how one chooses to articulate those pasts, how and when one chooses to respond to them, is not only a question of one's ability to disentangle stories but also a question that involves an assessment of risk.

Caretaking

As it turned out, Mario and I were not the only ones in Chacabuco looking to preserve the more recent story of the political prisoners. Walter Robertson is the caretaker, the man who had waved us in and whom we met again when we emerged from the theater and its "museum." A local man, he tells us he has stuck it out here where previous incumbents had had to admit defeat. He is happy to greet us, to welcome us, to extend his hospitality to showing us the sites of Chacabuco *qua* the detention center. We jump into his jeep and drive out along the dust road past several empty rows of little mud and brick houses, staring blankly out, one after another, to the first site on his "tour," followed of course by the dogs—one is Walter's own, the others are strays, driven to Chacabuco and abandoned there, Walter believes, because they know he's there: the caretaker.

We stop outside one of the little squat houses, to all appearances the same as those in their rows all around us. But inside, there is a surprise. One wall of the small front room has been transformed into a three-dimensional mural of a church amid a few small houses that resemble those of Chacabuco. It is made in mud and painted white and red (fig. 1.8). Walter explains that one of the inmates, whose nickname is "Caliche," returns to Chacabuco intermittently to repaint and repair this mural. A work of restoration, taking care of a past one might assume he would rather forget, which stands in remarkable contrast within the context of the whole complex, which is falling into ruin,

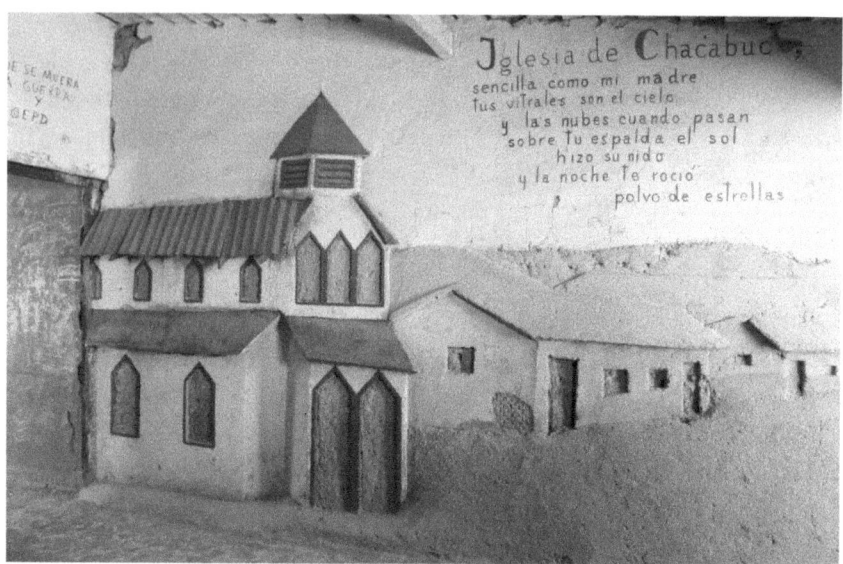

FIGURE 1.8. Caliche's church mural. Source: Vikki Bell.

mostly becoming rubble. The condition of the mural suggested the ongoing care that a promise to remember requires. We were moved by this endeavor, but we had questions. Not least, who was this inmate who found it so important to return to this remote setting to invest time in what appears as an artwork within a confined space of an abandoned town? They have become friends, Walter says, reaching into the car to retrieve some photographs of the two of them together. We are amazed at this returning prisoner, caring for the place that was his cell; we are surprised to see his photograph, him smiling and joking with Walter, sharing an *asado* (barbeque) at this site where he was held for the best part of two years. Walter is proud of his friend's artistic talents, also showing us photographs of the sculptures that Caliche made in the central square. Only later do we come to realize this is the same man who appeared with his sculpture in *Yo He Sido, Yo Soy, Yo Seré*. But in Walter's telling this is not a heroic narrative. It is a passing on of the joy of friendship. Walter wants to share this story; he is positively bursting with the pleasure of being able to tell these visitors from distant countries about their friendship. "You should meet him," he says. "I'll call him!" And he takes out his cell phone and calls the number. We are introduced and the phone handed over. We arrange to meet in Santiago the following Wednesday "at the new Museum of Human Rights," suggests Caliche. Such a story must be passed on, we agree, must be gifted, the task of preservation attempted and its passage facilitated.

The next stop on Walter's impromptu tour is more tricky, more testing of politesse, and of the positionalities we occupy. A short ride away from Caliche's church, another small house on an abandoned street bears a polished metal plaque, recently placed there by the detainees of Chacabuco survivors' association. An improbable little green velvet curtain, held up with pink plastic wire and tied with string, frames it. It tells a tragic story, as it commemorates Oscar Vega González, who was detained in this house and who committed suicide here on November 22, 1973. He was an older prisoner, aged sixty-seven at the time, and was, shockingly, also a former worker in the Oficina and had lived in Chacabuco with his family at that time.[14] The plaque names the various workers' organizations that he had been part of, but it also names the cause of his suicide as the depression that resulted from the physical and psychological mistreatment he received during his imprisonment.

Walter wants Mario to try to feel the ghost of Oscar. "Stand here," he says, positioning Mario in the center of the room. "Close your eyes," he instructs, "can you feel it?" Mario stands there a while, but shortly he has to step aside, gently shake his head and say "no," smiling, his negative response qualified and nuanced in gesture and tone. Mario understands that this is a scene in which a gift is being given, a story which Walter wishes one not just to hear from him, but to feel. It is not only the gift of hospitality from one to another who wanders unannounced, as we had, into his home; it is also a ghost story, and as such, it is a challenge to our modes of accounting for how the past, including how the dead continue to ask questions of us, how their stories can intensify our sense of our selves, achieving a connection and even a quickening of hearts.

The distinction at stake is not between the existence of ghosts and reality, but about how we express that "haunting." As Vinciane Despret would say of her work on how the dead are kept in relation to and by the living, there is no either/or, but an "and and": no either/or between "is it my desire or *really* the dead?"[15] Perhaps we need not impose any hierarchical order—certainly no dichotomy between rationality and enchantment—on the different ways we offer the dead another mode of existence? That is, the living continue to act toward the dead, whether that is by the "reality" of a life gone but remembered as stated on the plaque—"Su recuerdo permanecerá por siempre en nosotros" (Your memory will stay with us always)—or by the sense of a presence at the site of death implied by Walter's request. Or indeed the visual verification sought via the shadowy photos that he later shows us on his phone, sent by visitors who believe the images capture glimpses of ghosts. Even, one must surely add, the research project in which we are engaged, offering further passage for the stories to be shared in different forums elsewhere. This is our task, to preserve and to share, but also to put these things in relation in order to make our own propositions. Since none of this—the images I take, the "presences," nor the bald materiality of the place—will tell alone. The bullet holes in the walls of buildings do not tell the story of how they appeared there; we need Walter to weave the story—as told to him—for us. Similarly, the canteen area that has largely collapsed bar a few wooden poles sticking up out of the ground—together Walter and Caliche were beginning to rebuild it—is merely a collection of wood and poles until a narrative or proposition does that joining for us, until Walter explains it was the canteen, and until Caliche, as he will, fills the site with his memories of the prisoners gathering, socializing, and strategizing there. It is "rubble" until it becomes inscribed, animated, by and with those who care to sustain this past, those who take care of the words and images they make of it.[16] And, of course, those who care to listen. Each of these stages is slippery and complex, fraught with issues of composition, of how each element is put in relation, how it is brought to presence, of reception, how and where it is received and able to be preserved, and of ethos, the atmosphere and ability for an ethical subjectivity to be creatively inspired and forged in its light, as it were.

Before we leave Chacabuco, Walter shows us the sculptures in the square in front of the theater, made by his friend. Maybe it was at this point that we realized that Caliche was the very man who made the sculpture in the 1974 film. The arms of a small tree reach up and the head of a human figure has been carved from the tree trunk; the head tilts slightly to one side. It is somewhat reminiscent of Edvard Munch's 1893 *The Scream* and I see here the figure of a man being tortured (fig. 1.9). Yes, Walter confirms, it is a monument to those who went through that pain, a depiction of the military's behavior standing in the broad daylight of the square, one that Valdes was only able to get away with by insisting that it was obviously the figure of Christ. Carved on the sculpture is "Orlando Valdés 'Caliche' 1974": His sign, his (counter-)signature.

But *That* You Cannot Forget: The Interview

Those who read or listen to our stories see everything as through a lens. This lens is the secret of narration, and it is ground anew in every story, ground between the temporal and the timeless. If we story tellers are Death's Secretaries, we are so because, in our brief mortal lives, we are grinders of these lens. —JOHN BERGER, *Our Faces*

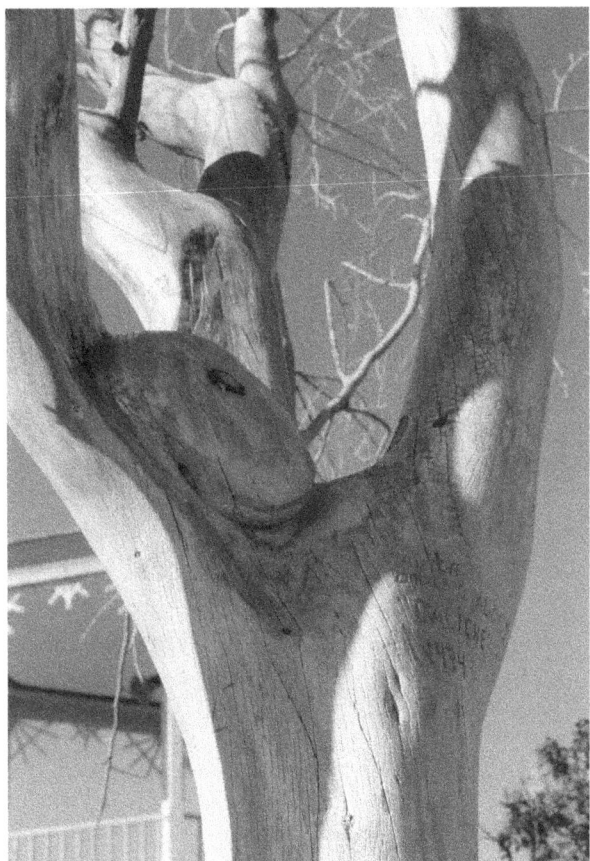

FIGURE 1.9. Caliche's tree sculpture. Source: Vikki Bell.

When Walter Benjamin suggested that the gift of storytelling requires not only the teller's many abilities—he mentions to "preserve and concentrate" the story's strength, to rid the story of any accompanying "explanation" or "interpretation," to coordinate eye, soul, and hand in the telling—he also proposed it as a listener's art, one which requires the somewhat surprising qualities of "relaxation" and its accompanying "self-forgetfulness."[17] Only by relaxing is the story impressed on the memory of the listener, such that, while all stories carry the traces of their tellers "the way the handprints of the potter cling to the clay vessel," the listener is able to retain the story and effortlessly pass it on in his or her own retelling. Benjamin writes: "This then is the nature of the web in which the gift of storytelling is cradled."[18] A storyteller receives a story, but the retelling is not an attempt to convey "the pure essence of the thing, like information or a report. [Storytelling] sinks the thing into the life of the storyteller in order to bring it out of him again."[19] Unlike novels, for

Benjamin, stories do not end, they are passed on, and they continue to provoke questions.

This web of receptivity and generosity, of attentiveness and relaxation, gifting and receiving in Benjamin's account of the storyteller also infuses Donna Haraway's recent writing, especially of her use of the metaphor of string figures, the "cat's cradle" game that becomes central to her argument, enabling her to weave her thesis together with the arguments of Isabelle Stengers, who writes: "[in cat's cradling, at least] two pairs of hands are needed, and in each successive step, one is 'passive,' offering the result of its previous operation, a string entanglement, for the other to operate, only to become active again in the next step, when the other presents the new entanglement. But it can also be said that each time the 'passive' pair is the one that holds, and is held by the entanglement, only to 'let it go' when the other takes the relay."[20] Haraway seeks to encourage a thoughtfulness about how we inherit the entanglements of our current times, seeing in Stengers's argument a resonance with her insistence that how we receive, our response-ability, can be thought not as a passive inheritance, but as a creative ethical enterprise.

Meeting Caliche outside the new, and very large, Museo de la Memoria y Derechos Humanos (Museum of Memory and Human Rights) in Santiago, Chile—the meeting place he chose—was an opportunity for his story to be told. He is smiling and jovial, and he has a surprise for us; he is accompanied by a friend of his, Luis Mondaca, who was also imprisoned in Chacabuco and who is going to help tell their story. Mario and I are keen to become "all ears," to be attentive and prompt as little as possible in order to allow the story to flow. This is our interviewers' stance, the element of passive "receiving."

As in my initial epigraph, Caliche retains an astounding ability to retain a joyous wonder about the world; these, his very first words to us—"the stars are amazing"—are infused with his openness to the beauty of the natural world, as he recalls the moon and stars that guided the men at night and that they even studied, during their time imprisoned in the desert. "[With the astronomy professor imprisoned with us] we'd even have astronomy classes at night with corresponding sticks laid out. . . . We would lie down on the ground and we would mark the movements of the planets."[21] His wish to connect with us through this experience of the constellations seen from the desert indicates his commitment to maintaining a sense of wonder in the face of adversity, something that has been said of critic John Berger.[22] Like Berger, one senses that Caliche has a strong attentiveness to place, and performs with his returning to Chacabuco a repair work which is not—or not only—a kind of therapy for himself, but is also an enactment of forgiveness for the place itself. Caliche forgives Chacabuco, and even cares for it, as if it is for him a sad misfortune that the old mining village was enlisted into this role. To give his time and attentions to the church and other structures, still, is not only to preserve something of their time there as a history lesson for future generations, but also an act of creativity motivated by something both more gentle and profound, a treasuring of a precious but transient life amid the timelessness of the stars and planets.

In the interview, it is striking that the two men settle into telling their story by reference to peoples and stories that one might consider on the face of it unrelated to their imprisonment, but that, having seen the film *Yo He Sido, Yo Soy, Yo Seré*, one recognizes as a similar gesture of connection—and of political solidarity—across temporal contexts. They speak about the contemporary situation of the Mapuche people in Chile, whose land rights are not recognized, and of past workers of the oficina *salitrera* at Chacabuco, who suffered hardships and injustices:

CALICHE: To come and work in any of those company towns was like working in a prison. Why? Because they would pay them with vouchers. They could only buy things that were sold there . . .

LUIS: So if there were wage increases, they'd simply put the price of sugar up . . . compared with the coup (the 1973 *golpe de militar*) there is freedom in the streets but you're taking away the workers' rights to better themselves, to demand better working conditions.[23]

The link with their own experience of the place is made by drawing the stories of these earlier lives and hardships through time, and through the shared experience of an attempt to survive, the infinitive becoming a mantra. Luis says, "Like those workers, we were living in order to survive. Our sole aim was to survive, during the dictatorship, to feed ourselves and to survive."

Luis and Caliche were taken to the National Stadium in Santiago in the early days of the coup, among the estimated 12,000 who were held there between September 11 and November 7, 1973.[24] This is where they first met, in the cramped conditions of the locker rooms where prisoners were held, some 150, in Caliche's estimation, in a four-meter-square space. "We slept like a collection of spoons" Luis tells us: "somebody would get cramp, and then they'd . . . shout out and we'd [all] turn over!" At the start of the interview, Luis and Caliche speak about the stadium in terms of these cramped conditions, and the lack of food: "There was insufficient food. We had to steal food that was meant for the soldiers . . . with the danger that they could shoot us if they saw us."[25] Caliche went fourteen days without eating, Luis ten days. It was only at the end of the interview, perhaps because the men trusted us or perhaps because they wanted to be sure we understood the seriousness of the crimes the Pinochet regime committed, that the men returned to the topic of their imprisonment in the stadium to tell us about the torture they suffered there. Luis recounted:

> They put me on the *parrilla* [the grill] and then the *submarino*. There was a barrel full of sewage, all the waste matter was there. What was I going to say? [to their request for names of others] Nothing. I would faint. I would just hold my breath and just faint. There was a doctor there, a doctor who would check us and would examine us if we were passed out. And the doctor would say—there's an expression in Chile—"this one is faking it!" [¡se está haciendo!] And they would do it again, and then leave me hanging.[26]

Luis says he tried to distract himself, to remove himself mentally from the pain: "When I was hanging, I would pretend that I was at the beach. My body was hanging but I wasn't hanging like that."[27]

This experience of extreme physical torture was followed by the deep anxiety of not knowing what was happening, whether the torture would be repeated, whether one would give in: "It was the uncertainty of knowing if they would return or not. Keeping that all inside you, questioning yourself, 'What will become of me? I am [to survive] or I am not. What condition will I be in? [Will I] spill the beans or keep things to myself?'"[28] Luis was adamant that he owed his life to those who did not mention his name under torture, and he tells us how he used his strategy of detachment to survive even the most extreme pressure, including mock executions: "[At the police station where I was first held] they said 'OK we're going to execute you, what do you want to say to us?' 'Nothing, nothing, I have nothing to say.' [At those times] my family did not exist for me anymore, because if I detached myself, through my thoughts, from my family . . ."[29]

Caliche also reports that he was made to suffer one of these simulated executions:

> When this happened to me in the stadium, I had my eyes covered so I couldn't see anyone, I heard someone say "OK with this one, execute him, this one has to die!" and they made me walk 10m to a wall. . . . And somebody beside me said "Son of mine, confess! Why are you going to die for others who are guilty? Say their names! You're going to get yourself

killed." So I would [say] that I know nothing, so don't ask me anymore. I was ready to die. So I hear "Aim! Fire!" And I hear the rifles fire. I hear the banging, the explosion, but I am still standing and I am still there! And I begin to hear noise. These guys haven't killed me!" [Laughs][30]

Caliche laughs at the end of this terrifying account—typically, as he laughs often. The two men work together like this, moving the story along by moving us through different emotional reactions. Throughout the interview, Caliche often speaks in this anecdotal form, recounting scenes and tales of how the prisoners "spoke back" to power, recounting how the men somehow forced the military guards to recognize their common humanity, or how they managed to laugh amid the worst of circumstances. Luis's role differs; he wants to be sure that they do not underplay, and that—despite his friend's emphasis on the resistance and the absurd, often perverse, situation—we understand those worst experiences, those that aimed at breaking their resolve. For him, the way he was forced to witness the torture of others was unforgettable:

They took me and made me do a tour around the stadium, around the *caracol* [a circular building known as "the snail" where torture was conducted]. . . . They would lift my hood for me to see and I saw children, girls of 16, 17, 18 years old. There were these milk bottles with a mouth like this [showing the shape with his hands] full of rats and they were placed against their vagina. Dogs on top of women, on top of men, sons on top of their mothers, on their sisters. I was seeing how they were all being sexually abused, made to do sexual acts, against the university girl students.

And they also made me see where they would yank the nails out, where the electrical prods were used [to electrocute people in different parts of their body, including] in the anus, women always in the vagina, on the breasts. They made me do this tour, and then they said, "Now we're going to massage you." I suffered more seeing [the others] than what they did to me. When they put me on the *parrilla*, when they beat me up, when they hung me. That was small. What hurt me most was to see [the others].[31]

According to Luis, it is the memories of such suffering that stay with him and also with others who were subjected to such witnessing, including those who have not been able to regain their mental health as a result, and many more who suffer inwardly and silently. Luis tells us: "Many of us who saw, [and] who lived, cannot leave our memories behind. [Some] go crazy. [There's no] forgetting. [Some continue] to say nothing of what happened in the stadium and when they were in prison. *Compañeros* . . . who accompanied me to Chacabuco, these guys haven't even told their children or even their wives all that happened. [Men held at] the Technical University, the Stadium of Chile, the National Stadium and Chacabuco, their families know nothing, nothing. They have remained traumatized. But *that* you cannot forget."[32]

As the two men share the telling of this tale, they confirm and add to each other's account, occasionally correcting each other, or breaking off to discuss the sequencing of events or updating each other on the current health or passing of a comrade. Theirs is a shared history, and the entwined telling—"two pairs of hands are needed"—suggests they are happy to help each other convey, check, and confirm its sense and sentiment. Indeed, it's as if they concur, performatively, that the telling of their story is too delicate an art not to craft together. It is a shared story, but it is also a shared life story, and as such requires an art that, as Cavarero has put it, should seek not to capture its meaning, but "to reveal the finite in all its fragile uniqueness and sing its glory."[33]

Upon arrival at Antofagasta, a town on the northern coast of Chile, and after an uncomfortable three-day journey by sea, the men were disembarked and then suffered another uncomfortable journey in cramped train carriages before arriving at the camp, where they were stripped naked and assembled on the football pitch, their clothes and few belongings in piles in front of each of them.[34] "We were received by Carlos Humberto Minoletti, then captain. And he welcomed us newcomers with punches and kicks. He beat the shit out of us," reserving particular insults for particular prisoners, striking each as he did so.[35] To the history professor, Mario Céspedes Gutiérrez, Minoletti said he was going to teach true Chilean history, not the "crap you teach on television and in the universities."[36] To Ángel Parra, musician and son of Violeta Parra, he said that he was going to teach them true folklore—"not the shit you sing" but the music of Los Huasos Quincheros, the neo-folklorists of Chile, who sang what Luis describes as "the 'postcard' version of Chile, about the *campesinos* sowing in the fields who had to toil so there would be blond shafts of wheat."[37] And to them all, Minoletti said that if anyone were to contemplate suicide, to be sure to use two blades: "'Be sure to cut your veins well because the desert has a thirst for communist blood. Make sure you cut the veins because otherwise we'll kill you ourselves.' That was the first day."[38]

After these insults and beatings, the men collected their belongings, now scattered around, and carried whatever they could—"some wore several layers of clothing" even in the heat of the desert—to where they were allocated their houses in the rows of workers' housing, wondering where they were and how long they would be held.

Oscar Bonilla, the minister of interior defense, visited Chacabuco and came to the men gathered in the canteen: "He told us, 'You're not political prisoners, you're hostages to what happens outside of this regiment. You'll be the first dead.'"[39] Caliche explains: "He said, 'If a military personnel dies outside, ten of you are going to be shot. For each one of them, ten of you will die.'"[40] The men recalled this as a moment of "honesty" but its effect was to send a wave of anxiety and fear throughout the prisoners: "Rumors spread: 'They are going to kill us.'"[41] The anxiety caused by these rumors was awful, Caliche remarks, but Luis is quick to explain that the men's response was to work to lift the mood; he gestures towards his friend with pride: "The ingenuity of the Chilean is represented in my friend, Caliche!"[42]

Caliche smiles and takes on the story, explaining that he had a friend, another Luis, called Luis Cabezas, who he had met at the National Stadium. Luis suggested that in order to lift the spirits of the men, they should perform some comedy sketches together: "make people laugh. Laughter is the best medicine for everything."[43] At first the men performed at meal times: "Every afternoon we would tell a joke and people would laugh. That's right. But we started running out of jokes [laughs] and we started asking other people to come up and participate. . . . There were people who could recite poetry. . . . we formed an orchestra, 'Sounds behind bars' [Sonores entre rejas]. . . . There was a lot of music, *cumbias*, music to dance to, but the principal part was the comedy . . . me and Luis Cabezas. We dedicated ourselves to it."[44]

The two of them were given stage names: "[Someone] said, 'Hey you can't keep performing without having a name, guys!' As the pampa produces caliche, so my *compañero* was called Pampa and I was Caliche. Pampa and Caliche. That became the act [laughs]."[45]

With much merriment, Caliche recounts the organizing of the shows with comedy and other sketches. Astonishingly, General Lagos, the first general in charge of the infamous "caravan of death," was interested in these shows, and called Caliche out of the camp—"calling me 'Calichito' with much affection"—to ask if the prisoners would also perform the show for the military troops in the old theater which was outside the permitted area for the prisoners.[46] Caliche agreed to repeat the show for the troops, but only if the prisoners could also attend the show for a second time in the theater. So it was agreed. The first show included a farce about Tarzan, Caliche remembers, and the *compañero* who was playing Tarzan swung around the theater on a rope, going higher and therefore faster than he meant to do, swinging out of control, to everyone's amusement. "As he passed by, he was calling 'Stop me! Stop me!'" chuckles Caliche. The prisoners also played tricks on the generals, fixing the raffle so that they would win the prize, which turned out to be fictive and worthless, and arranging a sketch about fortune telling which was making a joke out of the fact that the camp had informers (from the notorious DINA) within it.[47]

> We dressed up as gypsies who were going to predict the future. We invited people onto the stage to sit at the table [and] to ask us some-thing. . . . Whatever they asked, we responded, "You're going to soon be leaving, going to your freedom" or "Don't worry, you're going to be liberated!" or "Your wife hasn't cheated on you!" . . . Just things for fun. . . . But we had already prepared a bucket full of water. And we had arranged that someone would come on stage [as if he were a volunteer], and ask, "Has anybody infiltrated Chacabuco?" and we replied, "If any-body has infiltrated the Chacabuco prison camp, let a drop of water fall."
>
> So this guy sat at the table and asked, and we pulled on the string . . . and a bucket of water soaked the guy and even the general sitting in the front! [Laughs].[48]

The sketches were of course a means of survival in the camp, a group activity that reveals something of the negotiated relationship of the prisoners to the military guards, as well as of the mutual support, the improvised social-ity, the prisoners gave each other. In relation to the first of these, both Caliche and Luis offered accounts of how the prisoners were not infrequently kindly to the military guards, passing up kettles of hot water to those guards on duty in the watchtowers in the winter, playing a game of football together—which the prisoners easily won since they had professional players among them—and even trying to help save the life of a soldier who shot himself, as there were several doctors and surgeons among the prison population. Caliche re-marks: "We changed some of the military's minds about us . . . because we, the political prisoners, made a queue to donate blood, to save this military guy. It was impossible to save him, though."[49] The guards rotated every fort-night, however, and the official stance, that of officers higher up, would "re-adjust" the attitude that had become too friendly, so that the prisoners were again subjected to humiliations and "demoralized" by the military.[50]

As for the prisoners, their mutual support took numerous forms, as they tried to maintain their resolve. The sketch-shows were one such, music was another, as was the making of the wood-carvings such as those shown in the documentary (some are now held in the Museum's collections).[51] Caliche taught woodwork to many prisoners, and there was even a little industry that built up whereby the military personnel would sell the pieces at the market in Antofagasta.[52] But the prisoners also organized themselves in other ways, in order to maintain their sense of dignity and purpose. Luis explains the way they organized themselves into a political structure:

The logic of the army was "raise the morale and then drop them." To keep them just alive. . . . We, being conscious workers, being committed activists, being militants of different parties, nevertheless managed . . . to make a *consejo de ancianos* [agreement, as in the French revolution]. So the camp became organized into battalions—each of the rows, about ten houses, would be a battalion and each one of those had a representative who went to the *consejo de ancianos* to represent the battalion. There they elected a leader. And that was Mariano Requena [who had been Allende's personal physician], the first leader. . . . It was a democratic organization, it could have been anybody . . . but we had to be strategic. [Requena] was worldly and he knew how to speak to authority.

Such organization, and such commitment to surviving the ordeal of imprisonment, was also evident in the mutual care and concern the men showed each other in terms of mental health. Caliche explained that in the wake of Vega's suicide, the men became vigilant, and if there was concern about someone who was potentially falling into depression they would endeavor to lend him supportive companionship.

When he started forming and painting the church relief in his cell, Caliche reports, the men thought he was spending too much time alone, heading off as he did after midday lunch to continue his project. But when they discovered his endeavor, it became a communal project, and the men worked together to mix the mud and to paint the relief of the church on the side of the room. Luis was one of those who helped. It was, he explains, a way of surviving, of leaving a trace of something, creating a picture that they believed would help their story circulate. They would attempt to sustain and inspire the other men, saying, "The world is not going to . . . forget you. Throughout the world [people will remember] the prisoners of this concentration camp, the prisoners of Chacabuco. . . . That [church] is a postcard [*postal*] from Chacabuco sent out to the world."[53] It was, in other words, a form of archiving, a mode of preserving something from their experience, maintaining it so that it might be continually "posted" forward so that their stories had the chance at least to be considered into the future. Without explicit content, without being explicitly documentary, the making of the mural was a task imbued with an archival spirit.

A high boost to morale was received when the prisoners were visited by Cardinal Silva Henríquez, "the highest moral authority" in Chile at the time. He inaugurated and blessed the house where the church was constructed and received gifts from the men. "I gave him a crucifix made out of wood that Caliche helped me make and form," reports Luis.[54] Moreover, Luis reports that Silva Henríquez had defied Pinochet in choosing to be at Chacabuco with them, sending a delegate to represent him at an international event taking place simultaneously in Santiago hosted by the Pinochet military junta. This affirmation was felt intensely, because to have such an authority attend to them as valued members of a community reaffirmed the sense of belonging that the military regime was attempting to quash; the shock of the violence and expulsion meted out by Pinochet—the attempt to rescind their membership of the citizenry and indeed their very humanity by removing them en masse—was somewhat ameliorated by Henríquez's visit, affirming for a day at least their sense of being Chilean subjects of concern to its religious if not its political authorities.[55]

Furthermore, the visit was in the context of the work of the Vicaría de la Solidaridad, the important human rights organization set up by Silva Henríquez, who organized for the families of the detained to visit them in Chacabuco; the organization sought to defend their cause during Pinochet's regime. For this struggle and labor, undertaken on their behalf, the men feel profoundly indebted. Likewise they are in awe of the brave campaigning efforts by the families, especially by the women: "The most important combatants were our women—I'm speaking of my mother, my sister, Caliche's wife and the elderly women who cared and who fought during the whole dictatorship, with little money they . . . The elderly women were very combative. My mother, her relatives too I think, they marched in protest to La Moneda, were in front of La Moneda with the widows of those executed and disappeared."[56] While he himself survived by imagining himself unbounded by his intimate relations, Luis's relatives protested his plight not only as one of hundreds, but also in all his uniqueness.

Concluding Remarks

What makes a narration a political act is not simply that this narration invokes the struggle of a collective subjectivity, but rather that it makes clear the fragility of the unique. —PAUL A. KOTTMAN, "Translator's Introduction" to Adriana Cavarero, *Relating Narratives*

Although we don't imagine ourselves anything as accomplished as Benjamin's storyteller, Caliche and Luis's story felt precious, unforgettable, and certainly one beyond, as they put it, the knowledge offered inside the museum walls; it was meant as a gift to be gifted on to others. It is important, Luis remarked, "to get as many people as possible to know that Chile is not simply a remote long skinny country . . . [but] that we are people who have lived a history and that the survivors of the dictatorship are still combatting and continuing the struggle . . . our truth which cannot be negated . . . because we lived it . . . we shared it."[57] We keenly feel this responsibility to "take the baton" in Stengers's sense, not just for the story to be set against the ruination of the world (in Hannah Arendt's phrase), but also because its careful entanglement of affect, memories, facts, and calling out of named others must not be dropped because of a failure on our part. Sociology, typically, involves such retellings of stories; there is a necessary reweaving or reemphasis that writing about their story entails, a reorientation in order to "grind the lens" for readers to receive the story of Chacabuco, as gifted to us by Luis and Caliche.[58] To pull the story through the mists of time, away from the shadow of the destructive violence of the Pinochet regime that threatens to capture it, is central to the sociological task, especially as there are multiple stories about the camp of Chacabuco that risk not just fading in the course of time but being eclipsed by other accounts, as our trip there suggested. Caliche and Luis are acutely aware of this potential for resistance—which turns on the incommensurability of discourse and life, or discourse and a life—that offers the possibility of inserting a different account. Furthermore, insofar as they tell the story, together, and with such attention to detail, such honesty and humor and sense of purpose, helping each other do so, they simultaneously act as witnesses to each other, as much as do Mario and I. They imply something interesting about this period of their lives. They imply that although of course they can speak for themselves, they prefer that the story is recorded as a joint effort, they prefer in a sense not only to "speak for themselves" but to speak both *of* others—of the workers in the mine, the Mapuche, their fellow compañeros—*and in front of* others. Their stories articulate a profound ethical responsibility that arises from the implicit understanding that since one's existence is both a belonging and an exposure to the world, one's autobiography necessarily takes a relational form.[59] To tell one's story, as Cavarero has argued, is a form of self-creation that will be about others, and that requires others in order for it to be told, even as the telling produces a uniqueness for the self. Indeed, her thesis is that if there is a human desire to hear one's life story told—so that another might offer the confirmation without which the autobiographical impulse is suspect—nonetheless as the tale of one's life unfurls, one can certainly make a political intervention, archiving a collective experience, a collective struggle and subject that also contains the tale of a unique existence.[60] Similarly, one might understand Caliche's remarkable efforts to maintain the house-cell and its church mural at Chacabuco as a "repair" work that not only asks that the story of what happened there be told, that not only insists that the political prisoners' stories never be eclipsed by the story of the mine—nor indeed vice versa—but also affirms the uniqueness of his own person, his own endeavors. The work he continued to do to maintain it was not to preserve and maintain his mural as it was, as a static moment in his life or in the history of Chile, but it is about marking an experience through which individuals lived, together, at this place, as a reminder of the care and creativity that sustained them amid the darkest of times. As such, it is profoundly oriented to the future, a proposal to keep relating stories.

Caliche, Orlando Valdés Barrientos, passed away in 2019.

2

PAPER AFTERLIVES

On the Archive as Biopolitical Remains

The archive of the Vicaría de la Solidaridad in Santiago, Chile, collects the papers of the remarkable organization that came into existence within days of the coup of September 1973 to aid and support the families of those affected by the tumultuous and violent events. Those who sought its help initially were those whose loved ones never returned after the mass detentions that accompanied the military's actions—the detained-disappeared—and those who had themselves been illegally detained. As the regime's prolonged violent practices continued, the Vicaría helped those affected by kidnapping, imprisonment, murder, forced exile, and "disappearance." Established under the auspices of the Catholic Church by Cardinal Raúl Silva Henríquez, first under the name the Comité de Cooperación para la Paz (the ecumenical Committee of Cooperation for Peace, COPACHI); then, when Pinochet ordered the Committee to cease its operations, reborn as the Vicaría, the organization received the distraught families and victims, offering them legal advice, filing thousands of habeas corpus writs, and helping with housing and giving psychological, medical, and economic support. With its headquarters in the archbishop's palace next to the cathedral in Plaza de Armas in central Santiago, the organization was openly defiant, publicizing its data on the extent of the violence being perpetrated against ordinary people through monthly reports, and seeking national and international support to put pressure on Pinochet's military government. It became a trusted news source for those seeking to understand what was happening in the country, helping to challenge the misinformation that the military authorities sought to circulate. This vital work was sustained by a team composed mostly of lawyers, nuns, priests, psychologists, and social workers; committed and brave, they knew that they were putting themselves in danger. Their offices—some twenty came to be established across the country—were raided, workers were expelled from Chile or refused reentry, and were regularly harassed. The director of the analysis department, José Manuel Parada, was abducted in 1985, and his body, along with two other men, was found by the roadside the next day.[1] When the Vicaría finally closed its doors, in 1992, it became FUNVISOL, the Documentation Foundation and Archive of the Vicariate of Solidarity (Fundación de Documentación y Archivo de la Vicaría de la Solidaridad). The archive has continued to be a crucial source of data and information, holding around 47,000 individual case files and more than 80,000 legal documents. Together with other important archives, it continues to be consulted in legal cases, as well as by families of victims, journalists, and academics.[2]

The FUNVISOL archive is testament to the form of resistance practiced by its workers, a resistance that, in the face of the military regime's attempts to cast out swathes of people from the nation-state, repeatedly reinscribed the victims as members of the citizenry.[3] Maintaining a faith in the social and legal structures that had existed, the Vicaría responded to the dramatic and chaotic events *as if* the rule of law still pertained, filing writs and pursuing cases, acting toward the authorities on behalf of the victims as bearers of rights. Through the careful creation of records and case files that could, crucially, later be recalled, they anticipated the return of values of democracy and human rights that the Pinochet regime attempted to quash. This meticulous work insisted that the victims and their families would not be cast out across the caesura, and instead maintained a mode of biopolitical governance that challenged the regime to answer for its actions and its attack on its own people.

In this chapter I consider how this dramatic situation of violent social change felt from the point of view of those in whom the regime was disinvesting, as it were. Is it possible to read the archive for the traces of what was happening to the social body, to how that was experienced by the victims and their families? What were the effects of this violent period on those whose loved ones were caught up in it, and can we get a sense of their response to it, as well as to the solidarity offered by the Vicaría? In order to do so, I have chosen to focus on a particular case, one that I was introduced to during a visit to the FUNVISOL archive in 2019.

On that visit, the archive manager Marcela showed me a selection from a collection of portrait photographs of the detained-disappeared.[4] With white gloves, she carefully removed each set from its envelope, and laid them out for me, telling their stories as she did so. Eloquently, she explained the circumstances of each of their disappearances, outlining what was known of their cases and where they were related to one another, explaining what those relationships were. One of the first among the several cases that Marcela showed me was that of Carmen Cecilia Bueno Cifuentes, who was disappeared along with her partner Jorge Hernán Müller Silva in Santiago in 1974 when she was twenty-four years old. There were several photographs in Carmen's envelope, reflecting the full and happy life of a young woman: One shows her looking relaxed, sitting on a stool in a rural setting and smiling up at the camera (fig. 2.1); in another she is wearing a bikini posing carefree at the beach; others seem to be professional images, studio portraits taken with attention to pose and lighting. Alongside those of Carmen, Marcela placed those of Jorge, showing him looking smart in a suit, sporting an impressive moustache, or gazing moodily out at us, his curly hair framing his face (fig. 2.2). Intrigued, I requested Carmen's file and began to piece together her story.[5]

In this chapter I will argue that through Carmen's—and Jorge's—files one can trace the ways in which the coup radically attacked and reconfigured people's relationship to the state. Through the archived documents one feels the family's sinking sense of disempowerment, their fury as well as their determination. The family's struggle was a response to the regime's attempt to remove their very sense of themselves as citizens and to terrorize them into relinquishing their status as politically invested subjects. These were battles in which the military dictatorship was attempting to reposition the People, on the one hand, by exposing their flesh to violence through torture, murder, and disappearance, and on the other through forms of disinvestment, nonrecognition, and disentitlement. Read for these traces, I suggest, the archive testifies to the enormous pressure felt by ordinary people who were caught up in the "flash" of power, as Foucault once put it.[6] Having been the People, the bearers of modern biopolitical power, having experienced

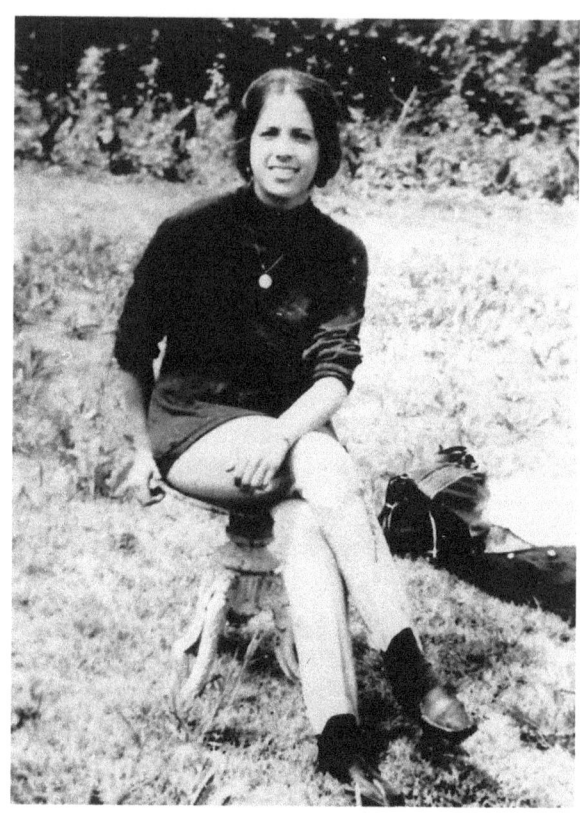

FIGURE 2.1. Carmen Bueno Cifuentes. Source: FUNVISOL, with permission.

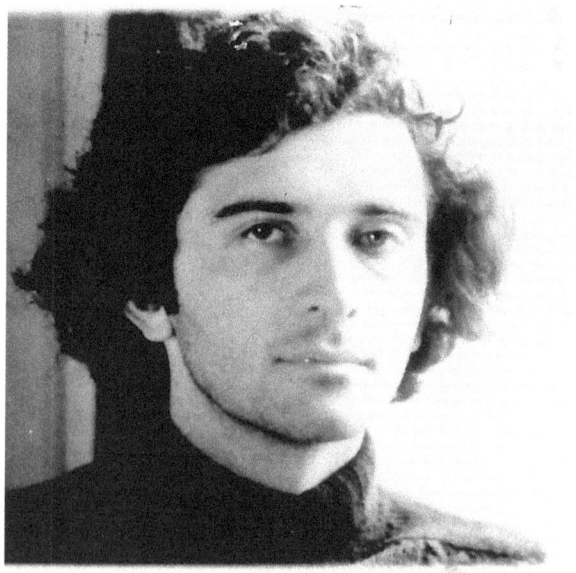

FIGURE 2.2. Jorge Müller Silva. Source: FUNVISOL, with permission.

a modern existence in which they understood themselves as the normative compass of a democratic state, people suffered the shock of the dictatorship's attack not only as the violence that it was but also as a profound distortion of their prior status.

In making this argument I am elaborating upon the suggestive arguments of Eric Santner, whose work has focused, both earlier and elsewhere, on the historical changes that modern governance wrought and required as the sovereignty of monarchs gave way to modern democratic societies. His thesis is that within modern democratic societies, modern biopolitical governance not only disciplines but also *invests* the bodies of those who constitute the People.[7] Indeed, it must so invest the People in order that they comprehend themselves as the bearers of the power that had once belonged only to the sovereign. Post-monarchical societies become modern only insofar as the People understand themselves as the normative compass of their state, as collectively adopting the mantle that had once been the sovereign's alone. Despite its anachronism in relation to the historical period at stake here, this thesis enables one to understand how, when a coup such as the one in Chile sees power "returned" to the hands of a dictator-sovereign, it also necessarily involves a scrabbling back of these forms of investiture. This retraction—like the dissolution of the king's body in Santner's analysis of the transition to modern sovereignty—was fraught and complex, because just as becoming the People required an adjustment to new forms of biopolitical governance, so too the violent removal of that positionality effected a profound change. An attempt to alter Chile at the level of political infrastructures and governance, the dictatorship simultaneously aimed at the level of the flesh in its reordering of people's sense of bodily security, their understandings and their expectations for life. It attacked people's intimate and embodied relationship to their nation-state, resetting it abruptly and thereby creating turmoil, distortion, confusion, and all manner of forms of exposure.

Yet as the dictatorship sought to renege on any democratic notion of the People, to make people relinquish their sense of their rights and most basic democratic values, organizations such as the Vicaría supported those most directly affected, the families of the murdered, detained, and disappeared. As the desperately affecting case of Carmen Bueno illustrates, they refused to surrender their sense of their status in relation to the state. They continued to demand that the administrative, legal, and political structures treat them as citizens and operate according to democratic norms and values.

Paper Afterlife: Carmen Cecilia Bueno Cifuentes, *Desaparecida*

An archive holds only what is archivable, and like the FUNVISOL archive as a whole, the file of Carmen Cecilia Bueno Cifuentes is dominated by legal documents, summaries of the case, and correspondence with governmental and other authorities as the family and the Vicaría sought help and answers. Derrida wrote: "The technological structure of the archiving archive also determines the structure of the archivable content even in its very coming into existence and in its relationship to the future."[8] Fact-driven, with dates and locations, the letters and legal documents are most suited to becoming-archival, and the legalistic narrative is reproduced across the several different forms and documents as the organization repeatedly presented the case. What we can gather from these documents about Carmen Bueno is what can be captured on paper. Indeed, within the archive, Carmen's life becomes a bundle of documents and she, a "paper cadaver," in Kristin Weld's memorable phrase.[9] Yet even within the file, one can discern something of the tremendous shock and torment that the crime of disappearance caused, as well as the determination of the families and the Vicaría workers as they sought to pursue their struggles with the authorities, determined as they were to resist and protest against the Chilean state's kidnapping of their own citizens.

A summary of the case, based on the facts contained across several of the legal documents, was produced by the archive for Carmen's file. It allows one to quickly understand the main facts of the case: "Carmen Cecilia Bueno Cifuentes, film-maker, militant with the MIR [Movimiento de Izquierda Revolucionaria], was detained together with her boyfriend, Jorge Hernán Müller Silva, film-maker, militant of the MIR, on November 29, 1974, around 9.30–10 a.m., in a public street, Calle Bilbao at the intersection with Los Leones, by people in civilian clothes who were traveling in a van."

Over several pages, the summary then pieces together what happened to the pair after their detention on the streets of Santiago and how the pursuit of their cases within the legal system fared. Through the sightings of Carmen and Jorge by other detainees who saw them first at Villa Grimaldi, the notorious detention center on the outskirts of Santiago, and later at another detention center called Tres Álamos, there emerges a sense of their movements and treatment in the first weeks after their detention. Witnesses at Villa Grimaldi confirm the account of where and how Carmen was detained, as well as the fact that she was tortured. Survivors from Tres Álamos reported seeing the couple there, and recall that Jorge and Carmen communicated with each other through signs when the women were taken to use the bathroom. The summary states that when their communication was discovered, Jorge was taken to the head of the detention center, Orlando Manzo Durán, who said they would be punished. Witness testimony states that Jorge had thought this was likely to mean he would be moved to another building within the camp known as Cuatro Álamos. But when he reported to Manzo's office, the situation was clearly worse. Although the witnesses could not hear what was said, they saw one of the officials say something to Jorge that made his body falter in shock: "They saw Müller put his hands to his face and support himself against the wall."[10] Carmen then appeared from the office, the testimony continues, and both were taken away. On December 17, 1974, or thereabouts, three members of the Dirección de Inteligencia Nacional (DINA) known for "transferring" people—a euphemism for murdering— were seen arriving at the camp and leaving with the couple. They were never seen again.

Reading Carmen's file enables one to appreciate the tireless efforts of the Vicaría's lawyers and her family, as they tried desperately to establish what had happened, despite the denials and obfuscatory responses they received from the authorities. As was a common experience, they faced the authorities' refusal to recognize the fact that she had disappeared, or even that she had ever existed. Shortly after her disappearance, on December 7, 1974, her father filed a writ of habeas corpus, a mechanism that is precisely designed so that the people may know that the state recognizes the existence of the body of one of its members, at the Court of Appeal in Santiago. On January 23, 1975, a month and a half later—even though the law stated that a habeas corpus receives a response within six days—the writ was declared "*sin lugar*" (without place) after the military and the Ministry of the Interior sent negative reports to the court, indicating respectively that they did not have her in detention nor had the Ministry ordered her detention. Given these responses, the court forwarded the case to the criminal court to investigate the claims around the "*presunta desgracia*" (presumed misfortune) of Carmen Bueno.

One begins to sense the extreme tension between how the family and the lawyers of the Vicaría approached the case, on the one hand, and how the authorities were responding, on the other. The former's pursuit of the case through the Chilean courts indicates their continued faith in the state's legal institutions to establish truth and to provide justice, despite each effort being denied and rebuked. In words and deeds, they maintained their sense of what should be, what *had been* until very recently, functioning systems of law and justice. And they did so even as these systems were being eroded, and their sense of what Santner calls their "existential legitimacy" was being simultaneously quashed. As the Vicaría and the families of both Carmen and Jorge Müller responded to an increasing desperate situation, following all available routes through the Chilean legal apparatus, the dictatorship undermined the very intelligibility of the social world, that which "touches . . . on one's sense of the coherence, continuity, and vibrancy of the form of life into which one is inscribed and from which one derives one's most basic orientation in the world."[11] Along with the crime of disappearance, therefore, came an attack on those who fought against these brutalities by appealing to the democratic legal institutions as if they would continue to function as they had previously, an attack that was bewildering because it removed the very sense that "one had a place in the world that entitles one to enjoy a modicum of recognition of one's words and actions."[12]

What is exposed, then, beyond the exposure of the physical vulnerability of the body, is the precarious fragility of the democratic order and its structures. Indeed, one could go further and argue that what is revealed is the "ultimate lack of foundation for the historical forms of life that distinguish human community."[13] Certainly the detainees were forced to exist on the threshold of abandonment, reduced to what Santner terms their "creatureliness" as the state retracted the biopolitical forms of "immunization" afforded to its People, and ultimately, in the case of the disappeared themselves, turned its full force upon them.[14] As one reads the statements by some of those who saw her in the detention camps, one has a sense of how—astonishingly—Carmen attempted to maintain her own sense of herself "on-side" in relation to that threshold.[15] In that space, where the "contingent, fragile, susceptible to breakdown" nature of human forms of life were made apparent, the witness statements nevertheless recall vivid examples of moments where, despite everything, the prisoners attempted to retain their hope, and their humanity, through the forms of community still available to them,[16] through friendship, shared communication, even laughter. Fatima Mohor Schmessane, who was twenty-four years old and still being held in the Tres Álamos camp at the time she gave her statement in November 1975, was detained by the DINA a week after Carmen, on December 2, 1974.[17] She was taken first to Villa Grimaldi, where she met Carmen. According to her statement, "There were about eight women, in poor physical condition. Among those I met in the cell was a thin girl, of regular height . . . dressed in blue jeans and an orange top, 26 years old and I knew her name was Carmen Bueno. I made friends with her."[18] Fatima recalls that in the few days they spent together before she was taken away, Carmen was still suffering from the torture she had been subject to some days before by the DINA: "She complained of pain in her vagina, and in her hands." Alongside this horror, however, Fatima remembers another detail that, due to its preposterousness, moved the women to laughter. Carmen told Fatima that she had been accused by the DINA of having bought a dog from Miguel Enríquez, the leader of the MIR (Movimiento de Izquierda Revolucionaria): "They presumed that something had to have been between her and Miguel Enríquez, an accusation that they were creating about her that made those of us who were with her laugh."[19] This image of tortured women sharing laughter confirms tales of solidarity in the centers of detention familiar from other sources.[20] And, I am suggesting, it can be understood as a mode of clinging to one's place within the "juridical order," of refusing to be abandoned to a reduced status.[21] Likewise, another witness, María Antonieta Castro Ramírez, also held in Tres Álamos at the time of the statement, declared that she had met Carmen Bueno in Villa Grimaldi, and on just one occasion, saw her again at Tres Álamos. In a statement that further implies that Carmen maintained some hope and, by attempting to record the duration of her detention and communicate it to others, engaged in practices that affirmed her own existence, Maria Antonieta testified that when she was transferred to a different cell in Tres Álamos, she found Carmen's name and surname "scratched onto the wall, apparently with a pin, and underneath her name there were around six lines, presumably indicating the days that she would have been in that room."[22] If she was reduced to a state of creatureliness, exposed to the "ontological vulnerability" that is not biological but permeates all human beings since we must live within our always fragile forms of life, Carmen was attempting to literally inscribe herself "back" into those forms.[23]

Despite these witness statements, so full of details of a human life, the legal authorities, the Ministry and SENDET—the Secretaría Ejecutiva Nacional de Detenidos, the national prisoners' "service" which was set up in 1973 to coordinate the military government's intelligence services and police—reiterated the negative response to the habeas corpus, plunging the families of Carmen Bueno and Jorge Müller into a peculiar zone where they too were asked to exist on a threshold, simultaneously within and without a state. The creative-destructive power of the sovereign's word is like God's, and when the sovereign figure returns—as, I am arguing, it did in the form of Pinochet—a state of emergency within which "the normal function of positive law is lifted in favour of the king's executive decisions" exposes not only the vulnerability of the rule of law, the exception that had remained within legal jurisdiction, but also the vulnerability of ways of life previously taken for granted.[24]

Remarkably, however, the families of the disappeared continued to act as if the normal functioning of positive law still existed, or perhaps would again exist, even when faced with the sheer mendacity of the authorities. Carmen's file contains a letter sent by the Minister of the Interior to the mother of Jorge Müller, dated July 31, 1975, that refers to an infamous episode in which Pinochet's regime attempted to spread misinformation. The letter was short. It states that in response to the request for information about Jorge Müller, the Ministry "has no register of him and has exhausted all requested lines of enquiry."[25] In reference to Carmen Cecilia Bueno Cifuentes, it continues, "It should be noted that on 23rd July of this year, the press reported that *this person figures in a list of dead extremists* published in Argentina, as reported by the UPI news agency in Buenos Aires on 22nd July 1975."[26]

The reports to which the Minister refers were published in three Chilean national newspapers—*La Segunda*, *La Tercera*, and *El Mercurio*—which carried the story, based on information seemingly coming from Argentina, that several "extremists" had been killed in Argentina. The story named them. The suggestion was that an organization coordinating revolutionary groups had released this information, with the implication that either their deaths were at the hands of members of their own group in a dispute, or that they resulted from wounds inflicted by Argentine security forces who had interrupted a meeting of these "guerrillas." But the circumstances of these reports were suspicious and were immediately understood by those searching for their disappeared as an attempt by the regime to deflect the blame from themselves by suggesting that those considered disappeared had instead fled the country to continue their "subversive" activities abroad. All the people named had been apprehended on different dates and in different parts of Chile, and all were names that had been given to the courts by their families. Moreover, these names were among those the families had sent to the Brazilian press to let the world know what was happening in Chile, and the Brazilian press had also published these names, known as the "119 disappeared," with the story reported widely. The source of the news of their deaths in Argentina remained anonymous and "curiously"—to use the restrained word that Carmen's father chose when he mentioned this episode in his submission to the United Nations later in 1975—the Argentine publication in which the names were initially given, called "LEA," vanished, having only produced just the one edition. As was suspected at the time, and was eventually proven, this was a misinformation strategy, the false report circulated as part of the DINA's "Operation Colombo." A newspaper clipping from 1976 in Carmen Bueno's file gives the sense of how Operation Colombo intended for this misinformation to work in their favor. Giving the names of four people who had reportedly been killed in Argentina, it states that these names are

> among those who appeared in a list of the "119 disappeared" that a Brazilian newspaper put out last year and that was reproduced around the world. There was no end of people who presumed to judge the Chilean authorities for these supposed deaths. . . . But the extremists were alive and agitating in our neighbouring nation. . . . This proves once again, the enormous anti-Chilean campaign. . . . [This year, 1976] the world in general has started to open its eyes and to concentrate its gaze on those who speak of social justice but who have no qualms dominating with blood and fire the people who they say they defend.[27]

It was, as Carmen's father, Señor Bueno, states in one of his letters in the file, a "sinister maneuver," accusing those it had murdered of killing each other.[28]

In a slip that revealed the lie, and must have been terrifying for Carmen's family, the list of those killed in Argentina actually gave the name of her sister, Maria Bueno Cifuentes, who had not been detained and was still living and working in Santiago. The file also contains reports that, without identifying themselves, state agents searched Carmen's mother's home under false pretenses and had arrived unannounced at her sister's place of work to check her identification documents and to intimidate her. The file does not record the family's reaction to the slip or these harassments, but a further official document from the Swiss embassy in Chile, a certificate dated May 31, 1976, suggests their response. It states simply that "Maria Olimpia Bueno Cifuentes has been granted permission to live in Switzerland permanently." Like many Chileans, Carmen's sister felt obliged to leave her country, a country that no longer offered her the "immunity" that modern biopolitical states promise, and chose to flee into permanent exile.

Undeterred by the failure of the legal process, in May 1976 Carmen's father submitted a new habeas corpus (*recurso de amparo*) to the Court of Appeal, this time including the supporting statements of Fatima Mohor and María Antonieta Castro that had not been available to submit with the first writ. And a few months later, in August 1976, the Vicaría asked the Supreme Court to investigate the cases of 383 people, including Carmen and Jorge, who had disappeared between September 11, 1973, and June 30, 1976. These actions both came, once again, to nothing, with the habeas corpus returned negatively and the Vicaría's request denied, appealed, and denied once again. Taking their appeal to a higher authority, to international legal processes, the family and the Vicaría wrote to the UN's High Commissioner for Human

Rights in November 1976, after the Chilean government blithely announced that all detainees held under the state of emergency had been freed, making no mention whatsoever of those who had disappeared. A typed statement from Carmen's father, detailing once again what had happened to her and all of the information about the various legal routes the family had pursued, is in her file. His despair comes through in this statement, despite its succinct and restrained legalistic nature. For example, he writes of the second writ of habeas corpus, recalling that

> the *recurso* was denied, and this on the basis of a single report from the Ministry of the Interior, despite the fact that we didn't approach that authority, since we knew in advance, as did the court, what the answer would be. No, we asked for the court to approach the DINA, since their agents were responsible for the detention of my daughter, and her presence in the centers that they are in charge of was proven. The court didn't want to officiate over the DINA. . . . Again the Court abdicated its responsibilities, [creating] a situation that *asks the most enormous questions about the fate of a young Chilean.*[29]

Señor Bueno seems close to breaking during the course of the writing of this letter. Toward its end, it is as if the realization that the entire legal structures by which he had hitherto understood his family to be protected, by whose norms they had lived their lives, within which even more fundamentally, their very existence was registered, had been spectral. Everything that had secured their sense of themselves, that had held the family together, was being destroyed. During the course of the submission of the second writ of habeas corpus, he writes, the president of the Court of Appeals in Santiago said there was simply "nothing to be done," prompting the profound and terrifying realization that the family could have been talking to "just anyone."[30] The symbolic status of legal authority, in other words, had vanished; the former experts had become merely people, with no more authority or knowledge than the citizens over whom they wielded their power. Exasperated, but still refusing to renege on the possibility of restoring moral rectitude and legal authority, Señor Bueno explains his attempt to reach beyond this nation-state and to appeal at the international level. When the highest authorities within a legal system become "just anyone," he writes, "there is no other course of action but to approach an international commission entrusted with upholding respect for the PRINCIPLES OF LAW."[31] This last phrase was typed in capitals, as if he wanted the typeface to carry the sound of his raised voice and convey the desperation that the meaning of words alone could not contain. Carmen's father's outrage at the loss of the legal system's first principles is clearly felt at the level of the body; it is a profound sense of abandonment. He wishes to bring his desperation to the attention of the High Commissioner, describing his wretchedness as a state that has made living an unbearable, endless struggle for him and his wife: "In Chile there is a denial of justice and an abandonment of those who need it most, the disappeared, those who, like my young daughter, were one day victims of the most illegal form of apprehension and whose fate is unknown to this day by her parents, whose lives have become a permanent battle."[32]

In December 1976 the International Commission of Jurists, based in Geneva, declared that there had been a denial of justice in relation to the case of Carmen and demanded that the clarification of her situation be pursued appropriately in Chile. Obliged to comply, but tardy in doing so, two years later, in 1979, the Minister Servando Jordán was appointed to investigate the disappearance of people detained by the DINA. But the investigation was far from satisfactory. Trying to understand the workings of the detention center Tres Álamos, where both Carmen and Jorge were seen, was met with various obfuscations, including by the former director of the camp, Orlando José Manzo Durán, who was interviewed several times.[33] Repeatedly denying any knowledge of the disappearances or any wrongdoing, he made perplexing declarations such as that they did not beat anyone in the camp "because we didn't have the means for it"; that he did not remember any of those who were disappeared; and that remembering them was not "authorized by the government." He could not recognize any of the photographs of the disappeared that he was shown, he said, because when they were in the camp they arrived "dirty, unshaven and emaciated." While he did keep a register of arrivals and departures, this, he said, had been given to the Centro Nacional de Informaciones (CNI), successor to the DINA, who in turn declared that the books had been destroyed "for security reasons." Faced with some new testimony from Nelson Aramburu, who was detained in Cuatro Álamos with Carmen and Jorge, Manzo denied remembering the couple or any of the situations that Aramburu described. Maybe, he suggested, they had been using false identities.[34]

Such flat denials and dubious suggestions repeated tactics already familiar to the relatives of the disappeared, ones certainly familiar to Carmen's family. A letter that was sent to Jorge Müller's mother, Irma Silva de Müller, in May 1976 sits in his file.[35] There, the Interamerican Commission for Human Rights sent to Señora Müller the answer to the questions they had received from the Chilean government. The government had stated baldly that the names the families had sent had not been detained in the country and neither were they currently detained. They can be presumed, the government continued, "to have gone into hiding voluntarily in order to conduct secret clandestine activities, since several other people apparently disappeared since 11th September 1973, have eventually been seen willfully engaging in criminal actions and some of them have asked for asylum within foreign embassies. . . . These claims are further evidence of an attack on my government and are the work, certainly, of enemies of Chile who wish to provoke concern within national and international public opinion, part of the campaign against the government organized by Marxist elements."[36]

In the press, too, such falsehoods were repeated. In her file, Carmen's case summary records the words of the military judge General Enrique Morel, who stated in an interview in the magazine *Hoy* in October 1977 that in relation to "the 119"—the list of names of detained-disappeared handed to journalists and published in Brazil—"many had been found alive or had been killed by the Argentinian armed forces," a statement about which he said, when Servando Jordán's enquiry later questioned him about its veracity, he had simply repeated from newspaper reports. The Minister of Foreign Relations, Lieutenant Colonel Ernesto Videla Cifuentes, also revealed his own earlier lies when he told the Jordán tribunal in January 1980 that he had not investigated the legal existence of Jorge Müller. Yet in 1976, after the Chilean ambassador Sergio Diez included Jorge's name in a report presented to the United Nations that stated that these people never existed, Videla had written to the German government, responding to their request for explanation, and stated that the inclusion of Jorge Müller's name had been a "lamentable error," promising to look into the reasons behind it.[37] Not least because the military officials closed ranks and feigned ignorance in these ways, the Jordán investigation stalled, and in April 1980 the enquiry declared itself unable to continue the investigation of the disappearance of Carmen Bueno and Jorge Müller, among others.[38]

It is my contention that we can read—and "reanimate"—Carmen's file as the story of the incredible tenacity of those who fought to know what had happened to her and to be sure that the truth of who was responsible became known to all. The fury and the determination that one can detect in even the most legalistic of documents in the file flowed from a sense of what was being taken away from the citizens of Chile at that time, a sense that the very meaning of being a citizen of a modern democratic nation-state was being rescinded. If the files—the affidavits, the letters seeking information, those seeking support, those trying to prove her very existence—construct a "body" of sorts, Weld's "paper cadaver" that lives on in the archive, it is constituted by the remnants of the ways in which citizens become enrolled into the biopolitical administration of modern societies.[39] Many of the archival documents are official documents, with dates and signatures and in some cases official stamps, referring explicitly to institutions and institutional processes that, as Maurizio Ferraris has persuasively argued, inscribe them—both the documents and the people to whom they pertain—within the social fabric more broadly.[40] Official identification papers abound in these files, since in the face of the military government's denials of these persons' very existence, it was necessary for the Vicaría to collect these proofs of the existence of each individual. Typically, one finds copies of passports, membership cards, wedding or baptism certificates, and so on, the various modes by which administrative, bureaucratic, modern societies register, acknowledge, and administer to a person as a member of its various institutions.[41] These are documents that confer membership of the nation-state and as such are the traces of the state's administration of the lives of its citizens; they facilitate what Santner terms the "symbolic investiture" that envelops each member of the citizenry, acknowledging them and making them more than their bodies. Indeed, these biopolitical documents indicate the symbolic constitution, for each citizen, of their citizenship. As such they are the scaffolding of the second of their "two bodies," a body that once only pertained to the king but belongs—or should belong—to the People in post-monarchical modern democracies. "Once the body of the king is no longer available as the primary incarnation of the principle and functions of sovereignty," Santner argues, the symbolic structures and dynamics of sovereignty described by Kantorowicz's famous thesis on the king's "two bodies" "do not disappear from the space of politics . . . rather . . . with all their paradoxes and impasses, [they] 'migrate' into a new location that thereby assumes a turbulent and disorienting semiotic density previously concentrated in the 'strange material and physical presence' of the king."[42] Within secular modernity, the flesh that once "fattened" the one who held power and authority, granting their body a status of sovereignty over all others, is passed to the discourses and practices named—by Foucault and others—"biopolitical," charged as they are with "the caretaking of the sublime (but also potentially abject) flesh of the new bearer of the principle of sovereignty, the People."[43] Thus is each modern individual—those so accepted and granted status as part of the People, that is—invested with an existence through the institutions aimed at giving and preserving life. This "symbolic body" facilitates a life within which one lives and moves, just as much as one's organic body. Each individual is registered at birth, and throughout their life is enrolled in institutions—social, financial, educational, medical—such that these registrations and records confer symbolic membership of that state, creating our social world.[44] And pointedly for our purposes here, this symbolic body inscribes people into normative relations and institutions, offering individuals an existential legitimacy within the body politic. That legitimacy, in turn, and following Lefort's formulation, constitutes the collective body that legitimizes the state, forming the body of "the People" that takes the place of the king's body.[45]

Since the files in the FUNVISOL archive contain these remnants of this symbolic body, the "second" body that biopolitical processes constituted for these individuals, consulting them is to confront how at this point in history, the Chilean state was attempting to render this subset of its citizens *beyond* the People that were its "nation," creating a caesura within the body politic.[46] The rhetoric of enemies of the Chilean state, of subversives, and so on that were repeatedly articulated, accompanied by the obfuscations and flat denials of the existence of these individuals, indicate that all former biopolitical promises, as it were, were broken, and with them any protection that these citizens may once have believed they had some entitlement to. As we have seen, while the families of Carmen and Jorge continued to follow the lines of seeking justice as if the state were still operating democratically—and biopolitically—the refusals and disengagement of the regime can be regarded as so many efforts to place the couple beyond the citizenry. The military dictatorship was withdrawing from the "modern apparatus," drawing back, if you will, into a political theology in which Pinochet embodied sovereignty as had sovereigns of old, leaving these individuals exposed.

The exposure of the couple was mirrored also in their families' exposure to the state's power, a situation that revealed to them the fragility of the biopolitical promise as they too were disposed from their previous, presumed, status as citizens, as protected bodies. The families were in their own threshold state, where although they themselves were not physically tortured, they felt exposed at the level of the flesh. In vain, they repeated their demand that the state give some account of its actions, but their treatment and torment served only to reveal that there was no "immunization" conferred by their citizenship.[47] For this reason they started, as did many others, to seek safety and reassurance by moving their lives abroad, as we have seen with Carmen's sister, who took exile in Switzerland. And since Jorge's father had German citizenship, the Müller family were also preparing to find him safe passage there. One of the most moving papers in his file is the official letter from the German embassy, dated August 1975, stating that if he were to be set free, he would be granted the permanent right to settle in Stuttgart, Germany.[48]

The family had heard that the military government was allowing some of its detainees to be liberated on condition that they leave the country. Clearly, they were starting to prepare another life for Jorge in anticipation of his liberation. This letter, which under different conditions could have been his entry into a new body politic and a new life, remains only a trace of that unfulfilled hope, lying in his file within the Vicaría's archive.

The People, an Impossible Incarnation

In his exploration of the pressures that arose at the historical conjuncture where people were obliged to embody the modern notion of "the People," Santner attends to how symbolic representations constitute a cultural response to the task of living within, or as, the locus of political sovereignty. The abstractions, deformations, and contortions of modernist artworks, he suggests, reflect the complexities of attempting to respond to this historical change. These have continued throughout modernity, as the task of becoming "the People" is never completed. Santner explores, for example, the paintings of Francis Bacon, where he suggests that the theatrical settings that Bacon often placed his most convulsive portraits within—the raised platforms, the railings and strange cubicles—are traces of the dissipating structures of courts and churches that the political and biopolitical structures of modernity were invading and reworking in its experiments with new forms of embodiment.[49] "Together they create a kind of experimental space in which bodies are subject to mostly invisible torments and the viewer is variously interpellated as scientist, tormentor, complicit bystander, voyeur. This theatrical set up becomes especially poignant—Bernstein would say 'histrionic'—when the forces moving through the figure's body seem to push their way out by way of a scream."[50] Santner continues: "Such images create the impression of a body under impossible duress. . . . What I am suggesting is that the pressure at issue here needs to be grasped as testimony to the fact that . . . every head now has a 'body' of its own, one in which the symbolic, imaginary and real elements of sovereignty push against the skin of its bearer."[51] Implicit in this argument is not only the suggestion that modern representations respond to the particular historical conjuncture within which they emerged, a conjuncture that in Santner's thesis initiates and explains modern—especially abstract—art as a response to the irresolvable impasse of how to represent the People, how to adequately "incarnate" their sovereignty without any individual body ever being able to stand in for such a concept.[52] But also, such representations take on an urgency insofar as they function as the means by which individuals make the attempt to inhabit a sense of being the People, creating the milieus in which to explore and experiment with how to comprehend what it is to live as modern beings, what it is to assume the role of the normative compass.

The story of Carmen and Jorge takes on a further important dimension when we consider that as well as being involved in the MIR, they worked in film production. Having met on the film set of *A La Sombra del Sol*, the film whose opening night they had attended the night before they were kidnapped, they were working together for Chile Films at the time of their disappearance.[53] In the context of the political tumult of the early 1970s in Chile, their lives, both as young adults engaged with the political dynamics that were escalating divisions in their country and in terms of their work as image-makers, turned on the fraught question of representation. Indeed, and intriguingly for the argument I am pursuing in this chapter, Jorge had been the principal cameraman involved in the best-known attempt to create a representation of the People during the extraordinary period immediately preceding the coup: Patricio Guzmán's now famous three-part documentary *The Battle of Chile*. Guzmán's team set themselves the task of capturing the political events engulfing Chile as they unfolded, from the bitterly fought elections in March 1973 in which the right attempted to oust Salvador Allende, up to the moment when the situation exploded into the violence of the military coup in September of that year with the attack on the Moneda, the suicide of President Allende, and the widespread use of detentions. As a response to the unprecedented situation, the film captured the chaos and the contortions wrought upon the social body. We will return to these films, but first, I will begin with a lesser-known and incomplete project that the couple undertook at the temple in Maipú.

In Carmen's file there is an unassuming little cardboard document the size of a credit card. It carries a small photograph of Carmen, a headshot, her name, and its date of issue, November 22, 1974 (fig. 2.3)—just one week before she was abducted. It is a work-pass, granting her permission—as part of a film crew—to enter the newly completed Votive Temple of Maipú in Santiago, dedicated to Our Lady of Carmen, in order to film its consecration that was taking place as part of wider celebrations of the Año Santo.[54] An accompanying note carries a logo with the words "Chile: País de hermanos" (Chile: Country of brothers).[55]

On Saturday, November 23, 1974, therefore, six days before they were detained, Jorge Müller was behind the camera and Carmen was with him at Maipú in her role as assistant producer. The ceremony drew large crowds,

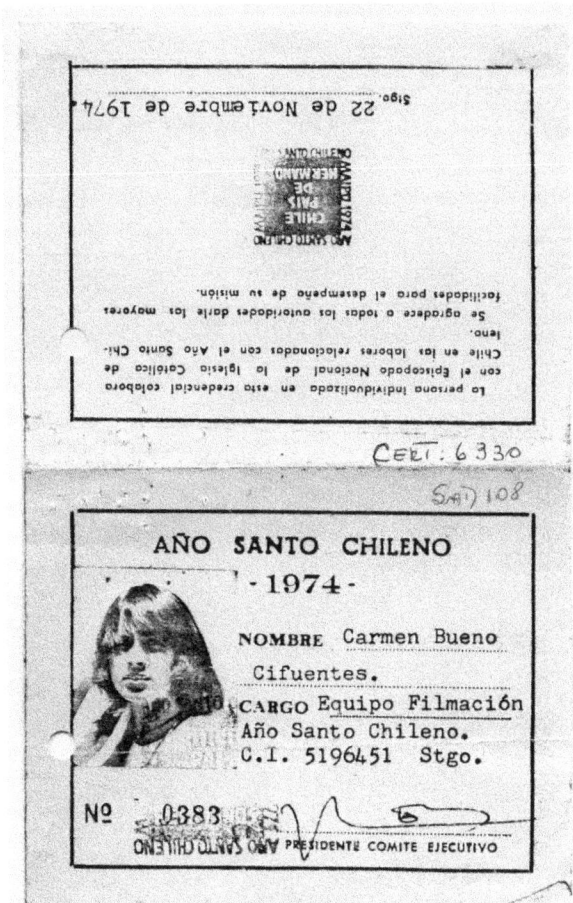

FIGURE 2.3. Carmen Bueno Cifuentes's pass for Año Santo Chileno event, 1974. Source: FUNVISOL, with permission.

and was presided over by the archbishop Raúl Silva Henríquez, who had established the Comité de Cooperación para la Paz just after the coup, which would become the Vicaría de la Solidaridad, the very institution, as we have seen, that would receive the couple's distraught parents after their disappearance. With the benefit of hindsight, it is deeply affecting to watch the rushes of the film that Jorge Müller shot that day, to see through the lens what they both would have seen, and we are able to do so because the footage, which was not edited in the aftermath of what happened, was stored by the sound engineer, Jorge Di Lauro, for several years until in 1989, a short edit was compiled for a television program; it is now available on the internet.[56] The camera follows key moments of the day: the priests laying their hands in cement to make a memorial of the consecration, the large crowd gathering outside the temple, the traditional crafts being offered by indigenous peoples, and the dancers whirling about. The camera finally comes to rest for several minutes on the construction of a towering cross in the square outside the church. In his commentary, Di Lauro attempts to conjure the atmosphere of the day for us, remembering among other things that, despite the fact that he was carrying his camera and filming, Jorge Müller was also singing the song dedicated to Mary, mother of Christ, "Virgin of Carmen, the Star of Chile," along with the crowd.[57] It was an extraordinary day, Di Lauro comments, a rare day of pure celebration, given that it was little more than a year after the coup. The smiling Silva Henríquez led the ceremony, greeting the crowd, and placing his hand on the heads of children as they passed by in procession. Behind him, one briefly catches sight of members of the military, in their uniforms and dark sunglasses. Between their shadowy presence and the celebratory crowd, a box is being carried in order to form part of the huge cross being constructed in the plaza. The camera lingers on the side of the box, which is painted with just one word: "Solidarity." At the end of the fourteen-minute edit, Di Lauro comments that the image of all of the hands of the crowds raised in a gesture of thanks was, and remains, a symbol of hope in the power of togetherness.

If this unity, the crowd as a sea of waving palms filmed by Jorge Müller, is understood as a hopeful representation of the People, it was a moment of collective self-representation that took place against the very particular set of political forces acting upon them at that time. They are depicted enjoying a communion conjured through a shared gesture and a shared Catholicism, enjoined also on this occasion by a national myth of the Virgin's part in Bernardo O'Higgins's victory at Maipú, a story that entwines Catholicism with the emergence of a nation-state against the backdrop of settler colonialism's violence and suppression. Constituted through gestures, faith, and myth, the fiction of the People was being performed and confirmed that day. But given that the people gathered at the Temple of Maipú, were living, like those across the country, in a new era of military dictatorship in which their political constitution as a self-governing democratic People had been dramatically retracted, the scene prompts reflection on how this performance of the People resonated for them within their new political reality. How were they feeling, a year after the coup? How were they responding to the Pinochet regime's claim to embody the true representation of the People's will?

If for the Catholic majority, the church was an enduring source of sociality, offering a representation of unification and a sense of common identity as a People with shared values despite the coup and seemingly beyond the political strife, its articulation of core Christian values of compassion, the sacredness of human life, and solidarity—that word that arises so poignantly in the film rushes—were highly politically charged in this context. That that religious unity also carried the potential to become a political force—including by implication an alternative leadership, one embodied at Maipú by Silva Henríquez—did not escape the Pinochet regime. Despite having the support of several religious leaders and organizations in Chile, Henríquez's ecumenical Comité de Cooperación para la Paz was forced to close its doors on the direct instruction of Pinochet in 1975. Moreover, the role of film itself as a powerful means of representing the People to the people and thereby a mode of serious challenge to the military government, was evidently considered a threat in the regime's eyes. This, one can only assume, is why filmmakers and other creative people were among the groups disappeared.

Jorge Müller was no stranger to these themes. As mentioned, from 1972 until the military coup in September 1973, the period in which the government was being torn apart as members of the Christian Democratic Party frustrated Allende's Popular Unity's plans for the country at every turn, he was the sole cameraman working as one of the small team of four with director Patricio Guzmán on the documentary film *The Battle of Chile*. The film is now a celebrated record of that extraordinarily volatile period in which people were variously called upon to represent themselves in the decisions that would guide the country's future. From all political sides, people took to the streets and engaged in the crisis through strikes, protests, and rallies. During that year, Jorge's very purpose therefore was to try to represent these struggles as the events unfolded, to capture their intensity and their decisive turning points. It was certainly a time when, in Santner's terms, the "surplus of immanence" that had once attached itself to the body of the king got "under the body of the People."[58] Returning to Chile from Madrid—where he had been studying film—after Allende's victory, Guzmán has recalled how impressed he had been by the extraordinary enthusiasm and happiness of the people as a result of Allende's Popular Unity agenda; in both the countryside and the towns, there was a kind of "permanent mobilization, full of joy," a "communal infatuation" that he felt compelled to film. "What is happening is unique, we have to make a film that follows reality to the last detail."[59] A photograph by the Portuguese photographer Armindo Cardoso, who accompanied the film crew as they researched and filmed, conveys something of the infatuation that Guzmán sensed; in it, a small group gathers for the camera in front of their home proudly holding up framed images of Allende and a United Party leaflet (fig. 2.4). Yet as the enthusiasm and happiness on the part of his supporters was met with the fierce opposition of the government's detractors, the resulting film became a portrait

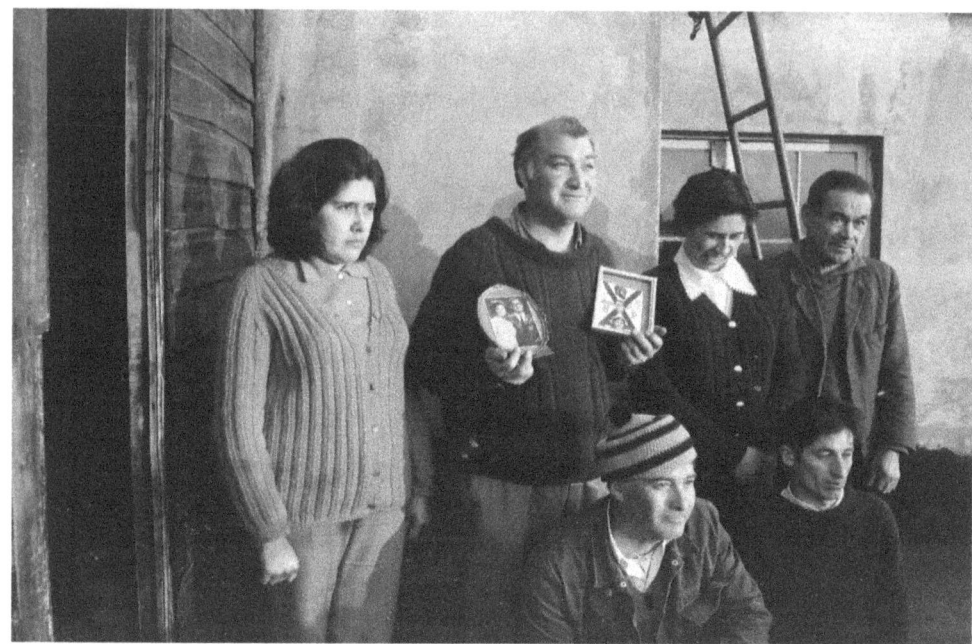

FIGURE 2.4. Family holding photographs of Salvador Allende. Source: Armindo Cardoso/SPAutores, with permission.

of the tensions and distortions as people sought to make sense of what was happening and what their roles could and should be.[60]

For Guzmán, the impossibility of complete representation "to the last detail" was a directorial problem. Unlike a king's procession, where the source of power is visible and embodied within one person, the notion of a People is elusive and dispersed.[61] Guzmán wanted to "let ourselves be led by what was happening around us," but this could not be without a plan, not without directorial decisions about which events were most important and would be able to carry the story. Certainly, he wished to convey "the different layers that make up the society," and to include those from both sides of the political divide.[62] As well as *what* to film, there were also practical and technical limitations: they were only a small team, with just one 16 mm Eclair camera and about one roll of film per day, allowing them just ten minutes filming each day. Despite these constraints, the crew managed to record an extraordinary number of events—demonstrations, union meetings, sessions in parliament, and scenes in the factories—that show key developments that preceded the coup. The cinematography combined long shots, frequently from a raised position

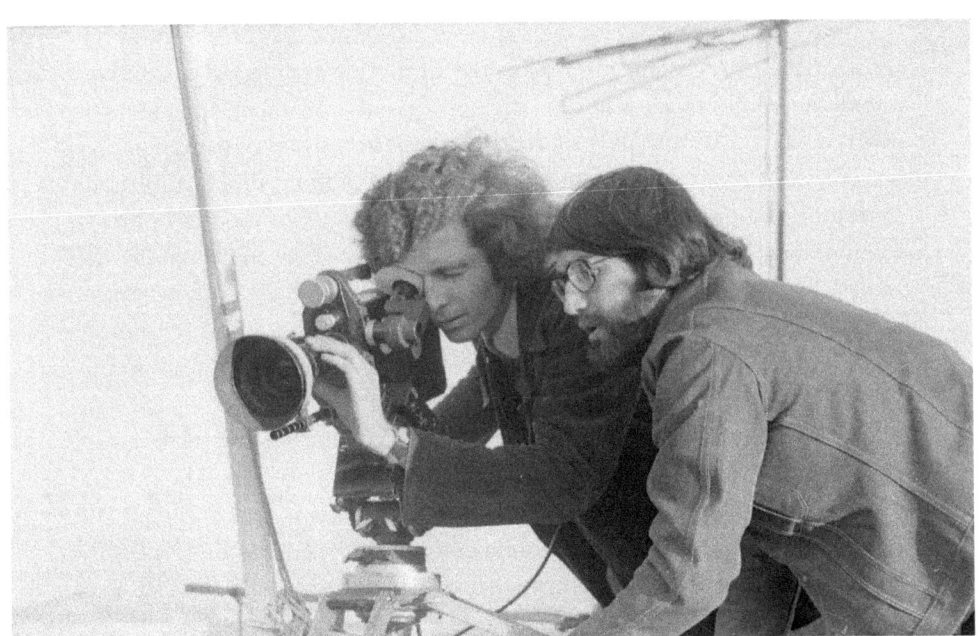

FIGURE 2.5. Jorge Müller with Patricio Guzmán. Source: Armindo Cardoso/ SPAutores, with permission.

that conveyed the scale of the scene immediately, with handheld improvised shots among the crowds. Whether these were groups gathering to make decisions about a shared interest, as with the striking workers, or demonstrations of support for Allende, or indeed protests from groups on the right, including the fascist group Patria y Libertad, many of the scenes in the film were of large crowds. Such demonstrations are by design representations of the People. They are *for* the camera, with banners written large so they can be read—and filmed—from a distance, accompanied by the soundtrack of collective chants, short and repeated, so the demonstrators' demands can be heard. Examples in the film include those for Allende—"We want Popular Power!" "Allende we are defending you!"—as well as the fascist group's call and response: "Chile— Great! Chile—Free! National Front—Homeland and Freedom! Nationalism— Here! Chile—Forward!" A photograph held in the National Library of Chile taken by the Portuguese photographer Armindo Cardoso, who was living in Chile at that time, shows Jorge with Patricio Guzmán filming on top of the Moneda (fig. 2.5); they are both crouched over the camera, concentrating on the task in hand, checking how best to capture the image of the crowd below.

Complementing the scenes filmed from a distance are those shot in the midst of the crowds and groups, as the film crew positioned themselves among the bodies to see and hear the opinions of individuals. This was not always an easy task, and in the footage we are often aware of the difficulties faced by the crew as the camera is jostled, the microphone drops visibly into the frame, and those being filmed react to the camera's presence. In an interview with Guzmán, he shows some photographs of the small team in the process of making the film, including of course Jorge Müller. Of one image, he comments, "I am pushing Flaco [a nickname for Müller meaning 'skinny'] to get him closer to the people, and he is pushing people so they are not in the way of the camera" while "Bernardo Menz [the sound engineer] is also guiding people away so they won't be obstacles for the passage of the camera."[63] These efforts to get closer are also those moments when the camera captures the ways that the political situation was playing out at the level of the embodied subject. Here, the uniformity of the chanting is replaced by various individual responses, and it is also where one approaches the stresses and strains, even deformations, that Santner sees in Bacon's art.

At the opening of the first film in the trilogy, for example, the film crew asks those in the streets of central Santiago for their opinions on the forthcoming election, in March 1973, in which the conservative opposition hoped to receive enough votes to disperse Allende's government. Several reply confidently, practiced in their answers, but a few are memorably overwrought and vehement, such as the woman in cat-eye sunglasses who wants to impeach the president and be rid of the "dirty communists" who are in her staccato words "degenerate, rotten, filthy!"[64] She is the most striking, her anger raising her voice to give sound to Bacon's scream. But there are others. And arguably equally as burdened were those who appear shy, tentative, even giggling at the notion that they are called upon to voice the nation's desire, to *be* the People. Throughout the film, moreover, tensions as to what "representation" means, and what it *should* mean, repeatedly emerge, not only between political opponents but within them, as for example at one demonstration organized by striking miners from one of Chile's important copper mines. When the police seem to withdraw from policing the demonstration, the strikers are confused about where to take their anger, and start to disagree among themselves. Should they keep marching toward the police, who now seem to be retreating, or should they reroute the demonstration toward the offices of the owners of the mine itself? They disagree about whose decision it should be. "Who represents the people?" one of them shouts at the other, immediately answering himself, "We do!," an answer that serves only to reveal the issue at stake.[65]

As a means of representation of the People and an articulation of their struggles and political imaginations, *The Battle of Chile* is not external to the dynamics it captured. Not only did Jorge Müller's task mimic the very problem that democratic systems face—the "technical" issue of how to represent people and movements, how to balance different factions, how to represent opposing political differences while not allowing the result to break down into fractious incoherence—but the film was also a part of the symbolic representation of the people and, insofar as that is true, a means by which people come to understand themselves in relation to the state. Since they were engaged in their own form of representing the People, Müller and Guzmán were operating on the same terrain as the more overtly powerful actors in the history they followed.[66] No greater proof of this is the fact that the film had to be smuggled out of Chile, and after it was edited, was banned in Chile and not shown there until 1997.[67] The film crew were aware of the risk they undertook and, as Guzmán comments, they knew they needed to be discreet, to be secretive about what they were filming and why; they tried to pass under the radar by appearing to be "just a few scruffy kids," not serious reporters. It seems their strategy worked insofar as they were able to gain access to key events, figures, and buildings. Indeed, another series of Armindo Cardoso's photographs shows them left to their own devices relaxing "backstage" in a room in the Moneda. They seem in high spirits between filming; in one Müller stands tall, raises his fist in a gesture of defiance and solidarity, but with a playful smile (fig. 2.6). Nevertheless, they knew they were in danger, and nowhere is this more explicitly conveyed than through the scenes during the attempted coup of June 1973 where they were filming very close to the now infamous incident—with which *The Battle of Chile* part 1 ends and part 2 begins—that shows a member of the military take aim, shoot, and fatally wound an Argentine cameraman, Leonardo Henrichsen, while he was filming.[68] Guzmán, Müller, and the others were only a block away from this incident when it took place.[69]

It is of course impossible to know whether Jorge Müller and Carmen Bueno were targeted for their sympathies and involvement with the MIR or for their work in the field of symbolic representation. Both leftist activists and film directors were targeted in the period the couple were detained, and for the couple, as we have seen, these commitments were bound up with each other. For *The Battle of Chile*, Müller filmed many various meetings of political factions, including a speech by MIR leader Miguel Enríquez. He appears in part 2 of the film, where on July 12, 1973, less than a fortnight after the attempted military coup, his speech was a call for a unity. Addressing a large

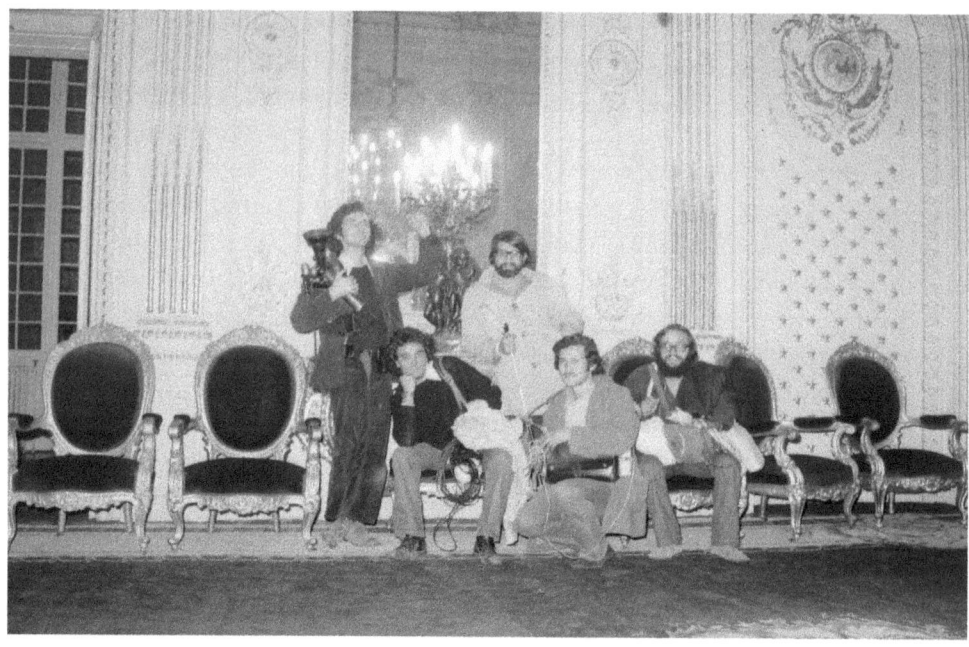

FIGURE 2.6. Jorge Müller raising his fist and smiling in La Moneda. Patricio Guzmán is standing to his left. Other members of the crew are seated: Frederico Elton (producer), Bernardo Menz (sound engineer), and José Bartolomé (production assistant). Source: Armindo Cardoso/SPAutores, with permission.

gathering, Enríquez says: "A single cry is heard echoing in the factories, estates, towns, and schools, in the bastions of the people. The call is to create, strengthen and increase popular power, the power of the community commandos, the power of the workers and the *campesinos.*" In addition, he appealed explicitly to those within the army to defect if fascist elements attempt to take power from the government once again.[70]

Although both Carmen Bueno and Jorge Müller were clearly committed to the aims of social justice, there is little trace of a deep involvement within the MIR in the FUNVISOL files. On an early form on which the Comité de Cooperación para la Paz recorded her case, now in Carmen's file in FUNVISOL, a worker has written in response to the question asking for information on "political activism [*militancia política*] before 11th September 1973": "Sympathetic to the left." But in another hand, someone has later added: "mother didn't know of activism."[71] Of course, parents often do not have full knowledge of their children's activities, but, together with the flimsy

nature of the "dog story," it does suggest that Carmen's activity was more ac-
curately "sympathetic" than militantly engaged. Carmen Castillo, the partner
of MIR leader Miguel Enríquez, has explained recently that the MIR was characterized by its lack of a violent "terrorist" agenda. Despite not taking part
in elections on principle, it encouraged voting for Allende and supported
his government. Under his presidency it became a legal social group that
sought to work for improvement in the conditions of those the MIR called
"the poor of the country and the city."[72] This social work was fueled by "the
desire for social justice" that was "very natural in a bourgeois-intellectual
social milieu," Castillo comments, one she herself came to "naturally at university, where contact with such groups was commonplace."[73] This may be
a description that also helps us understand Carmen Bueno's relationship to
the MIR. Likewise, Müller's parents have been quoted as implying that given
the choice, he would have preferred a day on El Quisco beach to a political
meeting, a comment which is echoed by filmmaker Carlos Flores in an interview in Guzmán's later documentary *Chile, Obstinate Memory*.[74] Flores recalls that "Jorge was not the militant type of MIRista who died in Pinochet's
torture camps . . . between the beach and a demonstration, he preferred the
beach. He liked clothes . . . he was frowned upon at the time when you were
supposed to give everything to the movement. . . . He talked about clothes,
women, wine, they were his little sins . . . he was really a little bourgeois. It
was part of his charm."[75] The director of *A La Sombra del Sol*, Pablo Perelman, ruminates that it was precisely these attributes, his nice, easygoing,
friendly character that may have made him a target: "He was the sort to be
'taken away' . . . to spread terror in a social circle where information circulated well. He was a filmmaker, with filmmaker friends. He was nice. He was
a prime candidate to disappear so people would know and be upset."[76]

The commitment to social justice and against hypocrisy was one which
another MIRista who was detained by the regime at Villa Grimaldi, Carmen Rojas, has suggested the younger generation of that time felt "in their
own bodies." The commitment emerged from struggles that were happening
in Chile and elsewhere: "They were part of a generation that felt in their own
bodies, the struggle of Vietnam, and that vibrated during the anti-imperialist
marches. They found their 'mestizo' and American roots, and thought deeply
about the terms of dependence in order to know why and with whom they
struggled."[77] Jorge's mother has also suggested that it was this goal of freedom and equality that moved him. In a documentary in which she spoke
about his disappearance, Irma Silva Müller (1920–91) remarked: "Jorge was
part of a political movement that wanted to discover the many faces of the

Chilean people."[78] After he disappeared, she decided to continue this social work of his: "I decided to work with poor populations where Jorge was no longer able to do his work. I understand what he was doing." To this end she taught folk music and traditional dancing, to continue his commitment. "I always used to have conversations with him, and he would tell me: 'Mum, they are killing people,'" she tells us. "Then," she continues, matter-of-factly, "they took him to a concentration camp."[79] In the face of the authorities' dismissive response to his disappearance and to thousands of similar cases, she recalls—chiming with the experience of Señor Bueno discussed in the previous section of this chapter—how she became angry: "When they said 'why don't you forget about your problem?' my indignation turned to rage."[80]

To Belie History: The Undead Image

History is hysterical. . . . It is constituted only if we consider it, if we look at it—and in order to look at it we must be excluded from it. As a living soul, I am the very contrary of History, I am *what belies it*, destroys it for the sake of my own history.—ROLAND BARTHES, *Camera Lucida*

In this closing section, I return to the photographs at the FUNVISOL archive that, as I described at the beginning of this chapter, were my first encounter with the cases of Carmen Bueno and Jorge Müller. To follow the places and moments when these images have reemerged is to trace how these archival images have become anti-archival—in fact, they never *were* archival—in the sense that they have themselves taken a role within the dynamics I have pursued here. Indeed, across the decades since they were kidnapped, these photographs of Carmen and Jorge have continued to appear, to participate, circulating in various events and moments, becoming more than records of historical lives. Refusing to be confined to the role of mere archival documents destined for a life as History, they have operated as the "undead,"[81] persisting symbolically beyond the lives that they record, intervening and provoking through their intensity. Throughout the 1970s and 1980s, they joined the many photographs that were an integral part of the families' efforts to resist the Pinochet regime, to circulate photographs of the disappeared in order to challenge the dictatorship's lies and obfuscations. To be sure, this is why they are in FUNVISOL at all. Photographs owned by the families, dislodged from their "proper" place in the domestic sphere,[82] circulated in the public not only to convey the wound that the violence was inflicting on quotidian life, but also I suggest, to insist upon their loved ones' place as precisely part of the social body. Beyond remembrance, since "the disappeared" were not simply those who had died but those who had been targeted by the state. As symbolic forms that persist beyond life, the photographs were deployed by the families who asserted their continuing legibility,[83] making the photographs bespeak their demands as well as their warning. Not least, I suggest, the images repeatedly posed the question of "the People." Who are we, as a society, as a body politic, if these outrages go unpunished? How will we allow ourselves—and each other—to be treated? Who will join us, who will help fight our corner? Who will speak up for us, who will represent us in the demand for knowledge, for justice? The photographs' circulation is not merely a fulfillment of the promise to remember the couple as individuals, therefore, but beyond this, a way of affirming shared commitments and shared denunciations. "Breathed back to life," these photographs are granted *survivance*; they have remained "lively" images with the potential to continue to act in the world.

Art historians may always have spoken of the vibrancy and the "liveliness" of the images they address, but their analyses traditionally embark on a journey away from that life, "deadening" the image, as it were. By contrast, and as I have argued previously,[84] W. J. T. Mitchell's question "What does the image want?" allows for a reorientation of the task, challenging us to focus on the desire of the image itself, asking what it might actively "call" for. Mitchell's proposal is that there is a poetics of the image that allows one to approach it as an "animated being,"[85] a proposal that carries a special resonance in relation to images of the disappeared. Thus while the images of Carmen and Jorge in the FUNVISOL archive are affective in the manner that Barthes famously described in relation to the image of Lewis Payne—photographed by Gardner before his execution, it causes us to "shudder over a catastrophe which has already occurred"[86]—that shudder is surely not the animation that these pictures "want." "What pictures want," wrote Mitchell, "is not the same as . . . the effect they produce." Indeed, he added, images may not know what they want and have to be "helped to recollect it through a dialogue with others."[87] My contention is that these photographs, as they have reappeared in different contexts and forums, have each time circled around the politics of representation itself.

In one of the professional portraits of Carmen in her envelope in the archive, she is looking up and into the distance, her lips slightly parted as if she is about to smile or speak (fig. 2.7). It is an image of a confident young woman, with an air of optimism about her. This photograph was used several times within the campaigns by the Vicaría to draw attention to what was happening in Chile. This image has therefore had a long "after-life," including

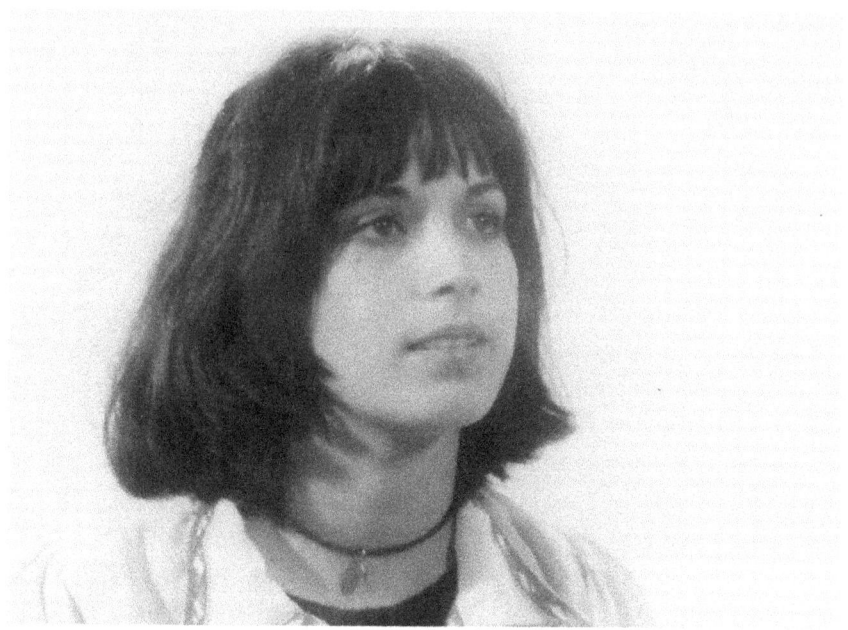

FIGURE 2.7. Carmen Bueno Cifuentes. Source: FUNVISO, with permission.

being reproduced on the cover of *¿Dónde Están?* the publication that listed the disappeared and that was distributed widely throughout Chile to inform people and to protest the growing numbers of people being disappeared. First produced in 1978, this publication reproduced letters from the Vicaría to the Ministry of the Interior, asking for action on the then 433 cases of disappearance; none of the cases was being investigated.[88] A photograph by Marcelo Montecino—the celebrated photographer who also took some important images of the political prisoners at the National Stadium—shows a woman, her own disappeared relative pinned to her clothes, displaying copies of *¿Dónde Están?* laid out in front of her at a meeting in 1979 (fig. 2.8). Asking for solidarity and support, the campaign approached people through their churches and on the streets, tirelessly demanding that these crimes be addressed as such.

The same image was also used on posters and leaflets throughout the 1970s and 1980s, as part of campaigns organized by the families, relatives, and groups including, centrally, the Vicaría. "What it wanted" was to maintain a visibility for these cases, especially since their passage through the legal routes, as we have seen through reading Carmen's case file, were being

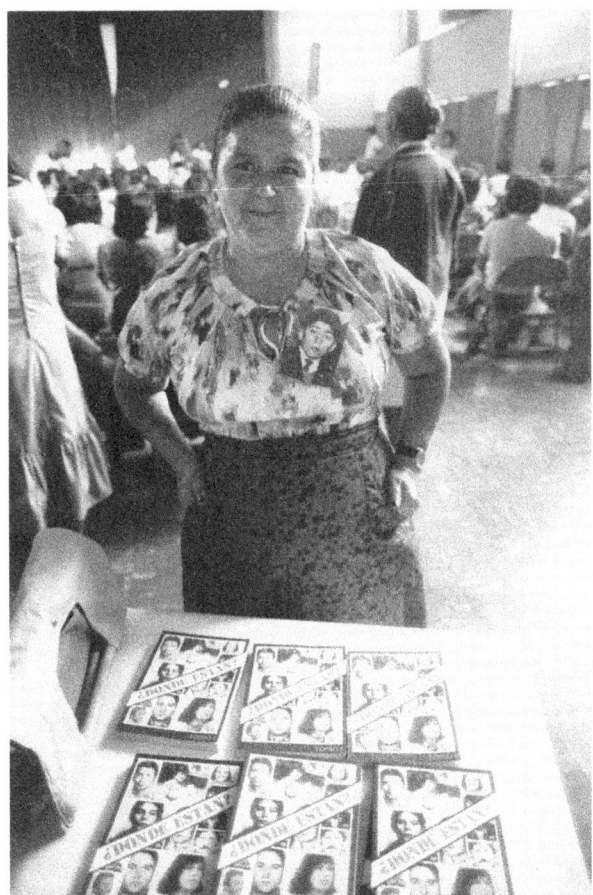

FIGURE 2.8. Woman selling *¿Dónde Están?* reports, with Carmen Bueno Cifuentes shown on the bottom right of the cover. Her son's photograph is pinned to her blouse. Source: Marcelo Montecino, with permission.

continually frustrated by the regime. Given that the lives of the citizens were being so blatantly disregarded by the state, the image appeals to the people beyond—or despite—the state's forms of intimidation. Seeking to maintain a social bond that had been fractured, the photograph requests commitment between people as citizens, as the elusive "social body" that Santner describes. Today, searching the digital catalogue of the Museum of Memory and Human Rights in Santiago, one will find, for example, a photograph of passersby considering a poster pasted to some boardings on a street in the 1980s; testament to the continuing campaigns, under the words *¿Dónde Están?* are photographic portraits of the disappeared, with Carmen's image visible on the third row. A similar photograph of her, presumably taken in the same photo-shoot, was also used on the poster that the Agrupación de Familiares de Detenidos-Desaparecidos (Association of Relatives of the

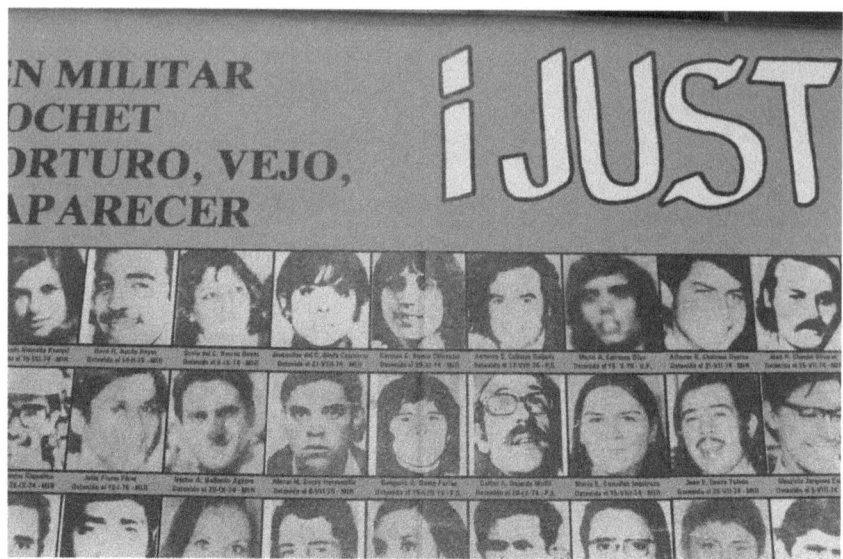

FIGURE 2.9. Poster by the Agrupación de Familiares de Detenidos Desaparecidos in the Museum of Memory and Human Rights in Santiago, Chile. Carmen Bueno Cifuentes appears near the center of top row. Source: Vikki Bell.

Detained-Disappeared) made in 1987 as part of their ongoing campaign to keep the issue in the public eye (fig. 2.9). It reads: "Pinochet's Military regime detained, tortured, abused and disappeared them: Justice!" Underneath it notes that the people depicted are those listed as disappeared in 1975 and 1976, "the 119" as they became known, but that hundreds of other "compatriots" had also suffered the same fate.

At the Museum of Memory and Human Rights, this second poster appears as part of a display concerning the role of the media during the dictatorship, to explain the contested context in which the images had to assert themselves into public space; it hangs alongside reproductions of the newspapers that printed the misinformation about the dead Marxists and "MIRistas" I discussed earlier in this chapter. By contrast to the newspapers, the 1987 poster describes the photographs as precisely "Chilean *citizens*," enfolding the disappeared into the social body. That these campaigns were challenging citizens to continue to include those targeted by the regime is also explicit in the use of Carmen's photograph in the early 1980s when handbills were distributed in the streets of Chile's cities with the question: *¿Me Olvidaste?* (Have you forgotten me?) (fig. 2.10). As the museum catalogue shows, Carmen's photograph

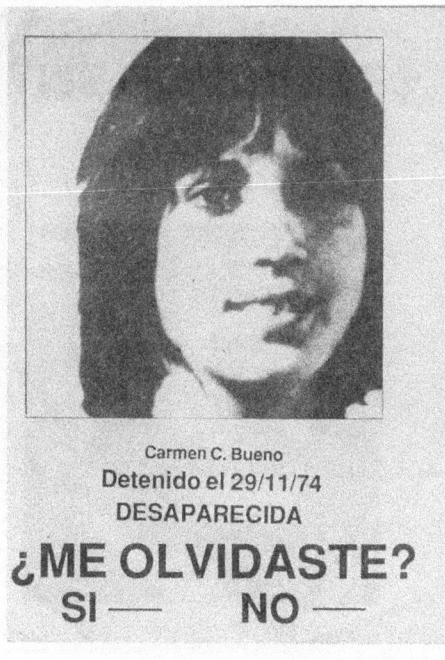

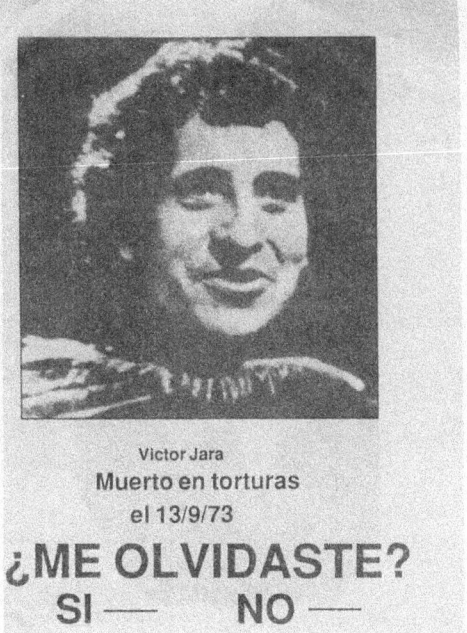

Carmen C. Bueno
Detenido el 29/11/74
DESAPARECIDA
¿ME OLVIDASTE?
SI— NO —

Victor Jara
Muerto en torturas
el 13/9/73
¿ME OLVIDASTE?
SI— NO —

FIGURE 2.10. Leaflet in the Museum of Memory and Human Rights, Santiago, Chile. Source: Vikki Bell.

appears on one side of the leaflet, and Victor Jara, the famous folk singer, murdered at the National Stadium on September 16, 1973, on the other.[89]

Arguably, the museum as a whole is premised upon the need for such a refolding of the disappeared and all of the victims of the Pinochet era "back" into the citizen body, an attempt to claim their place and their value to Chilean nation that was never only about remembering them.[90] In proposing and pursuing the project, then-president Michelle Bachelet was keenly aware that Chilean society was still deeply divided, with many still articulating their support for Pinochet. In Andermann's words, the mission of the museum was and remains "at least in part to materialize through its display the veracity of the allegations against the dictatorship on behalf of survivors, relatives, and human rights organizations."[91] While the museum seeks not only to convey historical information but to envelop the visitor-witness within an affective journey beyond a solely educational purpose, and is "performative" in that sense, it also needs to remain tethered to the truth of the archive.[92] Photographs are perfectly suited to this dual task,

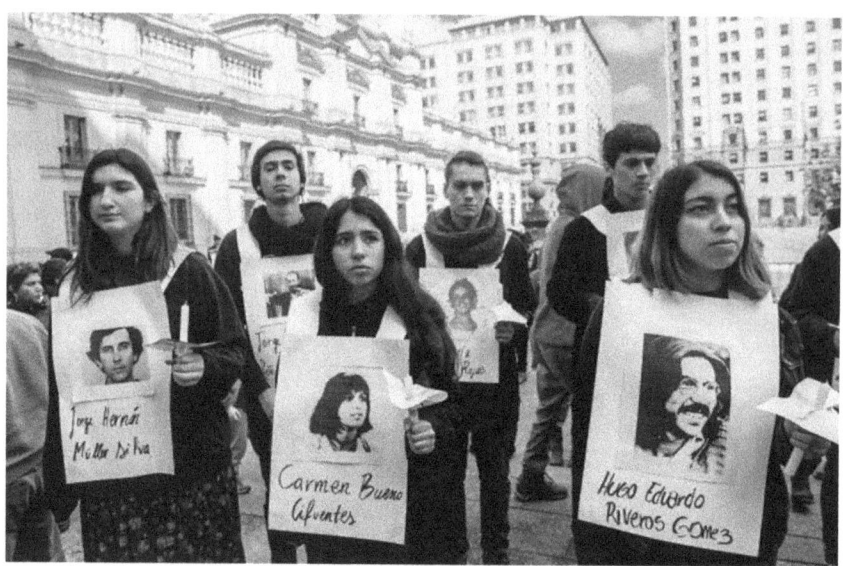

FIGURE 2.11. Young demonstrators holding photographs of Carmen Bueno Cifuentes and Jorge Müller Silva. Source: *El Nuevo Diario*. elnuevodiario.com.ni.

of course—archival and affective, both—and are displayed in many ways across the museum, including the impressive *velatón*, the wall of images of the disappeared and murdered that reaches up the double-height wall in the central room of the museum. Carmen's and Jorge's photographs hang here amid the many others, and one can stand before this wall and search for their names in the digital database, calling up their visages once more in digital version presented on the screen alongside brief accounts of their cases.[93] This special status of the photograph, its ability to be from another time but not be historical, is confirmed in the audiovisual section of the museum, where a documentary celebrates Carmen and Jorge's lives and their work, featuring several colleagues of the couple involved in film making.[94] Midway through the film, a woman starts recalling the night and morning they were kidnapped, and as she speaks a sequence shows their photographs being repeatedly ripped in half and thrown to the floor. The scene emphasizes that on one level the photographs remain merely paper, but this gesture creates a disturbing companion image to the words that are being spoken. Even if the violence of the ripping is minimal compared to what actually happened to Carmen and Jorge, it upsets the viewer to see these photographs mistreated and discarded. It is as if their purpose, their role, is not over; "we" are not over them.[95]

In contrast to the becoming-historical image, therefore, which "lives" only in the archive, these images of Carmen continue to be vital images, reproduced and circulated, digitalized and deployed within a political landscape. For example, in 2019, at the march and protest that takes place annually on the anniversary of the coup on September 11, the protests included young people wearing tabards with the photographs of the disappeared, among them Jorge and Carmen (fig. 2.11). What these images "want" in this context is not merely to be displayed, for the disappeared to be remembered, but also for the political conditions of that time in history to be analyzed for the caution they continue to sound. And furthermore—insofar as it was also a time when the attempt to fracture the People was met by the solidarity expressed in work of the Vicaría and others—for the reservoir of hope they might constitute. However imaginary, even impossible, it is to live as a People, these young people are poised to try; like Rojas's comment above, one suspects that "they feel it in their bodies."[96]

PART II

Colombia

3

COLOMBIA'S PROPOSITIONS FOR MEMORY

The Spirit of the Archive

Is it possible to create an archive of a conflict situation that is ongoing? How can one begin to imagine producing something as ordered, as logical, as an archive in the midst of the messiness of violence? And what would be the purpose of such an attempt? Unlike the FUNVISOL archive in Chile, or the Memoria Abierta archive in Argentina, the Colombian archive that is discussed in this chapter was initiated in the midst of ongoing violence, and by the state itself. As part of its attempt to embark on peace-seeking processes even before the armed conflict is over, and showing a remarkable faith in the very notion of the archive, it was established by law and reflects an ambitious vision, attempting to bring together an extensive resource composed of all existent archives of the violence from around the country. The daunting work of gathering and organizing this "archive of archives" fell to a group of academic researchers within the Centro Nacional de Memoria Histórica (CNMH), as one of the central projects with which it was tasked. This chapter draws on interviews with several members of that group and explores how the group set about their work, and how they imagined the archive and responded to the conceptual and practical challenges its establishment entailed.

What resulted, I will argue, can be understood as a spectral archive-body, pieced together from the remnants of Colombia's horrific experiences. The intention and hope was that the materials gathered, the hundreds of stories they contained, would retain the potential to be animated in the future, be able to rise up, as it were, to both preserve the truth of what had happened and to protect the ideals that fueled the archival endeavor. Through their speculative labor, the group attempted to imbue the archive with what I'll term, drawing on Derrida, an "intentional spirituality." As cryptic as that sounds, it conveys my argument that the care taken by the workers as they went about their work reflects the seriousness with which they sought to produce an archive that embodied their hopes for Colombia's future. The archive had to respond to the complexity of the armed conflict, and to avoid the pitfalls awaiting those who attempt to reduce that complexity. Since the promise of memory is not fulfilled by an archive that collects documentation for its own sake, the hope was that the archive might facilitate better understanding of Colombia's experience of violence. As such, the archive was a key part of the group's wider work investigating and articulating key dynamics in the armed conflict; these projects contextualize, complement, and help explain the hopes for the archival project. Before and alongside the archival work, the group produced many book-length reports on different cases and aspects as well as the most comprehensive and widely known report on the conflict ¡Basta Ya!¹ And furthermore, when the Centro was later delegated a further major task, to design and curate a national museum dedicated to memories of the conflict, their initial skepticism—and anxiety—was related to the tension between, on the one hand, wanting to fulfill the promise of memory and tell as comprehensive a story as possible and, on the other hand, the problem of telling the history too precisely, of ordering its elements too neatly and too authoritatively. Its plans for the museum became an attempt to negotiate precisely how such an institution might be able to sustain and reflect the spirit of the archive as they had attempted to conjure it: how to make the imagined museum open, diverse, mobile, inclusive, sensitive but defiant, with a spirit oriented toward peace.

The Centro Nacional de Memoria Histórica

The establishment of the Centro reflects an approach and a central concern that distinguishes the Colombian story. Whereas many countries have implemented transitional justice mechanisms through which the truth is heard via testimonials delivered in quasi-legal settings, attempting to "deal with the past" in a dedicated forum and within a set timeframe, Colombia's approach implicitly questioned the idea that truth could be so straightforwardly articulated. Thus they included, alongside the legalistic processes, a parallel process of research intended to offer "clarification" to the wider society. The concern was that there was no shared understanding of what had happened, and that merely hearing and collecting testimonies of the conflict would not suffice, simply allowing a cacophony of voices without offering requisite comprehension. To facilitate what is termed historical memory, research and analysis was needed.

Indeed, attempts to speak about the impact and experience of violence in Colombia are often prefaced with a hesitation that confesses the challenge of putting the history of this armed conflict into words. Due not only to its intractability, its scale and ferocity, but also to its complex causality, the difficulty of telling the story is understood as the first hurdle along the way.[2] Colombia tends to be portrayed as a fragmented country, where, with no one stable friend-enemy distinction to ease our understanding, violence seems to erupt of its own accord.[3] Oftentimes, violence itself becomes personified, as the French sociologist Daniel Pécaut has noted, written as it is in capital letters (especially when referring to the period of la Violencia, from the assassination of the Liberal presidential candidate Jorge Eliécer Gaitán in 1948 through to the 1958 power-sharing agreement between the Conservatives and the Liberals), becoming figured as a natural and omnipresent, even metaphysical, destructive force.[4] And yet, complicated as this armed conflict is, Pécaut argues, the facts of what have happened are—in the majority of incidents—*known*, something, he suggests, that makes the Colombia context differ from the experience of clandestine state violence in post-dictatorship Argentina and Chile. If the facts are known, then this must also mean that, however challenging the task, they are narratable, if one listens with care. It is important not to resign in the face of the task, Pécaut argues, and to understand that we do know what is behind the violence: the complex of historical legacies of previous violent events and discord, persistent social inequities, and deep social problems.[5] These, he implies, not violence per se, are what "pull the strings" of Colombia's experience of conflict.[6]

Something of Pécaut's sociological approach, and his insistence that to understand the causes of violence we must resist the temptation of reductive explanations, is reflected in Colombia's "transitional justice" and peace-building measures. In order to elevate the mere *collection* of accounts to the status of a *collective* account, to have any hope for a shared comprehension of the armed conflict, careful expertise was required to research, analyze, and present the facts of what had occurred. The key institution assigned with this formidable task was the Centro Nacional de Memoria Histórica.

Initially called the Grupo de Memoria Histórica, their work began in 2007 as part of the measures put in place to fulfill the requirements of the "Justice and Peace" law of 2005 (Law 975). That law arose from the government's negotiations with the paramilitary groups, and it aimed to facilitate the peace process through its principal focus, which was the reincorporation of the combatants from these illegal armed groups, mainly paramilitaries, back into politics and society. The Grupo was set up as a unit within the Comisión Nacional de Reparación y Reconciliación in order to facilitate key aspects of the legislation, the most important of which were, first, to enable perpetrators to deliver their public statements in which they accepted responsibility for their actions in order for them to be able to receive legal and other benefits.[7] As we will see, the process of hearing these statements was problematic, and the members of the group felt extremely uncomfortable about the way they sidelined the victims' experiences. In part to address their discomfort with the first, the second task given to the group became their focus: to produce a report that explained the rise and development of the illegal armed groups in Colombia. This was a tall order, presenting many challenges and entailing many methodological and analytic decisions, and ultimately the group produced much more information than the legislators no doubt imagined, as well as the important *¡Basta Ya!* report, to which I will return below.

With the 2011 "Victims' Law" (Law 1448), the Grupo was renamed the Centro Nacional de Memoria Histórica (CNMH), acknowledging its achievements and the centrality of its role. The members were guardedly optimistic about this law, seeing it as a "watershed" moment, according to Andrés Suárez, member of CNMH until 2018, because it addressed the imbalance created by the 2005 legislation that had focused on perpetrators, focusing instead on the needs of the victims. "We now had a new mechanism of transitional justice focused on the victims and that sought reparation for victims, all victims, including those victimized by the State," he explained.[8] Within a transitional justice framework, the stated aim of the Law was to offer victims their "rights to truth, justice and reparation with a guarantee of non-repetition." Law 1448 created the Centro and gave it specific tasks.[9] In an acknowledgment of the complexity and widespread ignorance of what had been happening mostly in the more remote, rural areas of the country, these tasks were explicitly focused on creating understanding of the conflict for the wider Colombian public. First, the archive project. They were to seek out and bring together all the documentary materials, including oral testimonies, relating to violations that have occurred, and make this material available to investigators and citizens in general, through exhibitions, pedagogic activity, and other means, in order to "provide and enrich knowledge of the social and political history of Colombia."[10] Second, this law charged the Centro with the task of designing, building, and organizing a museum of memory in order to "strengthen collective memory about the facts of Colombia's recent history."[11] With the new transitional justice structures established through the 2016 Peace Agreement, the Centro was retained and works most closely with the Commission for the Clarification of the Truth, Coexistence and Non-Recurrence (CEV).[12]

How to Narrate the Past? Truth Agreements and Emblematic Cases

From the outset, and for many years, the ethos of the CNMH reflected an approach to history that was deeply aware of the dangers of giving historical accounts. It heeded, one might say, Walter Benjamin's warning in his "Theses on the Philosophy of History," that how the past is cited, and how it is deployed, is always partial and problematic. Not only will the fullness of what has happened defeat any historical account—such fullness only ever being imaginable, Benjamin wrote, if we delusionally consider that we have reached Redemption Day—but also, as a result of present forces and inclinations, any account will be a partial account: "as the flowers turn toward the sun, by dint of a secret heliotropism, the past strives to turn toward the sun which is rising in the sky of history."[13] The first director of the Group, Gonzalo Sánchez, was an academic historian who had worked for many years on issues of violence. In an interview that I conducted with him in 2020 together with my research colleagues, he reflected on his time with the Center. He began by explaining to us his initial reluctance to take on the task as director, not least because of a concern about being able to maintain autonomy; he knew, in other words, that history "turns to the sun," or can be made to turn, and he was adamant that he did not wish to write the history of Colombia's armed conflict under constraint or duress. Sánchez attempted to protect the autonomy of the Group (and then of the Center) in order to have the freedom to approach the issues as he wished, attending to their complexity and addressing the roles of the different actors without political pressure. Under his directorship, the Group and the Centro considered this autonomy paramount, anxious not to be seen as an arm of the state.[14] They sought financial independence, but more importantly here, they sought to establish a way of working that would embody their principles, be reflexive and responsive.[15] From the beginning, the Group discussed and developed ethical principles, a schedule of research and a methodology that sought to put the victims at the center of their work.

Yet specific legal demands and constraints that the laws placed on the Group meant their own agenda was initially somewhat frustrated. The first of these immediately took them away from their victim-centered approach, since it concerned the *Acuerdos de la verdad* (truth agreements). These were declarations of fact that demobilized paramilitaries—those who were not deemed to have committed serious human rights violations and who declared themselves committed to becoming reintegrated into their communities— were obliged to make as part of the demobilization process in order to access the reintegration program and receive the judicial benefits that the state offered through the 2005 law (Law 975, and then also by 2010's Law 1424). With the law's emphasis on the *clarification* of the history of the conflict, the Group was given the role of confirming that these declarations did indeed constitute contributions to knowledge. By comparing the information to other sources, including the victims' recollections of what had happened, the Group was asked to verify the information. While the Group was not in a position to verify the veracity of the information as such, since theirs was not an investigative or juridical role, the task was to confirm whether the statements did "contribute to historical clarification and offer specific facts." If they did, a "Memorandum of truth" was signed between the demobilized person and the Group and a form of amnesty could then be granted, allowing a reintegration process to commence.

The Group was also involved to some extent with the declarations of those who had committed more serious violations, where the perpetrators would confess and give accounts of their crimes at the public prosecutor's office, with the public prosecutor, the prosecution, and the defense lawyers present. These perpetrators were not offered complete amnesty, but in return for their declarations they received relatively shorter prison sentences.[16] These declarations meant the public airing of what had occurred, and through the perpetrators' own accounts, they revealed the brutality of the events as well as the identities of the perpetrators and complicit relations between criminal groups and other sectors of society. Despite the clarification these accounts offered, the members of the Group felt uncomfortable about these confessions, as did many others in Colombia, not least because the media's reportage of them was so focused on the perpetrators. Although the victims of the crimes also submitted their own accounts of events—in their thousands—to the public prosecutors' office and these were recorded, these accounts were collected only for the limited purpose of checking what the perpetrators said when the latter spoke. It transpired, in fact, that most of the victims' testimonies were not used at all, since many perpetrators did not appear for their allotted time to testify, or because the crimes reported by the victims were ones committed by groups that were not covered by the 2005 law.

The CNMH shared the victims' sense that they were being sidelined by this process. Moreover, unlike many transitional justice mechanisms elsewhere, when the perpetrators spoke, the victims were not allowed to be present. Not that they were necessarily asking to be brought face-to-face with the perpetrators. "[The victims] told us that they would be concerned to be in the same room as they would be likely to kill [the perpetrator]," one of the Group members told us; but "they also felt, as they put it, 'we couldn't even pinch him.'"[17] The process was deeply painful for them, but that pain went unacknowledged. Instead, they were obliged to listen to accounts that not infrequently began with self-justifications of the violence meted out, often couched in the familiar terms of defending the nation against guerrillas or communism. And although the victims were not present in the room when the perpetrators gave their accounts, they were frequently gathered nearby, and were sometimes even asked to help the perpetrator remember events by passing on notes delivered between the rooms. CNMH member Andres Suárez recalls cases where the perpetrators claimed not to recall events: "[They asked] 'can you give me more information to [see] if I remember if I participated directly?'" But then, when information was delivered, they claimed not to recall the specifics. In another case, Suárez recalls, photographs of the disappeared were taken to an ex-paramilitary who was giving his account, who then dismissed them, saying: "Don't bring me any more photographs; they don't mean anything to me."[18] The dismissal of the photographs, so precious to the relatives and survivors, was deeply upsetting for them. For the perpetrators, Suárez comments, "the scale and dimensions of what had happened were such that, as one of [the paramilitaries] said: 'There is a moment in the war when you lose count and it is better to do so. . . . It is not as if we were keeping records of all those that we killed.'"[19]

According to Gonzalo Sánchez, the *Acuerdos*, and Law 975 as a whole, were "shameful" in relation to the victims: "There was only the voice of the perpetrators, [shaping history] according to their free will and telling whatever they wanted to tell."[20] While the authorities and society in general were able to understand more of what had occurred, the process continued to silence the victims. As Martha Nubia Bello, member of the Grupo, recalls:

"It was terrible that it was only through the words of the perpetrators that the victims' accounts" of what had happened, given many years before—the forced disappearances, the murders, the taking of children as child combatants, the massacres—were "recognized."[21]

In order to change this and to develop "possibilities for questioning the solitary voice of the perpetrator," as Sánchez puts it, the Grupo decided to make the second task that they were mandated by the 2005 law the main focus of their work.[22] As mentioned, they were to produce a report that explained the rise and development of the illegal armed groups in Colombia. Here lay the opportunity to put the victims at the center of the account and to fulfil their commitment to listening to the victims' stories. On one level this request for the Group to undertake what amounted to a writing of the history of the conflict appeared to be a straightforward task for a group of academics, several of whom were trained and experienced historians, anthropologists and social scientists, familiar with carrying out research. They understood that in order to be able to grasp the complexity of what had occurred, and to give the stories they gathered the chance to be heard, they would need to undertake several research projects in different parts of the country. But this task was so vast, that they needed a strategy to approach it, and for this reason they chose to focus on what they came to refer to as "*casos emblemáticos*" (emblematic cases). Through a series of carefully selected field-based research projects, studying particular territories or events, the Grupo hoped to be able to carry out in-depth research while also showing the broader and deeper dynamics that were also at stake elsewhere. Thus each emblematic case was chosen for its potential to reflect upon a larger issue, such as impunity, land dispossession, or political exclusion. For each, a team of researchers went to the chosen territories affected by violence, and spoke to victims and local organizations in order to gather as much and as detailed information as possible.[23] Through "inductive reasoning," Sánchez explains, they tried to speak to the overwhelming number of instances of violence "while giving close attention to fewer."[24]

This work began with the Trujillo massacre, a difficult and complex case not least because it involved atrocities committed by both the paramilitaries *and* state actors. State involvement had been confirmed by the Inter-American Court of Human Rights, and the Colombian government had accepted that responsibility. The Grupo chose the case in part in order to test how much true autonomy their research would be allowed.[25] The Trujillo massacre was a period of continual violence—mostly targeted murders and forced disappearances—that occurred over several years between 1986 and

1994 (and also continued afterward), with the most intense period of violence in 1990. Some 245 people lost their lives. The group gathered information from relatives and victims, local community groups, and international organizations who had followed the events, including Amnesty International and Human Rights Watch. Long-term CNMH member Luis Carlos Sánchez recalls: "Initially people did not trust the researchers nor the institution because it belonged to the national government. Only by working hard and carefully, and with the aid of key connections in the communities, was trust established, allowing the rich materials of the research to emerge and be collected."[26] Starting with smaller, more intimate conversations, then gradually gaining enough trust to conduct workshops in the affected communities, the team worked there over a period of a year or so.

The resulting book-length report, *Trujillo: Una tragedia que no cesa* (Trujillo: A Tragedy Without End), published in 2008, gave the facts and analyzed the dynamics of the massacre, with ample space to detail the victims' stories of the impact that the violence had had on their social and economic welfare, their social networks, and their everyday lives.[27] The stories give voice to the accounts of victims, relatives, and the survivors, including children who had witnessed their relatives being killed, allowing them to articulate their enormous pain and grief. Even the landscape, including the Cauca River, where most bodies were found, now held painful memories for them. "The drama that the violence unleashed is an open wound. Each time it returns, so does the bleeding," one survivor recalled.[28] In Trujillo, speaking to the communities through workshops and individually, the Grupo developed their research method, premised on the notion that one must "build from the very local, so that from the detailed work with the communities, one could raise the voices of these people, so that theirs became the key interpretations of the armed conflict. [The aim was] to empower them . . . in the dialogue [about how to build narratives and a memory about the conflict]."[29]

Over the following years the Group undertook several such investigations, developing shared methodological reflections so that new cases could be undertaken with fewer people and in parallel. There were around twenty workers involved in these investigations (ten researchers, each with a research assistant). These detailed reports, with their focus on careful, sensitive fieldwork, were received with overwhelming positivity by the communities studied, and the team remain proud of them.[30] The team was always careful with what information they requested from people, conscious that their role was to document the memory of the conflict not to act like a judicial enquiry. Gonzalo Sánchez explains: "We never asked for information that we thought could be dangerous for the people to give, just because it would be academically interesting. We asked them 'what should we say? [But also] what should we *not* say about this?'"[31] Again, the care the Group showed was attuned to the fragility of the ongoing situations, and the potentially damaging effects of their giving an account of the violence. While the reports certainly "demanded answers," it was not their intention to become part of legal prosecutions, and they kept a guarded distance from judicial process.[32]

¡Basta Ya! Enough Already!

Legally, the Grupo had been mandated by the 2005 law to produce just one report offering a single account that would detail the origins, formation, and rise of illegal armed groups. This was the history that the law understood as in need of "clarification." The Group decided to fulfill that mandate through the publication of their general report *¡Basta Ya! Colombia: Memories of War and Dignity*, published in 2013, which drew upon the almost forty investigations that the Group had by then carried out.[33] The report went far beyond its remit; it incorporated much more than the legal requirement, reflecting the careful conversations and detailed investigations of the Group. As well as a chapter on the formation and rise of illegal armed groups, the report discusses the types of violence that the Colombian conflict has suffered, the responses of the changing justice systems, and details the impacts of the violence on the victims. A long final chapter centers on the memories of the survivors, showing the legacy that violence has left in its wake. The report remains the most comprehensive document of the contemporary armed conflict in Colombia and has become the key reference for those seeking to understand the origins, dynamics, and the toll the conflict has taken.

The report also incorporated a strong visual component, including, along with several maps and graphs, an impressive selection of photographs by the Grupo's photographer, Jesús Abad Colorado, who worked with them from the outset of their work. With his affecting images, one sees the impact of the violence, captured less through dramatic images of war than through small gestures and moments in the aftermath. The image of a young boy of about ten years old buttoning up the shirt of his dead father, murdered by paramilitaries in San Carlos in 1998,[34] for example, or the despair on the face of the Red Cross worker, her T-shirt marked by blood, in Medellín in 2002.[35] Images show whole villages and towns turning out to bury their dead, or else to march in defiance and commitment to rebuild their homes, as happened in Granada, Antioquia, in 2001, after an attack by the FARC destroyed 250 houses.[36]

Moreover, in addition to the written report, an accompanying film was commissioned. *No Hubo Tiempo para la Tristeza* (There Was No Time for Sadness) allowed the Group to explain key dynamics, to enable the viewers to "travel" to the regions where the violence was at its most intense, and allow victims and survivors to speak directly to camera about the violence in their regions.[37] The affective atmospheres made possible through film helped to address one of the principal issues that the Group sought to overcome: that because the conflict happened mostly in rural areas, and because victims tended to be in small numbers over long periods of time—a "high frequency and low density" form of violence, as one of the Grupo members describes it in the film—with dramatic and catastrophic events occurring less often, the huge numbers of people killed, disappeared, tortured, mutilated, raped, displaced, and affected in other ways, were somehow hidden, or as it is articulated in Spanish, "invisibilized," from the urban populations and the wider world in general. For city dwellers, the armed conflict felt "almost like a fiction," says the narrator. And when the conflict is "invisibilized," Andrés Suárez comments in the film, it means that by the same token "the importance of efforts towards peace are minimized."[38]

The film puts the stories of key communities at the forefront. One horrific story it tells through the commentary of the local priest, Autún Ramos, is the infamous massacre that occurred in Bojayá, Chocó, on May 2, 2002. As a result of fighting between the FARC and a paramilitary group, a bomb landed on the roof of a church where some 200 people from the town had taken shelter; 79 people were killed in the explosion, 48 of them children. The camera follows Ramos as he takes a walk around the old church grounds, now becoming overgrown as the town has been relocated and rebuilt nearby. "There were many pregnant women," he explains, adding the awful detail, "We found their babies stuck on the walls, dismembered."[39] While the fighting continued, Ramos ushered the people out and onto a boat. Fearful that they would be attacked, they shouted in call and response: "I called: 'Who are we?' And they all answered, 'The civilian population,'" as they made their escape.[40]

Neither the report nor the film shies away from such details, attempting to convey the extent of the suffering inflicted on communities through what Suárez calls the "perverse creativity" of the forms of violence. But the Group was mindful not to portray the violence as divine violence, nor to personify it in the way that Pécaut described. Thus, even in the more limited space of the documentary, the dynamics of the historical and political context of violence are referred to by several commentators. Colombia's history of extractivism, the role of land-ownership, the history of political exclusion, the inequities of exclusive agrarian development and the responsibility of the state are all explicitly mentioned. Equally, the commentary suggests that these communities have been caught between the conflicting interests of drug traffickers, mining and energy projects, agro-industry, and the corruption of alliances between paramilitaries, the political class, public officials, and economic elites. The documentary challenges the political ideologies that have been promoted and—it implies—distorted in the service of sustaining conflict. Ramos, the priest at Bojayá, reports that he met the young son of a guerrilla, a boy of nine or ten years old, who was carrying a gun. He asked the boy, "What are you doing? Why are you in this war?" to which the boy replied, "We have to liquidate the oligarchy." Ramos was shocked; he says the boy's words stayed with him. "What oligarchy? In these conditions, in this poverty in which people live?"[41] The implication is that children were being trained to think and speak in the terms of the guerrillas' ideologies, without the maturity to understand or evaluate them. One of the leaders of the indigenous Uitoto group, Ismael Fajardo, comments that the leaders had had to work to "destroy the military idea of revolution" that the guerrillas were promulgating in La Chorrera. On the other hand, comments CNMH member Marta Nubia Bello, the paramilitaries were dangerous for a different reason, which is that they operated without a political program: "The paramilitaries didn't have a political project. They were armies of mercenaries in several cases. Sometimes they didn't even know who they were working for, in whose name they were committing these crimes."[42] Where they were present, she continues, the distortion of political dreams and ideals meant that "noble ideas" were claimed to justify the most vile and horrific of violent methods.[43] Often the idea of the People somehow justified the violence. Ramos puts the conundrum thus: "All the armed groups—all—turned at times against the people that they said they fought *for*. We would say, 'But we are *part* of this People!'"[44]

As mentioned above, with the so-called Victims' Law of 2011 (Law 1448), the Grupo was taken decisively into the state apparatus and became the Centro Nacional de Memoria Histórica. This law asked the Centro to continue its previous work but also added two more significant tasks, both relating to the question of how to maintain the work of memory into the future.[45] First, the Center was required to establish an archive, the "archive of archives" mentioned in my introduction, that would gather documents relating to human rights violations committed during the conflict, to be made available to researchers and to the public. Secondly, it was asked to establish a national museum of memory in Bogotá, which was described by that law as a pedagogic undertaking that would enrich and "strengthen collective memory."

Survivance: The Intentional Spirituality of the Archive

The ambitious task that the 2011 law gave the Centro of building a comprehensive archive of the armed conflict meant that it was charged with the collection of all the various evidence that individuals and communities had in their possession. It was an enormous undertaking to catalogue and arrange them systematically, and to make them available in a digitalized and searchable archive for the future. The task explicitly intended to speak to the future, and to present the experience of violence for future eyes. If Benjamin's angel of history is blown forward but is frozen looking backward as the detritus mounts up, the archive is by contrast an active endeavor that gathers up and sorts the sky-high pile that calamitous historical events have created.[46] Although it seems to look backward like the angel, and like transitional justice mechanisms, the archive's activity is fundamentally futural, concerned with making a body of sorts to offer those in the future the chance to make sense of what has happened historically. Indeed, insofar as an archive is a body that remains behind after death, the trace of lives lived and lost, it is an entrusting that evokes Derrida's term *survivance*. In his lecture about this term, Derrida suggests that *sur-vivance* speaks to the possibility of a sur-vival beyond death, or better, an existing in which the opposition of the living and the dead "must lose all pertinence." He discusses occasions on which the past is reanimated, made to live again. Among other examples, he considers the book *Robinson Crusoe*: "The survivance of a book, from its first moment on, is a living-dead machine, sur-viving, the body of a thing buried in a library, a bookstore, in cellars, urns, drowned in the worldwide waves of a Web, etc., but *a dead thing that resuscitates each time* a breath of living reading [*sic*], each time the breath of the other or the other breath, each time *an intentionality intends it and makes it live again* by animating it."[47]

The archive of the CNMH, I suggest, displays an intentionality in this vein. Without seeking to ensure a particular version of the future, it aims to offer the possibility of sur-vivance to the archive, the possibility that the archival body might live again, and might even be able to rise up and provide a defense of sorts, protecting the future against the return of violence. No doubt the notion of an archival body can become a personification that is just as lacking in nuance as the personification of violence. Yet the archive of the CNMH certainly fits Derrida's description of a trace that is "shot through with intentional spirituality."[48] Quoting Edmund Husserl, Derrida argued that the trace-book-body is "a *geistige Leiblichkeit*, a body, a spiritual corporeality, a body proper (*Leib* and not *Körper*), a body proper animated, activated, traversed, shot through with intentional spirituality."[49] The intention of the CNMH archive is to become spirit. It *intends* to haunt the future with these past events and their consequences, to allow voices of those affected by the violence to carry forward and whisper into the ears of the future. Even the text of the 2011 Law noted that other countries emerging from conflict had constructed such archives, implying that there was a need for an archive and an efficacy about them, such that these international institutions may serve as models for the CNMH, and for Colombia, where such an archive was a novel concept.[50] To have such an archive, it was implied, would be to offer the future a vast body of knowledge and lessons learned. Moreover, it was clearly understood as a body that was to perform a job, and was intended to be active—once activated through usage in the manner of Derrida's "living breath"—so that it might rise up in the name of peace.

The task of constructing such a formidable body, one that might hold such promise, saw the Centro team work carefully with communities all over Colombia, seeking out the many ways in which people had recorded the violence. The team worked especially with social leaders of communities in the territories, who very often were already organizing their own archives, spurred on not least by reparation applications. The Centro spoke to these communities in order to see what their priorities would be for the Centro's archiving activities in relation to their own, negotiating the relationship between local projects and national bodies.[51] Through their gathering and listening, the CNMH archive emerged as a sort of spectral archive-body, pieced together from the remains of the horrors of the conflict.[52] Its construction has required the Centro team to act not only like collectors, gathering existent archives, but also like detectives, uncovering archives where they may exist "unbeknownst" to those who own them. Miriam Loaiza explains: "The word archive tends to make people think of paper, no? But when one asks 'how did you register that? How did you document it?' they start to talk about photographs, videos, quilts, drawings, maps so that the concept of the archive becomes richer."[53] Loaiza describes one important example of the Centro's work, that began in 2016, which was with the Arhuaco group in the Sierra Nevada de Santa Maria. This group believed they had no archives of their community, but through careful discussion with researchers from the Centro they came to realize that they did in fact have quite extensive archives, comprising the handwritten documents of their land made during the period of colonization by the Capuchin monks, including sketches of the land and former buildings, as well as those archives they had created that describe their modes of education and the materials gathered for the reparation requests.[54]

The depositing of one's documents, artefacts, crafts, and other modes of registering the conflict is not, from CNMH's perspective, about achieving power beyond life. The intentional spirituality of the archival-body is not a "haunting of the future" in the sense of frightening the future, of terrorizing it with a violent past that asserts its continued presence. Instead, the desire for preservation is a response to a fear felt now. It is those in the present who are—not unreasonably—fearful, and the archive is a way of stilling their fears. Thinking of Crusoe's obsessive fear of being buried alive or being eaten alive by cannibals, Derrida writes, the fear that concerns what may be perpetrated against you by one's "own," which is to say *by your own lineage*, those who have responsibility for you "after your lifetime." (Indeed, Derrida comments, since crimes against humanity can only be committed by humanity, they have an auto-immune, or suicidal, structure to them.)[55] There is a crucial sense in which the project of the archive accepts that the future is a place in which we cannot "live," passing instead to "one's own" not the demand for the continuation of the past but the *choice* about what to do with it.

An archive only ever gifts the *potential* to make the past "live," hoping that through the "lessons of the past" the suffering of the past comes to assume a purpose in a calmer, and kinder, future. This hope requires therefore that the archive be put to use, and it is only through its use that it achieves a vitality of sorts. Certainly, the Centro's archive has already been given "life" through the educational, artistic, and academic uses that have been made of it.[56] It has also, like FUNVISOL in Chile, had important legal uses.[57] One example of the use of the archive in a legal case was in the investigation of the murder of social leader Temístocles Machado in January 2018. The Centro holds the archive of his community of Buenaventura, a community on the Pacific coast that has suffered much from the conflict, and with whom the Centro had worked two years earlier on a research report. As archival team member Dora Betancourt explains, the Centro was able to make that archive available to his lawyers. She says, "For me, it was very rewarding to be able to defend the cause of a leader who had worked his whole life to defend the land, and who was murdered [for it]."[58]

Certainly, if those in the future are to understand the archive as a gift from prior generations, something not only to preserve and consult but to cherish and to spend time with, it must be known to have been freely given. Any notion that it was an imposition, or a stale "depository" without the care and good wishes of the previous generations embedded in it, would dissolve the all-important relationship of the future users to the very concept of an archive. In recent years, some of the groups and individuals who have deposited their archives with the Centro have threatened to withdraw them. They have publicly declared their doubt about the uses to which they fear their archives may be put; they have articulated the vulnerability they have felt when, following a change of government, the Centro was placed under new directorship. In June 2020 MAFAPO, the group of Mothers of Soacha and Bogotá, whose sons died as a result of the "*falsos positivos*" scandal and who have become a mutual support and a well-known campaign group, stated that they no longer wished to cooperate with the CNMH.[59] Having previously collaborated, freely giving interviews about their stories for the archive, publications, and for use in the Museum, the Mothers were angry and concerned about certain declarations made by the second director, Rubén Dario Avecedo, expressing his views on the conflict.[60] In particular, they were worried that his expanding notion of who constitutes a "victim" might mean their stories were to be placed alongside narratives that celebrated the "heroism" of the armed forces.[61] This "withdrawal" caused some bemusement insofar as the archive's digital nature prevents physical withdrawals. All of the archive's holdings are digitalized and the Centro does not hold physical copies of the more than 300,000 documents that are listed.[62]

However, the gesture to remove the archive's MAFAPO holdings makes perfect sense as an effort to deny *vitality* to the archive, to mark displeasure through a refusal to breathe life into the archive. To evoke Derrida's argument again, it is a refusal to grant sovereignty to the archive, to recognize *these* guardians of the archive as the "fellows" to whom this gift was bequeathed, and thus an attempt to seek a different mode of giving the traces of their loved ones a chance at living "beyond death." This was a battle about sovereignty therefore, that attempted to "kill off" the archive through a withdrawal not of the documents, interviews, and photographs but of the vitality that the archive *could* have, the living-beyond-death of the mothers' stories, their survivance. By articulating their discontent, the mothers signaled that they would not allow this institution to "be" their archive-body. It was as if the mothers were saying, we would rather just die than live as part of a beast created like this, with our own precious stories mingled with *these* parts and living under *your* sovereignty.

The Museal Proposition: Body, Earth, Water

If the beauty—and the fragility—of an archive is that it offers content without the imposition of permanent narrative or form and instead invites returnings and re-entrances, a museum, by contrast, requires curation and direction. A museum guides its visitors and traditionally makes its contents "speak." For this reason, when the 2011 Law added as a second major project the creation of a Museum of Memory, the team was surprised.[63] At first blush, the idea of creating a museum was in tension with their ethos, asking them to present the past, to make executive decisions about how to tell the history of the armed conflict, to curate it both visually and experientially. As team member and a former lead on the project Luis Carlos Sánchez remembers, "Even for us the idea of making a museum was not comfortable. That is, when we were first told that this [our work] was going to become a museum, it was like: 'A museum? A museum! For real?'"[64]

Their initial concerns, as Luis Carlos Sánchez explained, were—as with the research reports and archive—whether a museum could be sufficiently capacious to reflect a "diversity" and a "versatility" around what memory means to Colombians.[65] As opposed to the archive's open and humble stance, could a national museum escape a sense that its purpose is to provide a singular definitive account? Could all the careful decisions they had taken around the archive and the reports be translated into a public museum? Through discussions they concluded that only if they could construct a museum that was open to many ideas and modes of memory, to many different communities across the country, *and* accommodate additions to those in the future, would they be able to commit to it. With an understanding that memory would—and should—always exceed whatever the museum contained, it could be thought "as an operator in a process [of memory] that is much broader than itself."[66] Thus the work went ahead, and from 2013 the Centro set up a series of "Dialogues on Memory": meetings with local community groups, artistic workshops, and the like that sought to probe what memory means for people, and to develop discussion and support for what a museum could be.

Out of these discussions, as well as from discussions with existent museums in other countries (including Argentina, Chile, Germany, and Peru), the Wilson Center, and the ongoing conversations with community groups and leaders, the main "script" for the permanent galleries of the museum was created.[67] Elaborated from ideas gathered by the "Dialogues on Memory," this guide is organized around three themes or "axes": Body, Earth, and Water. Explicitly eschewing a form of narration that attempted to tell the history through naming political groups and affiliations, the choice of these axes as a way to approach the history has been explained by the team working on the museum project in a thoughtful document available on the museum website.[68] As we will see, this conceptual guide is an attempt to set the conceptual basis for the museum, reflecting the Centro's many years of research.

The document is remarkable for its foregrounding of the difficulties of the task of the museum, discussing the risks of petrifying memories, of privileging certain voices over others, and of being swayed to speak about certain cases and not others. There is, moreover, a principle of sorts set out at the beginning of this document, which is that any museum should not allow tales of war to overwhelm the presentation of what Colombia is: "The history of the country is woven not only through war and violence, but also, just as much, from initiatives for peace, resistance, political change and peace processes."[69] This sense that violence should not dominate the narrative at the expense of all that constitutes the country flows through the document, and underlies the choice of taking three axes by which to weave a journey for the museum visitor. Each axis is interconnected with the others, but each offers a particular lens through which to consider the history of what has happened: the body, the earth, water.

Approaching the issue of memory obliquely through these themes, the conceptual guide articulates an ambition to draw the visitor into the museum viscerally and poetically, without diminishing the shocking facts and stories of the armed conflict and its reverberations for the country. To address its three suggested themes briefly: first, the theme of the body. The stark statistics on the armed conflict illustrate the sense in which the violence targets the body through its dehumanizing practices. Drawing on the work of the CNMH, the authors state that at the time of the writing of the guide there were 220,000 dead, 10,189 people who were victims of mines, 17,610 forcibly recruited children and young people, 15,552 victims of sexual violence between 1985 and 2016, and since the 1970s, 78,202 people had been "disappeared."[70] But the guide insists that the museum must show that beyond these numbers are stories of individual bodies and suffering. These must be heard, both in order to create that imaginative "bridge" of connection with the visitors—a bridge that can interpellate as well as "interrogate" the visitor—and to underscore the how ongoing conflict inscribes *all* bodies into its "repertoires of violence."[71] With this comment, the guide gestures toward possible analytic avenues. Asking not only "What does war do to the body?" but also "What does the body do in war?"[72] it suggests a phenomenological approach through which the museum might speak to technologies of power in a Foucauldian sense. To show how the militarization of life that erases the distinction between civil and military life is sustained at the level of the flesh, the museum should give attention to "the ways the war orders, disciplines, and inscribes itself on the bodies of the combatants . . . operating on their bodies, emotions and ideas."[73] The conflict not only marks, dehumanizes, and breaks bodies, therefore, but also makes bodies, fashioning them into its web, so that modes of embodiment—the body's very postures, its adornments, its ways of walking—bespeak the intimate ways the conflict has insinuated itself and is sustained.[74] Living within conflict means constant negotiations with perpetrators, where survivors are forced to choose "sides" within families and communities, and where "grey zones" repeatedly emerge between victims and perpetrators.[75] Through this axis of the body, the guide hopes that the museum might be able to address this complexity, inviting consideration of how the armed conflict has taken hold even as communities have continued to resist attempts to dispossess them of their humanity, often putting their bodies on the line to defend life and rescue dignity.

Under the second axis of the earth, the conceptual guide suggests that the museum should seek to show how territorial relations have been at the epicenter of the conflict, with the use of massacres and forced displacements in particular seeking to control territories by controlling the movement of populations, resources, and routes within and through them.[76] Again, the statistics give some sense of the size of this problem: up to August 2016, 7,757,157 people have been forcibly displaced, 87 percent of them from rural areas.[77] The rise of drug trafficking in the 1970s and the widespread illegal planting of cocaine in the 1990s intensified power struggles and inequalities of land ownership and use.[78] For those having to flee their lands, there is a situation of social degradation, what the conceptual guide terms a "social death" as they fall out of social networks and the social contract.[79] In the museum, the struggles of indigenous people, those of African descent, and rural workers (campesinos) should be highlighted, the guide argues, to show the importance of these battles for the restitution and right to return to their lands.[80]

Once again the guide hints that the museum space should complicate any reductive readings of this situation, emphasizing that relations to territories are not merely natural. On the one hand, the very notion of territories delimits people's sense of imagined borders and situates them within networks of power. In these senses, they are problematic. On the other hand, territories give people their sense of communal existence and give meaning to their shared lives, organizing their modes of survival.[81] Memories of the conflict are bound up with the story of extractive industries and larger agricultural industries that have brought their notions of "development" into many rural areas, leading to further exploitative inequities and struggles for rural populations.[82] Moreover, quoting a participant from an indigenous community in La Chorrera, Amazonas, who participated in one of the consultations over the future museum, the axis affirms a spirituality that for indigenous groups is tied up with the Mother Earth.[83] It acknowledges, furthermore, that the land has itself been targeted by the conflict, suffering its own harms and violation. When land is attacked or misused, so too is the biodiversity, as animals, forests, and plant life are harmed, abandoned, displaced.

The third axis proposed for the museum, water, is presented as another lens through which to view the conflict as well as an apt metaphor, insofar as the guide suggests that the museum should itself maintain an open and fluid account of the history of conflict.[84] Water speaks to the image of Colombia as itself a country necessarily connected by water, referencing the sea, ports, rivers, and marshes in many diverse areas of Colombia—from Caribe, the Pacific, Magdelena Medio, to Cauca, Amazonas, and the Llanos orientales— that serve to connect people, lands, territories, and other living beings. For riverside, costal, and fishing communities, water is at the center of life and culture, sustaining ways of living on many levels, and is therefore associated with a sense of community and belonging.[85] Yet "during the more than five decades of armed conflict, Colombia's bodies of water have become receivers and witnesses to acts of violence." In particular, the guide reminds us, since 1980 more than 3,000 of the "disappeared" were thrown into rivers and tributaries such as the Cauca, Magdalena, and Atrato.[86] Water that was once at the heart of communal activities and brought joy as people gathered to wash clothes, to chat, and to bathe has become tainted by these atrocities. Indeed, the guide notes, the suffering of the rivers themselves was acknowledged by the sentence in an important case in 2016 (known as T-622), which recognized the Atrato River as a victim in its own right, having suffered from the impact of the exploitation of the forest and from illegal mining, developed against the background of the conflict; such recognition was unprecedented in Colombia.[87]

As the choice and justifications for these axes suggest, the authors of the conceptual guide are proposing that the museum explicitly embrace an approach that acknowledges the partiality of accounts of history.[88] More than this, the guide is an attempt to learn from critiques of history as progress, and of violence as personified, both essential Benjaminian themes. Indeed, the approach is reminiscent of Judith Butler's reading of Benjamin's "Theses on the Philosophy of History," which explores how remembrance might be opposed to telling a history or monumentalizing the past. Remembrance in Benjamin can be said to work against history, to undo a seamless continuity. In a close reading, Butler argues that it is possible to read Benjamin's complex text as a wager that "some forgotten set of histories, those that belong to the history of the oppressed, flashes up and makes a sudden claim" against the homogeneity of history.[89] On this analysis, there is the possibility of a sudden illumination, an interruption that reconstellates the time of the present that might otherwise be understood as unrelenting progress, marching on. The guide is impressive insofar as it proposes not only the principles that the museum should embody so that it be "wholistic, relational and attentive to diversity," but it also offers the axes as a method for inviting what has been cast as "nonhistory" from the point of view of those effaced by history, to precisely flash up in Benjamin's terms and disorientate the very terms of the telling. Benjamin's argument implies that another history might make itself felt, could make its demand against the history of the victor. It seems, as Butler points out, to arrive as a flash and in fragmentary form, only to fade once again.[90] Insofar as the conceptual guide seeks to maintain a fluid and heterogeneous approach to how history is told, insofar as the axes are mobile and remain open to novel modes of interpretation and connection from the audiences at the museum, it can be regarded as an attempt to offer the conditions of possibility for such novelties to arise. It invites a new fragment or a flash to interrupt the history being presented there. Moreover the guide states that there should be changing temporary exhibitions and that each visit to the museum should offer a different experience through its program of events, initiatives, and the new work arising from explorations of the archive.[91] Certainly, the guide embraces an expansive approach to the armed conflict in Colombia that seeks to avoid what Benjamin called "overnaming," about which Butler remarks, "There is such a thing as naming too much or naming too well. . . . the name seeks to capture its object and so risks its erasure."[92] Here it is the erasure of the conflict—an ongoing live conflict—that is risked if the museum were to seek to name it too well, too precisely.

Remaining true to their commitment to consulting with communities across Colombia, moreover, the Centro mounted an itinerant exhibition employing the three axes which was shown in different parts of the country in order to test the modes of exhibiting that were likely to be employed in the permanent rooms of the museum. Launched in Bogotá at the 2018 international book fair, *Voces para transfomar a Colombia* was designed to "test out" the ideas for the permanent museum.[93] Comprising displays with testimonies, photographs, songs, and objects, the exhibition sought to offer a taste of the museum's approach, traveling beyond Bogotá to gain feedback and to encourage the engagement of those beyond the capital in the project.[94] This last point was crucial, as—according to our interviewee Monica Álvarez, coordinator of the Red Nacional de Lugares de Memoria—many have articulated a preference for "a public policy of memory that really supports the territorial initiatives that are already working on [memory]."[95] Indeed, several have argued that since the conflict has mostly taken place in rural areas and towns, and little has touched the cities, and particularly in Bogotá—which has suffered violence but in ways that are rather distinct from those characterizing the majority of the conflict—the museum or museums should be where they make more sense.[96] The risk is that "a museum over there in Bogotá that does not dialogue with the territories, [could become merely] a way of embellishing Bogotá, rather than a conversation" with the sites of memory established around the country.[97]

The *Voces* exhibition intended therefore to offer a taste of the sorts of events the eventual museum will host, so as well as its installations, there were guided tours, workshops, plays, concerts, and film screenings to create a multisensory experience.[98] It was an approach that, according to Sofia González-Ayala and Alejandro Camargo, extended Nicholas Thomas's notion of a "museum as method."[99] Where Thomas argued that progressive museal practice involves practices of discovery, captioning, and juxtaposition, González-Ayala and Camargo emphasize that the *Voces* exhibition added a practice of "ramification" that explicitly sought to take the museal propositions beyond the exhibition space, to make spaces and conditions within which alliances and mobilizations may form.[100] Thus the curators explicitly set out to make the exhibition employ a curatorial methodology aimed beyond the communicative tasks defined by Thomas, reaching, as they state, "for meaning making as part of symbolic reparation," but without attempting to predict how the exhibitions' provocation would facilitate those connections and mobilizations.[101]

Having initially been highly skeptical, Luis Carlos Sánchez, former director of the Museum project, now sees the museum as "perhaps the most visible or strongest measure of symbolic reparation that the law of victims brings."[102] And while the very idea of a museum was controversial from the outset, it could be understood, he suggests, as a positive legacy for the Center. Moreover, insofar as the museum has generated the interest of young researchers, pleased to continue the work around memory begun by such key figures as Gonzalo Sánchez and fellow academic Rodrigo Uprimny, it could be a real achievement. But it will only be such a legacy if it can truly act as what he refers to as a "visibility platform" for the victims.[103] This crucial point, of how the Center's ethos can be guaranteed going forward, was underlined by the controversies that surrounded the itinerant exhibition, which was closed early in Cali in 2019 when the new directorship of the Centro was accused of changing the text of the exhibition guide and information that accompanied some exhibits, removing references to the word "war," for example. In May 2020, the JEP adopted interim measures to protect the exhibition as a "collection" after they received a complaint that the victims' agreements with the CNMH—and indeed their rights under the 2011 law—had been contravened, since the changes to the exhibits were made without consultation.[104] The implication is that the changes reflected the Center's new directorship's controversial understanding of the conflict, and the JEP ordered that the guide revert to its original version, as well as be protected from further alterations.

Of course, we will have to await the museum's opening to evaluate whether it fulfills the Center's initial ambitions as articulated in the conceptual guide and their research reports more generally, or whether it will suffer a similar shift in language and approach as that attempted in Cali. As I write, the site for the museum has been allocated—it will be in Calle 26 at the cross-section with Avenida Las Américas—and the Centro has also overseen the architecture competition for the museum building. The winning design, announced in 2016, is by architects MGP Arquitectura y Urbanismo + Estudio Entresitio (Bogotá/Madrid), and incorporates spaces for education, for reflection, for the archive and documentation center, as well as the principal exhibition halls. After delays due to the COVID-19 pandemic, the construction of the building has now begun, and in the meantime, the museum has developed an active web presence, presenting digital content on the museum building, its planned contents and uses.[105] In the next section, I will close with a brief consideration of a museum that already exists, the Museo Casa de la Memoria in Medellín. Although it is a smaller endeavor than the planned museum in Bogotá because its ambition is principally to serve the needs of the people of Medellín, it shares many of the ambitions of the conceptual guide discussed above, and so provides us with an opportunity to see how the proposition to build a museum that can be reflexive and self-critical, open to new voices and new accounts, might fare.

Sheltering Debate: Medellín's Museo Casa de la Memoria

Reflecting on the name of the Museo Casa de la Memoria in Medellín, Museum Director Cathalina Sánchez Escobar told us, "It is a museum that is a house, it's not a house that becomes a museum. . . . It is a museum that has a spirit, and that spirit is those testimonies, those stories, those experiences. If a museum is a building that exhibits, the house instead is something that keeps, that preserves, that allows dialogue, dissent, consensus: it is a tool."[106]

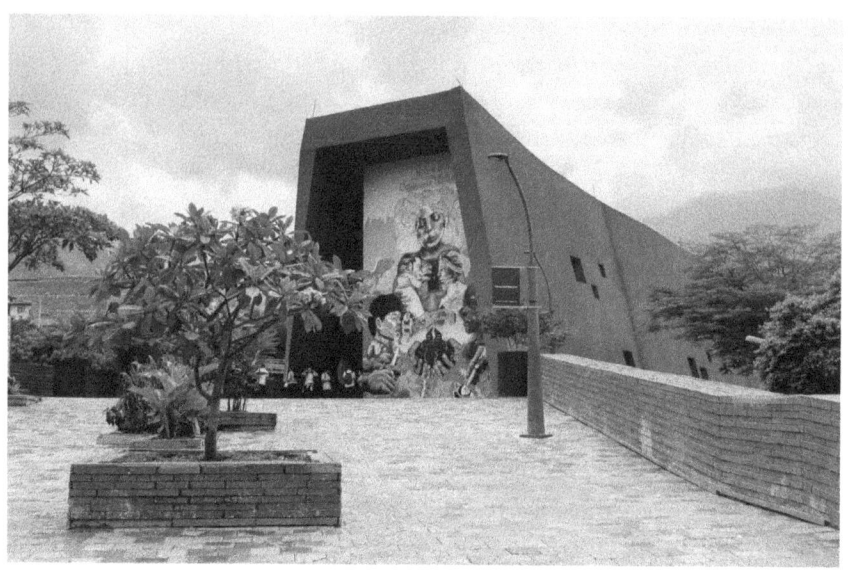

FIGURE 3.1. Museo Casa de la Memoria in Medellín. Source: Vikki Bell.

Opened in 2016, the modern architecture of the Museo Casa de la Memoria is a bold, angular building painted dark, with a high frontage—now adorned with a colorful mural by graffiti artists from the city—sitting on an elevated spot.[107] It is a statement by the city of Medellín and its citizens that the stories of violence that have occurred in and around the city, deserve to be housed (fig. 3.1). It is a promise to do so, to give them a *casa*. So too the survivors and relatives need a place to gather, to discuss, and to feel "at home" in the city. The choice of name is explained by the director with reference to preserving rather than exhibiting, to creating a space for dialogues whether they be heated or conciliatory. *Casa* also suggests a sheltering, the need for a shelter from an outside that is less homely, where the commitment to living together, to shared lineage, and to future fortunes cannot be assumed as it is in a home. And as Cathalina Sánchez suggests, it is a shelter for a "spirit," resonating with what I have termed the vitality of the archive. The people invest in this body of memories, they hand it over to the future so that it will continue to "live." In our interview, Sánchez told the story of a man who "just yesterday . . . came here carrying his own file in his backpack . . . he told me: 'Justicia y Paz told me to bring this here to testify. I need this to be kept in here. I need this to be known.'"[108] Sánchez comments that people not only seek to tell their stories in formal legalistic forums but also wish to share their stories elsewhere, precisely because they understand that their stories have a life beyond those formal processes: "They need [their experience] to be known, to be kept, to be saved, to be part of a general archive where they [the stories] can be consulted, because they are aware that their history is only a little piece of a bigger history that we need to know."[109] The Museo Casa de la Memoria seeks to be this place, the home for stories, for welcome, and for discussion of experiences past and present.

Yet this edifice is also a museum, the two terms—*museo* and *casa*—sitting up next to each other in a slightly awkward meeting, which makes it a rather different institution from a home. It implies and even requires an element of *display* of stories that otherwise, told within a family, are held close, kept as secrets. An exhibition is a showing and sharing, an exposure. Indeed, Mieke Bal opened her influential book about museums, *Double Exposures*, with a reflection on the terms "exposition, exposé, exposure," which she traced etymologically.[110] More clearly in classical Greek than in English, the verb *apo-deik-numai*, meaning "making a public presentation" or "publicly demonstrating," can also be connected with a noun meaning "opinions," in order to refer to the performing of those things that deserve to be made public.[111] But as discussed above, this entails decisions that render the task of the museum complex and problematic, as the humanities' critique of the museum has argued over several decades. In Colombia, putting accounts of the conflict into the public realm, and in front of "the public," positions them as authoritative, carrying ethical and political responsibility.

Bal's interest was in how the concept of exposition integral to a museum entails a gesture of exposing. It points to objects with a "Look!" that exposes them and implies a declaration of "that's how it is." Of course, a gap yawns between the mute object and the speaking or gesturing authority, and that gap is precisely where critical humanities situates its critique of the lines of power and the epistemic authority of the museum. It also, Bal notes, makes the contemporary museum a fascinating institution since it must now seek to incorporate the critique of critical humanities into a self-critical discourse while maintaining an "integrative" agenda.[112] What I have termed "the museal propositions" of the guide for the new museum constitutes such a discourse, one that is, as Bal describes, necessarily "constative"—affirmative, demonstrative, and if not authoritative then analytic—while simultaneously deconstructing, negotiating, and questioning its limitations and potential complicities.

The Museo Casa de la Memoria carries its awareness of this critique throughout the exhibitions and implicitly invites the deconstruction of

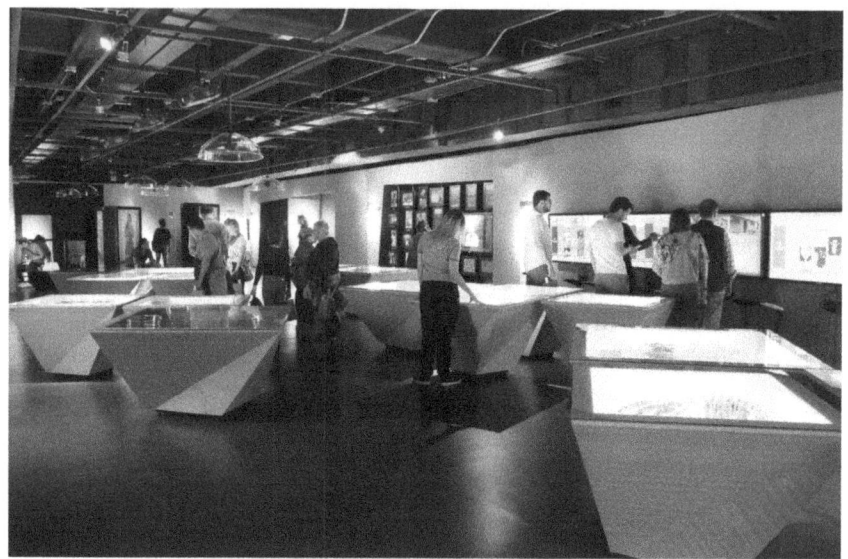

FIGURE 3.2. Interior of Museo Casa de la Memoria in Medellín. Source: Vikki Bell.

authority, its own and others, through its modes of display. As has been noted of museums elsewhere, it displays not just information but a simultaneous reflection on the limits and restrictions of the museum's enterprise.[113] Even the permanent displays embrace an ethos of the provisional and incomplete nature of an exhibition. For example, the commitment to questioning modes of narrating violence works its way into the language used in the "Look!" moments, to use Bal's terminology. In the central exhibition hall, named "Medellín: Memorias de violencia y resistencia," for example, a screen shows facts under the title "Violence in Antioquia," and announces that the following screens will show the statistics of violences committed in the region under the rubrics of the different forms of violence that are frequently employed in Colombia (fig. 3.2).[114] But immediately, the same screen notes: "This is only one dimension of the harms [*daños*] suffered by the population. There don't exist, perhaps *could never exist, precise registers* that could convey the magnitude of the harm occasioned by the war in our lands [*territorios*]." The point is repeated and fleshed out by a notice on the wall that is worth quoting in full:

The statistics that are presented here are incomplete, they are inexact. This is as much a result of the concealments, inefficiencies and omissions of public institutions as of the lack of knowledge about processes and the fear of the victims. Perhaps we will never know the dimensions of this tragedy. Nor will we know the magnitude of the intangible harms: the loss of confidence, the fears, the changes in social behavior, the mental illnesses and the cost of the loss of social ties, among many others. The cases presented here are to remind us of the value of life and the importance of continuing the search for truth, justice and reparation.

While the museum offers a lot of information through multimedia displays and installations consisting of objects, photographs, archived newspaper reports, and a detailed timeline, this marked question over the status of knowledge suggests that the long history of violence demands close and critical attention. Maintaining throughout an emphasis on the forms and routes by which knowledge comes to us, the museum avoids easy summaries or simplistic logics. On the one hand, there is clearly an ambition to tell the history of "what happened." For example, one of the museum's own guides reflects on this central hall's exposition as "seek[ing] to contribute to overcoming the indifference *and the lack of knowledge about the facts* of violence and grief, to seek understanding, social transformation and respect for life, moving towards a horizon of peace."[115] On the other, there are reminders throughout that knowledge is incomplete and in question, can only be collected piecemeal, and can hardly be "presented" in a museum, and that as a result, the journey toward understanding and toward this "horizon of peace" will be complex and difficult.

Some spaces within the Museo approach this horizon less through knowledge than through an explicitly aesthetic and affective approach, where the facts are minimal and "knowledge" is not presented as such. A darkened room situated beyond the central hall shows photographs of those who have been killed or disappeared, using mostly family photographs that are shown twice, once in color, then again altered so that only the person killed or disappeared remains in color, the others faded into monochrome. While the name and the dates of the person concerned are shown on the screen, no stories or analyses are provided. Faces smiling unknowingly, screens brightening then fading away into the cinematic darkness, names appearing briefly—a constellation of images calling for attention from all directions—the effect is immersive, cinematic, heart-wrenching (figs. 3.3 and 3.4). An almost shrine-like experience, this room requests silence, a respectful sharing in the sense of sorrow for the families of those lost to the conflict. Here then, the Museo Casa leans more toward the "casa," if you will, of grieving and consoling than the "museo" of exhibiting and informing that is the central hall.

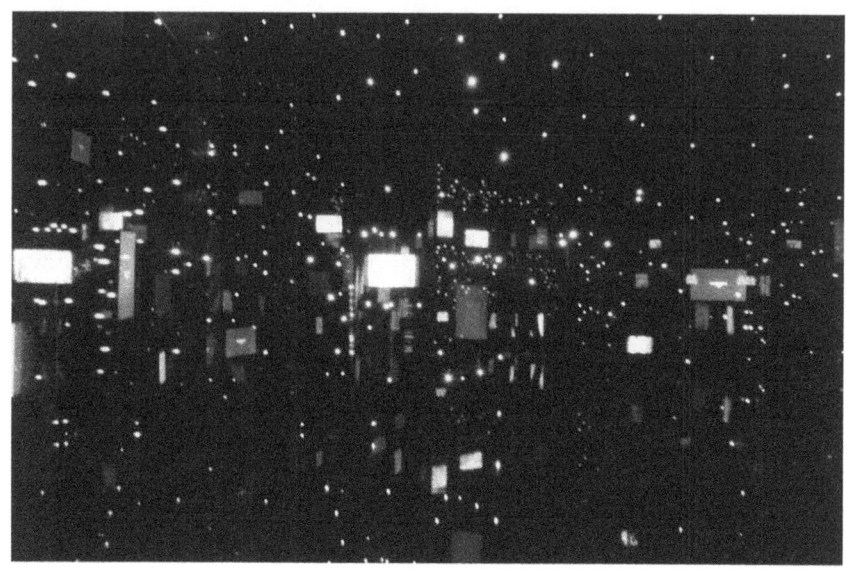

FIGURE 3.3. Museo Casa de la Memoria in Medellín. Source: Vikki Bell.

FIGURE 3.4. Museo
Casa de la Memoria
in Medellín. This
image relates to the
disappearance of
Everardo de Jesús
Carvajal Rodríguez
(*right*). Source: Vikki
Bell.

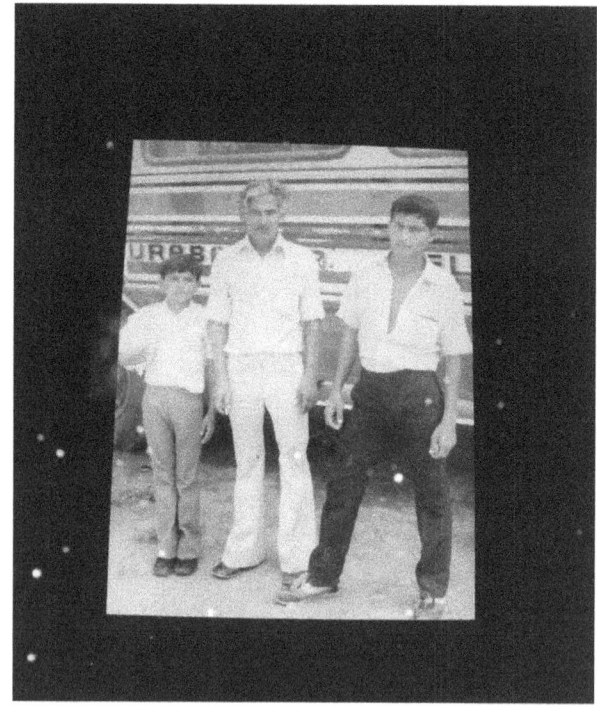

Perhaps it is through the use of its temporary exhibition space, educational program, and talks, where the museum at Medellín seeks to invite the local community into the space, that it dares to hope that it will be able to foster the conditions of possibility for a shared horizon of peace. No shared understanding or sensibility can be assumed, of course, so this ambition must repeatedly contend with the complexity of its audience and their present situations, emotions, and affiliations. On the occasion of our visit in October 2019, a new exhibition—*La Voz de las Manos*—was being launched. Under threatening skies, a little marquee and stage had been set up in front of the museum, and a discussion panel about the new exhibition was underway.

A central theme of the exhibition was reconciliation, and for this reason, the conversation with the invited speakers turned on what the term meant to them. Something of the complexity of affiliations was underscored by the intervention of one of the speakers, Ferley Ruíz Moreno, who shared his remarkable story, in which he explained how he was forced to participate in the violence, becoming a member of the Autodefensas Unidas de Colombia at the age of twelve when they came to demand that his family give something to their cause. Since his family were not in a position to pay the "tax" demanded, his father was asked to offer up one of his children. Having lost one sister who had been murdered in an attack, and in order to prevent them taking his other sister, Ruíz Moreno offered himself in her stead. Now "disengaged" (*desvinculado*) from the conflict, he offers his story to try to help others understand the complicated loyalties that surround the conflict.[116] Audience members were also invited to participate, and many did so. The woman sitting next to me stood and was invited to approach the stage. She unveiled a string from which three white squares hung, like handkerchiefs along a small washing line; on each there was pinned a photograph with a name and a few facts painted alongside them (fig. 3.5). She was handed a microphone and told us her story. Her name was Rosalba de Jesús Usma Patiño. The white panels showed both of her sons—Duber Andrés Barrio Usma and Adrian Jovanny Barrio Usma—who were both disappeared, Duber in 1998 by guerrillas, and Adrian by paramilitaries in 2002. Her daughter, whose image hangs in the middle panel, was nineteen years old when she was murdered in 2004, leaving two small children and, as the panel reads, "a mother without the love of her daughter." Rosalba's husband and three brothers had also been murdered. I took a photograph as Rosalba was sharing her moving story, and later, when I sent her the photograph, she sent me a voice message to explain the ongoing struggles of the organization Madres de la Candelaria to which she belongs. The latter organization has existed since 1999, supporting the

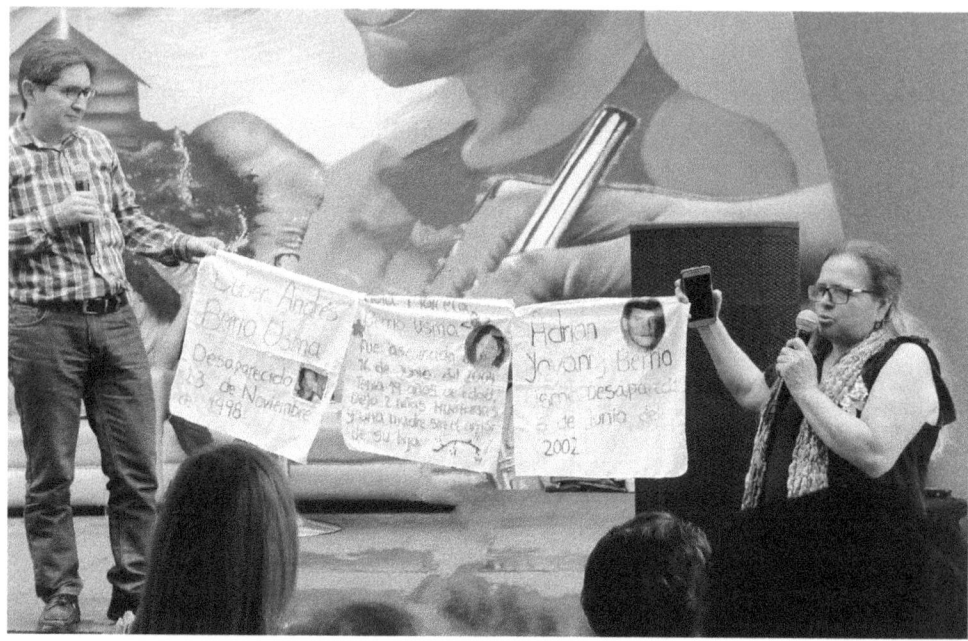

FIGURE 3.5. Rosalba de Jesús Usma Patiño at the Museo de la Memoria. Source: Vikki Bell, with permission.

relatives of those disappeared and murdered, and all who have suffered as a result of the conflict. It was, as she put it in her voice message, in order to try to "move the hearts" of those who would listen, that she continues to tell her story and those of hundreds of others, to speak up for human rights and bring attention to their continued suffering. I thought about how she had stood and literally made herself into a display, a little one-woman museum, creating a visual intervention to accompany her words. She needs her story to be exposed and retold across the world. Yet she also wants to make connections and to impress on the world how so many people beyond her have been touched by this conflict. And this is an urgent issue for present-day Colombia. Via WhatsApp we communicated back and forth over several days, a conversation during which she also sent me also the poster that was produced to express pain and indignation (*dolor y indignación*) at the murder of indigenous social leader Cristina Bautista just days after we met at the Museo Casa.[117]

By bringing together various groups and inviting people to use the museum as a safe space to tell and share their stories, to hear new dimensions and to find connections, the Museo Casa attempts to provide shelter without imposing one narrative solution upon them. It attempts, in other words, to realize its commitment to its "spirit" as described by director Sánchez Escobar in the opening of this section. I note how similar this ambition is to that which animated the CNMH's endeavors with the archive as well as its conceptual guide for the "not yet" national museum. It seeks to hold and preserve, like a house, but also, like a home, to welcome new visitors, to facilitate connections, to allow dialogue and dissent within a shared "horizon of peace."

Concluding Remarks

To reference Benjamin as I have done in this chapter was not an arbitrary choice, insofar as his work and arguments about the narration of violence and of history have been cited many times by others writing about memory politics in Colombia, including key members of the Center.[118] Yet even if that were not the case, the ethos and sensibility of the Center's work resonates profoundly with the questions Benjamin raised in the key essay I have been quoting here. If the Center's role has been to attempt the "clarification" of the history of the conflict, their ethos has been developed in order to avoid the problems Benjamin associated with the narratives of History. That is, to avoid becoming caught up in the winds of a notion of progress, insisting that the path out of violence is not as easy as documenting what has occurred. The task the Center was given by law cannot be understood as an objective, neutral task of description. Thus their central proposition, and their promise, was to approach the armed conflict through a focus on high-quality research that attends to the voices of victims as central, documenting the events and the effects of the conflict through research methods routed in their ethically attuned methods of research. But they have done so while insisting that documentation is not sufficient, that those in the future will continue to need to attend to the past and to reimagine its lessons. For this reason, they elected to arrange the "pile of debris" the conflict has left and continues to leave in its wake not only through the writing of the reports but also in the construction of the archive that it is hoped will allow and invite re-entrances. There is, I have suggested, drawing on Derrida, a "spirit of intentionality" to the archive. A fragile but crucial aspect of this spirit is that the archive is received in the future as a freely given resource, and one that invites new additions, new users and new insights to emerge from it. Moreover, the notion that the Center's work would culminate in a national museum—an idea that was received by the team as somewhat counter to their intentions, for all the reasons museums have been critiqued by humanities scholars—has been approached in a manner that resonates with central aspects of Benjamin's critical thought. As Butler muses in her reading of Benjamin, the latter implies that we might retain the hope for histories of the oppressed to be able to "flash" up and effect a "reconstellation" of the "time of the present," and that such a possibility would allow those effaced from a narrative of history as progress to make their presence felt and to exercise their demands.[119] I have suggested here that the "not yet" national museum has been imagined in the "conceptual guide" in such a way that it aims to organize its offerings thematically, using the axes that operate at a high level of abstraction in order to allow both a comprehensive expansive understanding of relevance to the conflict as well as a fluidity as to how its parts connect and allow new insights and relations to emerge. If we take the Museo Casa de la Memoria in Medellín as a model for much of what the national museum proposes, it is fascinating to see how the Museo Casa has created spaces that inform without claiming narration, how it includes affective as well as narrative spaces, and how it explicitly invites a range of voices into its space through talks and projects across the city and its diverse populations. One cannot plan for the "entrance" or the "flash" of a new memory from the past, but one can attempt to provide a place of shelter for the remains that exist as fragments in the present, and a place for debate into which all visitors are welcomed. If Benjamin posited a memory of suffering from another time that "flashes up in a moment of danger," it belongs, as Butler argues, to no one person or group; indeed it "cannot be understood as anyone's cognitive possession."[120] I have suggested that there is an optimistic reading of the institution of the museum insofar as it might embrace the task of attending to the past, sheltering stories that arise but without collecting nor assembling them too swiftly into new forms, to allow it to remain "undone," and to give a welcome to interruptions and to chance. This is what Butler calls the "wager" that Benjamin expresses. As for the "not yet" national museum, we await its opening to see whether the same sensibility can be sustained.

4

NEGOTIATING THE FORCE OF ART

The Work of Erika Diettes

Decades of academic interventions have debated the possibility—or other-wise—of art after mass atrocity. Exploring themes of witnessing, responsibility and ethics, of trauma, memory and the unimaginable, such debates have given rise to a rich library of work through which to consider images of and after violence.[1] In Latin America, as Steven Stern has argued, the "era of the dirty wars" meant that "Adorno's dictum in its more nuanced and paradoxical sense has come roaring back to life."[2] That is, not the oft-quoted aphorism that "to write poetry after Auschwitz is barbaric" but the philosopher's later formulations that concerned whether art could avoid the absurdity of thinking that cultural life would repair and restore humanity to pre-Auschwitz innocence, while using its creative forms to embark on the necessary task of exploring the world's "unconscious history."[3] As Stern expresses it, in Latin America, as elsewhere, the refusal to believe in art as a redemptive project of closure "does not cancel out the imperative to imagine the harrowing gap between what humans become and what they are meant to be. In entering that gap, art invites us to see and somehow take in as truthful experience that which is otherwise too difficult to stare at."[4] Certainly in Colombia, these concerns continue to resonate in relation to art's role in responding to the ongoing armed conflict, and the debates now unavoidably constitute the milieu within which contemporary artists produce their work.[5] How do artists approach their work in relation to these issues? How do they negotiate the dangers of art's interventions, its possessive tendencies and complicities? This chapter focuses on the work of the Colombian artist Erika Diettes (b. 1978), whose artworks have addressed themes of absence, disappearance, and memory after the atrocities of the armed conflict for several years now.[6] In order to explore her work and her working process, I interviewed her on several occasions, both in person and, during the COVID-19 pandemic, via Zoom. For Diettes, it became clear, there is an imperative to produce art in response to the devastation that the country has experienced not only because *not* to do so is to contribute to a sense of abandonment felt by many whose lives have been devastated by the armed conflict, but also because the work is a way to enfold the "too difficult" issue of the ongoing violence into public spaces. As one would expect, however, and as the chapter will explore further, there are challenges in pursuing this work, in seeking to respond "appropriately," which is to say in a way that, without ever being able to *give* justice, nevertheless "does justice." Every decision the artist makes wrestles with the *force* of art, its potential gift but also its potential failure, its ability to focus attention, to edit, frame, and choose the distance from which we engage with the issues it treats. It wrestles with the risk inherent in making images that may—monstrously, as Jean-Luc Nancy phrased it in an argument to which I will return below—grant violence its innermost desire to see the mark of its impact both on those it has targeted and, through the ripple effects of its devastation, on the world.[7]

The Sigh of Sorrow: *Sudarios*

Panels of delicate silk are hanging in the quiet space of a former church, suspended from the high ceiling. On each is printed the face of a woman, a close photographic portrait in black and white enlarged to seven feet. In all bar one of the twenty panels, the woman has her eyes closed and her brow furrowed as she seems to suffer an internal anguish that we witness but cannot share (fig. 4.1). For this installation, named *Sudarios* (Shrouds), Diettes spent many hours listening to the stories of victims of Colombia's armed conflict. Each of the women photographed for the *Sudarios* project was a victim in the same specific way: each had been forced to witness atrocities enacted against her loved ones. While she watched, a father, mother, husband, or

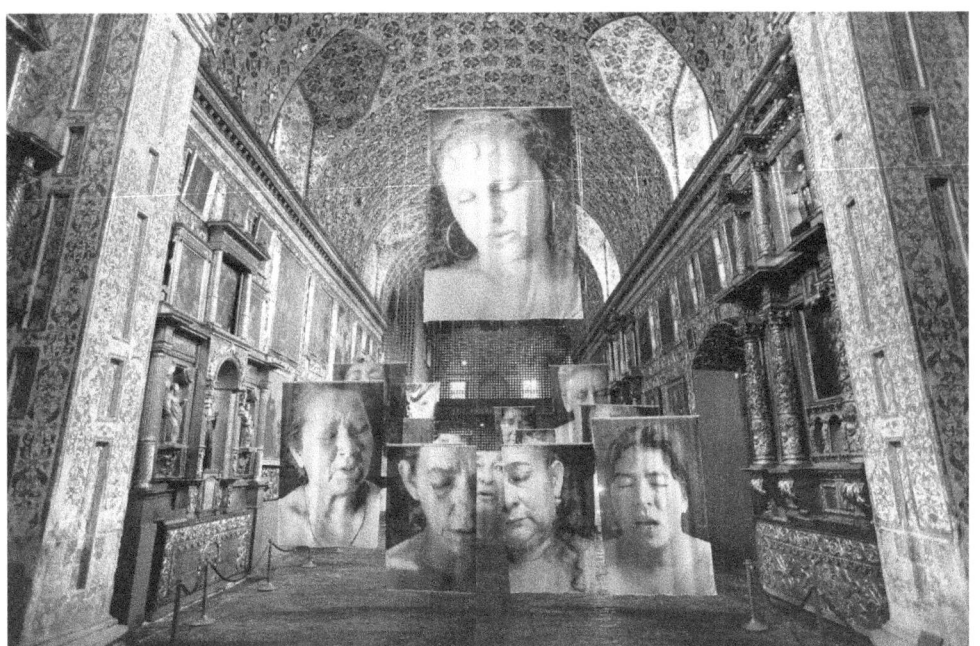

FIGURE 4.1. *Sudarios* installation at Museo Iglesia de Santa Clara in Bogotá, 2011. Black-and-white digital photography and silk printing. Source: Erika Diettes, with permission.

other relative was brutally tortured and killed in front of her. The shrouds do not depict those who have died, therefore, but those who are obliged to remain behind, the ones who survive, who must keep living. Although there is no accompanying text at the exhibition to give the shocking detail of these women's experiences[8]—like Doris Salcedo's work, the artwork arises from hearing these stories and is not intended as an illustration of testimonies but rather as an "exposure" of vulnerabilities in the wake of violence[9]—this use of grotesque violence as a spectacle and warning has been a common feature of the violence perpetrated by armed agents in Colombia's years of conflict.[10] Diettes's piece provides a meditation on the aftermath of this violence and the difficulties of being able to speak of and through the pain of these memories. The exhibition has been mounted several times across Colombia, as well as internationally in Australia, the United States and the United Kingdom, where Diettes has sought out places of quiet contemplation, mostly churches.

Diettes's portraits were taken while the women recounted the atrocities they had witnessed. They convey the intense embodied experience as they try to find the words to tell. As we look up at their faces, exposed as they are to our gaze, their eyelids fall, enclosing them within their selves, beyond us and beyond communication (fig. 4.2). They are undoubtedly what has been termed "haptic" images, meaning those that do not invite identification with the figure so much as they encourage a dynamic visceral communication between viewer and image.[11] The women seem to be fighting an internal battle in which we cannot join, and one which, in this moment, we fear they may be losing. They are paused in their speech, but one senses that they are watching the devastating scenes once again in their mind's eye. *Sudarios* gently asks that our attentions be on the isolation of their struggle, one of remembering, recounting, surviving. With their sorrow, the women are at the limits of language and at the limits of what they can bear.

As the breeze catches one of the ethereal panels, it flutters and twists as if the woman were moaning, while the others ripple and float like kites in a chorus of mourning. If we can attend to it, there is a "complex musics of the photograph," as Moten has suggested, a soundscape that precedes the image, and that requests our attention even though what we listen to "is also unbearable."[12] These images of desperate mourning certainly evoke that moaning, an absent sound that precedes, accompanies, and "augments" them, contributing to their "force." In fact, at the first exhibition of *Sudarios*, in Bogotá, Diettes included a looped audio recording of one of the women sighing at the end of her telling the story. After that show, however, she decided the audiotape was superfluous, since the spaces themselves, chosen for their quiet beauty, were somehow already able to provide—to provoke—the soundtrack.[13] To enter the spaces was to enter a meditative and reverential space of reflection. Faced with the images' own "musics," the mourning/moaning, the visitors stopped talking, Diettes recalls. Their own breath became a point of awareness and its gentle sound the only audible response, as if the spaces themselves were sighing. A response to the devastation etched on the women's faces, and to a sense of inadequacy in response, the sigh was all that remained.

Like Bill Viola's video works that have restaged scenes from old masters, mostly those depicting the story of Christ's suffering, *Sudarios* focuses attention on the minutiae of bodily and especially facial movements that emotion produces. "The body is the storm-centre, the origin of co-ordinates, the constant place of stress in all that experience-train," wrote William James more than a century ago.[14] In both Bill Viola's *The Quintet of the Astonished* (2000), inspired by Hieronymus Bosch's painting of Christ's executioners, where five performers move through a range of emotions, and his *Dolorosa*

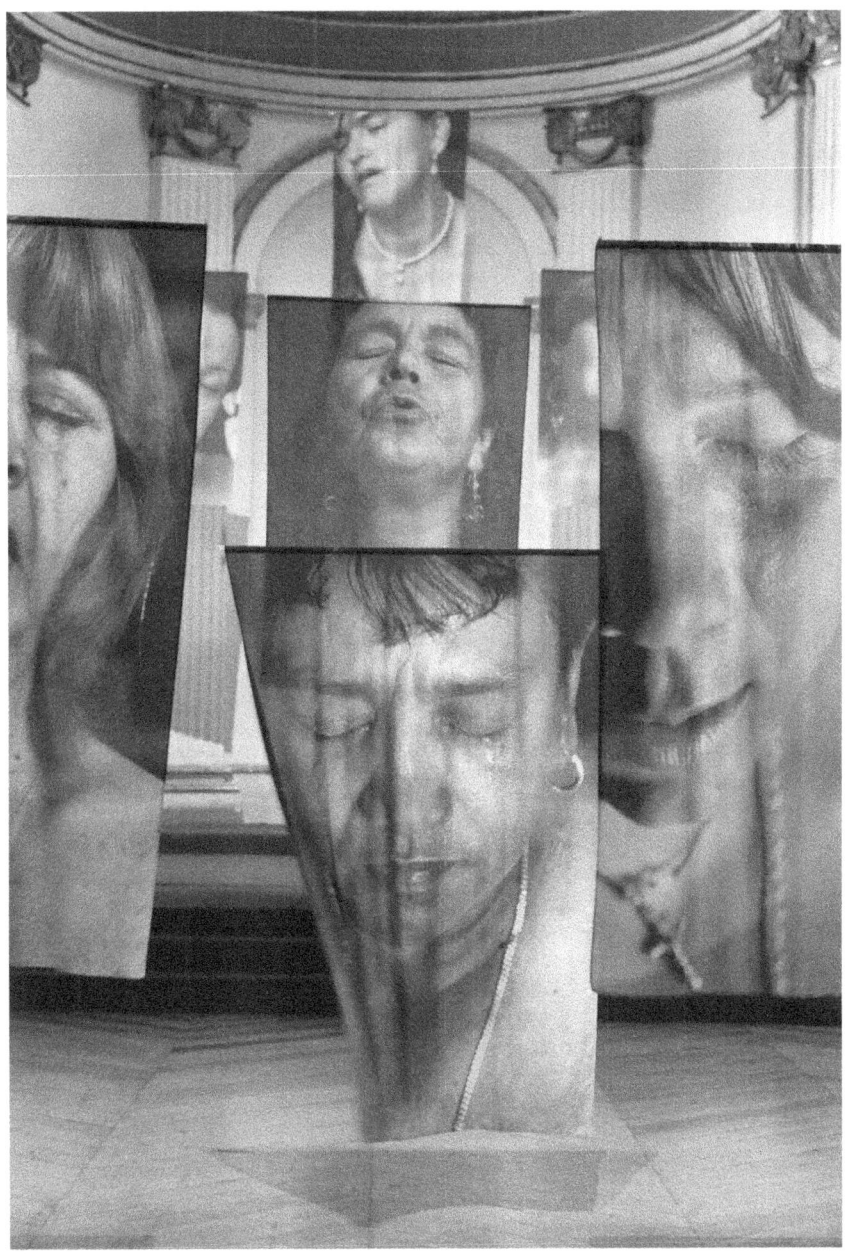

FIGURE 4.2. *Sudarios* installation at ex Teresa Arte Actual in Mexico City, 2012. Black-and-white digital photograph and silk printing. Source: Erika Diettes, with permission.

(2000) in which, in a response to Dieric Bouts's fifteenth-century panels, a man and woman very slowly and perpetually grieve, Viola digitally slowed their movement to effect a peculiar deceleration.[15] Consequently, as Mark Hansen has described, the figures "appear to undergo extremely subtle . . . shifts in emotional, or better, affective tonality."[16] Of the intensification that results, Hanson has written: "By presenting normally imperceptible facial cues that signal the body's very aliveness, the affective shifts on the faces of the represented figures trigger richly nuanced resonances in the body of the viewer."[17] The work "puts perception into the service of affection . . . opening perception . . . to its own radical imperceptible—affectivity."[18] Likewise, I would argue, Diettes's images capture the contortions of the face as emotions move through embodied subjects; while each image is a still photograph, the movement is provided in other ways: by the sense of memory-images moving across the women's faces as they "see" the awful memory once again, by the breeze catching the diaphanous material on which it is printed, and by the series, the fact that they move together in the space, suggesting the shared milieu of this violence and grieving.

That the images that compose *Sudarios* acknowledge the ongoing impact of the violence on these women's lives is significant enough in Colombia, where the Peace Accord brokered in 2016 is under pressure from many directions, where "listening" is a highly uneven enterprise. The scale of the task—over 262,000 have been killed across the years of armed conflict—tends to diminish hopes of Colombia reaching a full collective understanding or even proper acknowledgment of the impact of its armed conflict.[19] While the institutions of the SIVJRNR (el Sistema Integral de Verdad, Justicia, Reparación y No Repetición) set up under the Agreement continue to function, and many victims' organizations have participated in them—by, for example, offering their submissions to the JEP (Jurisdicción Especial para la Paz)—it is difficult to find optimism around the process. In this space and time, "before" the law, if you will, where there is no real sense of whether or how the thousands of injustices committed will be addressed, art plays a very special role. Art cannot *do* justice, it certainly cannot *give* justice, but existing in the messiness of the present, where those who have suffered from the violence of the conflict are obliged to carry on, it is a realm able to provide an attention of sorts. It constitutes a work of response, albeit it an aesthetic response. And insofar as this is the case, one can certainly suggest that it facilitates debate around justice, on many levels, including around the "justness"—the aptness—of the image.

If, as Mihaela Mihai has recently argued, artists can make interventions that practice an "aesthetic care," it can be understood as a care built upon an attention to relationality, routed as with Diettes's work through a feminist ethics.[20] There was certainly a central principle of care within the *Sudarios* project, with ethical principles and considerations informing each stage of Diettes's process of making art, beginning with the relationship between artist and subjects. Diettes spent several hours with these women listening to their stories, establishing relationships. She worked alongside her friend, a sociologist called Nadis Londoño, who was experienced in leading workshops with groups of people traumatized by the conflict from the Antioquia area. Over the course of several sessions, as the women talked, the portraits were taken, although Diettes took surprisingly few images—only around twenty of each woman—to reduce her intrusion. Conscious of the ethics of photography in relation to trauma, Diettes explains that although she wanted them to be unposed images, taken during the course of the conversation, she was careful to ensure that the women knew that photographs were being taken. She wanted them to feel that they were collaborators in the production of the image, so that the results were not "stolen."[21] For this reason she installed the camera and full studio apparatus, including lights, in plain sight so that the equipment was obvious to all. As the theorist Ariella Azoulay has emphasized, the photographic image is the result of an assemblage that includes not only the human relations between subject and photographer, not only the physical apparatus of the camera, tripod, and, lights, but also the "agreement to be seen."[22] To remember this, to keep uppermost an expanded awareness of the processes by which an image is created within the analysis of photographic images, is to maintain awareness of the civic relations of what Azoulay terms the "civil contract" of photography. Speaking of photographs that show the marks that violence leaves on human bodies, Azoulay argues that the civil contract is made between the photographed, who agree or even in some cases demand to be photographed, those who take the photograph, and those who, in looking upon it, also enter the relations of obligation that the contract sets in train. Here, where Diettes seeks to create photographs that speak of the unbearable pain caused by armed conflict in Colombia, where the relations between citizens and the state as well as between citizens themselves have fallen apart, her photographs work not only as an acknowledgment and reminder of the conflict but also—through its riposte to the violence that has been visited upon these women—as a call for a sense of civic obligation toward those who have suffered such profound losses. It is an attempt to facilitate the potential of the photograph to act *for* those it captures, to call out the failures of the state and the peace process through its request of the spectator as a citizen of photography.

Yet Diettes knows that these are processes that are not in the hands of the photographer alone, and she shies away from grandiose statements about the impact that the work might have. By the same token, perhaps, she seeks to give something more immediate (back) to those she photographs. The care she shows for her participants has been noted by others. Indeed, her work has been described as itself a shroud-like wrapping, constituted through gestures of care and comfort; Ileana Diéguez writes in her essay that Diettes's work is itself "the fabric of an extensive and intimate shroud with which to wrap, consecrate, bid farewell, and provide a final resting place for bodies not yet laid to rest."[23] Beyond the immaterial—time, care, consideration— aspects that the project offers through the process of making the work, she always also gifts a piece of the project to each participant, a framed portrait for example, individual artworks that the participants value highly. She continues to share with them also the pleasure of seeing the work installed in beautiful settings around Colombia and internationally.[24]

Mihai's thesis was that artworks also have the potential to complicate how violences are remembered, to question "the *grands récits*" that risk retaining the exclusionary accounts of community held by its perpetrators.[25] The care of which she writes therefore is a care that refuses to simplify, that cares enough to resist the simplified narrative, and that does not demur from allowing incomplete, messy, and complex aspects of past violence to remain part of the process of remembering. I would add that if visual art can nurture the possibility of a complex and plural memory-making, it is in part because it is released from the need to provide an account. Unlike a truth commission, then, or a trial, their presence is not given in order for us to garner knowledge. Rather than being absorbed into knowledge, rather than being turned to a purpose, *Sudarios* offers no explanation or account of the violence. Instead, it offers the installation as an opportunity for the contemplative consideration, as with Diettes's images of the women's internal struggles in the shadow of their memories. Andreas Huyssen has written recently in a similar vein about the work of Doris Salcedo, the most well-known contemporary Colombian artist, whose installation works are less about conveying the content of the stories from the armed conflict than they are about the process of memory, prompting the viewer into considerations of the politics of how memories appear in public space.[26]

Undoubtedly, Diettes's portraits recall the Roman Catholic tradition of Marian art, like so many instances of our lady of the sorrows. And yet these women will not be assimilated to historic representations, for they are clearly photographed, of "our time." And they are unabashedly fleshy. No collars or scarves cover the skin of their faces or necklines, their beauty in the realistic details of their human forms, unadorned or else only sparsely so by a simple chain or earring. These women are most assuredly here, living here on earth, "with" us, breathing the same air. Real as they are, however, the women in these portraits are also undeniably removed from us. To receive these images is to experience them at once before us and simultaneously receding, like the participant who, Diettes recalls, said of her struggle to continue living: "I am alive, but I am a ghost."[27] Flooded by the pain of remembrance, overwhelmed by their memories, the women seem to be caught in their "absence," turning in on themselves as they drift away, a sense further emphasized by their delicate material form.

Perhaps every photograph takes flight. Perhaps every attempt to "acknowledge" through portraiture requires a negotiation of a gulf that opens up. Jean-Luc Nancy has suggested that "every photograph is an irrefutable and luminous 'I am,' whose proper subject is neither the subject nor the photographing subject [who are forever united in the 'eternal instant that trembles in the photo'], but the silvery or digital evidence of a *grasping*. . . . This grasping presents itself and says to us 'I am.'"[28] The photograph declares itself as a form of presence, but crucially, at the same time, Nancy argues, this *I am* says "nous autres."[29] There is a gap therefore, that opens up as the image, any image, withdraws from those who gaze upon it, asserting its alterity *as* image. The sense of the women in the *Sudarios* photographs being "taken," then, the intense sorrow that constitutes the pathos of these portraits, only deepens the withdrawal and distancing that accompanies every photo-image as it "strays into strangeness" and in doing so "estranges us."[30] Indeed, in the showing of the *Sudarios* we are continually reminded, as I've eluded, that a curtain, however delicate, separates each of us. This is accentuated when Diettes hangs the *Sudarios* low to the ground so that the visitors walk close to and between the panels. The women are so close, available for our scrutiny. Yet because they are turned inward, detached, their eyes closed, they are like sleepers, they are not in communication with us, even as we may consider them so closely. Everything that comes to them comes from themselves "without any distance to travel, without any performance to present," as Nancy wrote of sleepers.[31]

Interestingly, Nancy's thoughts on the photograph's flight into strangeness, its removal or withdrawal from the viewer, is accompanied by the thought that ultimately every "I am" is "laden in the depths of it-self with innumerable we-others" so that perhaps this is what "the photograph charges itself with uncovering, suggesting."[32] He writes: "Each 'subject' in the photo refers tacitly, obstinately, to all others, to this prodigious universe of photos (in)to which we all take ourselves and one another, at some time or another. This colossal and labyrinthine phototheque in whose depths there stalks— like a Minotaur—monster, the monstration, and the prodigious image of our strangeness. The encounter is always monstrous, or monstrating, ostensive and threatening, invasive and evasive in the same moment, straying in its capture, released in being grasped."[33]

This is an alarming passage, one that suggests that perhaps whatever care is taken, whatever attempt we might make to receive a portrait in its uniqueness, its forceful, declarative "I am" will ultimately be undermined by the references it cannot but simultaneously make to all other subjects, all other images. Moreover, to look at the portraits and to see their resonance, as I have done with innumerable *Mater dolorosas* or with Bill Viola's works, is to treat them superficially, even monstrously. As Emmanuel Levinas wrote, to take someone's experience "in," to hear her story and to assimilate it to our knowledge, is bound to fail before the ethical challenge of meeting the other, halting the encounter's potential reverberations.[34] What is lost as one becomes lost in this labyrinth is the sense of the unique suffering and the story of the individual before us, as well as the obligations that are being requested of us. We are wandering in image-genealogies that will entice us deeper into the archive while avoiding the very specificity of each portrait, each experience. Like art history as a discipline, which refers newly encountered images backward, comforting itself by receiving contemporary work by uncovering within it references to previous images, it is an approach that fails to ask, as Mieke Bal's critique of art history suggested, the specific conditions of possibility of *this* image.[35]

In *Sudarios*, each woman—one feels it—has gathered herself and asserted her own story (her "I am"). And if there is a profound force to this assertion, as Nancy suggests, one that the image attempts to gather and present as a gesture of acknowledgment that can even be celebrated as "survival," it is also a force that creates the "*nous autres*," an asymmetrical relation. In the context of the armed conflict in Colombia, moreover, one cannot but also hear Nancy's lurking "monsters" less metaphorically. For the asymmetry that is the condition of possibility of the image is also its accusation. Before and beyond the making of the image, that is, there is the irreducible fact of the violence. These women—all from the Antioquia region of Colombia—have stories that are uniquely horrific however much they share aspects with thousands upon thousands of other instances of human cruelty in this conflict. Moreover, since, as Nancy writes in another passage, violence is intrinsically bound to notions of monstrating, as violence—the violent person—desires precisely

to see the marks that it makes on the other, and consists of the imprint-
ing of such a mark on its target, any image has to negotiate the potential it
carries of gifting violence precisely what it seeks, an image of its impact on
the world.[36] This is where the monstrous resides, in the repetition of human
monstrosity. One cannot receive the force of the assertion of the image as
unique, as the "I am," therefore, without also acknowledging the vulnerability
exposed and always already thematized, if you will, by violence.

To Shape the Unimaginable: *Río Abajo* and *Relicarios*

Diettes's work is born out of her sensitivity to these issues, ones that all
photographers are obliged to negotiate and that become acute in projects
such as hers. Her previous project, through which she met the women of the
Sudarios, was focused on objects rather than portraiture. With a lyricism
that acknowledges the unique story of each individual without compromis-
ing the identities of their families in what is an ongoing situation of fear, *Río
Abajo* (2007–8, which she chose to translate as "Drifting Away") began in
response to an article in the Colombian newspaper *El Tiempo* entitled "Colombia Is Searching for Its Dead." The article reported on the district attorney's office's request for people to help identify pieces of clothing in order to
identify bodies.[37] Deeply moved by the photographs of clothing reproduced
in the newspaper—bones with the footwear still attached, shoes and other
clothing—Diettes became intrigued by the idea that these materials that had
molded themselves to the individual's body, that had protected them, were
being called upon to identify the missing person.

Through the contacts of her family and friends, Diettes reached out to
relatives of people who had lost loved ones in the conflict. She included as
many different groups and sectors of those affected as possible, wanting the
work to speak to the whole country rather than to particular groups within
it, in an attempt to allow the possibility of communication across political
differences.[38] Moreover, Diettes worked again in the tension between the desire to honor the memory of the specific person and gift a work of beauty to
the relatives who had introduced her to that person's memory, while eschewing the impulse to give an account of the violence that they or their families
suffered.[39] The work started, as did *Sudarios*, with Diettes listening to each
of their stories in depth, as an important part of the process, giving time to
receiving the gift of the story. Only once the relatives knew Diettes did she
request the loan of articles of clothing—shirts, shoes, caps—or other personal
items, such as spectacles, that had belonged to their loved ones. These were

items that they had preserved, that they may have grabbed as they had to flee from their homes, or kept in hopeful anticipation that their relative might return. As time passed, the items had been kept as mementos, taking on a status as quasi-relics. Diettes's gathering of them constituted a special archive, one that as Ann Laura Stoler speculated in her remarks on archiving as dissensus, used saved clothing as a humble material object that "condense[s] accretions of relation," approaching it as an idiom that fits awkwardly into the established archival idioms but that to which we can, and should, attend nevertheless.[40]

Each item bears the imprint of its owner in some real or abstract way, and Diettes knew, even before she had a sense of what the artwork would be, that she was being trusted with precious objects, invaluable to their donors. One woman told her that she had sewn the shirt of her loved one into her pillow and slept on it every night; only for Diettes's project did she remove it.[41] Charged with such treasured belongings, the photographer documented each donated piece carefully and stored them safely while they were in her care. Indeed, such was their sacred status for the relatives that Diettes says she waited some time before she decided how to photograph them, taking them out only to look at them "as if awaiting permission from the object itself to take its picture."[42] No doubt she was wondering—one can understand her hesitation—how to negotiate the potential she had to be part of Nancy's labyrinthine "phototheque," how not to repeat violence's monstrous "monstration."

In the case of the crime of forced disappearance, the pain of grieving is compounded by the cruelty of the victims' bodies' status as unknown or unrecovered, many buried in mass graves by perpetrators or in unmarked graves by those who find the bodies but cannot identify them. For many relatives, the relation to the very landscape of one's region and of the country is irreparably altered. Not least the rivers. Throughout Colombia's conflict, bodies have been thrown into rivers, rendering them cemeteries for untold numbers of victims.[43]

Eventually Diettes was obliged to make her decision. One might even say that she was forced or had to force herself to decide. As Derrida has written, despite and amid the dangers, we must speak of the unspeakable; one cannot *not* speak, without "forming the worst complicities,"[44] without being irresponsive. But that decision to speak will both *require and be a force*. Hence Diettes's hesitations and care; she felt the need to tread carefully. These negotiations— which arise from an awareness and acceptance of the risks of the force one wields—are unavoidable. In art as in law, the attempt to "do justice" to the experience and situations at stake will ultimately require the decision to cut across the contemplation and the process.[45] Despite the difficulties of bearing witness, one has to *force* oneself to save something. Primo Levi wrote in *If This Is a Man*: "We must not become beasts. Even in this place one can survive, and therefore one must want to survive, to tell the story, to bear witness; and to survive *we must force ourselves* to save at least the skeleton, the scaffolding, the form of civilization."[46] The importance of recognizing the force that is required—and that also makes one's wielding of it risky and even dangerous—is made by Colin Perrin, who also writes beautifully in the same piece about the breath as the "silent 'foundation' of human rights," an argument that resonates with my point above concerning the sigh.[47] In her own essay for the *Memento Mori* book, Diettes opens with a quotation from Georges Didi-Huberman's *Images in Spite of All*: "Seizing an image from it, in spite of itself? Yes. It was *imperative* to give shape to the unimaginable whatever the cost. The possibilities of fleeing Auschwitz were so scarce that the simple release of an image or some kind of information—a map, some numbers, some names— became the necessity itself, one of the last gestures of humanity."[48]

For *Río Abajo*, Diettes's decision was to photograph the pieces of clothing and articles beneath water, acknowledging the disturbing role that rivers have assumed in Colombia's conflict (fig. 4.3). The water lends the objects a sense of movement once more, giving an element of chance and even "freedom," if you will, to the objects. Diettes printed the images large, so the clothing was at least life-size, onto glass panels.[49] The glass allowed the images to retain the translucence of the clear water and the vibrancy of the colors of the objects, something that Diettes decided was important after listening to one of the first mothers who gave her a red shirt belonging to her son.[50] The mother had chosen this particular shirt, she told Diettes, because "in this [red] shirt, my son looked so handsome. When he put on the red shirt, he looked divine."[51] The resulting image becomes an understated, vibrant celebration of his life, a bold color suggestive of his youth, gently floating yet animated by the swirl of the water. Color also meant, Diettes notes, that the images resemble stained-glass windows, especially as they were displayed upright, away from the walls within self-supporting frames, and the light passes through the colorful images accentuating the colors, working with the water's patterns to accentuate the sense of gentle movement as one moves around them.

In this way, Diettes's decisions remained aesthetic while they simultaneously sought to retain the specificity of the memories and the quasi-religious status given to the clothing by the families, who had often been treating them like sacred objects, including through rituals such as washing them on an anniversary or at Christmastime. Indeed, following her first exhibition in Grenada, Antioquia, where people were taking part in La Marcha

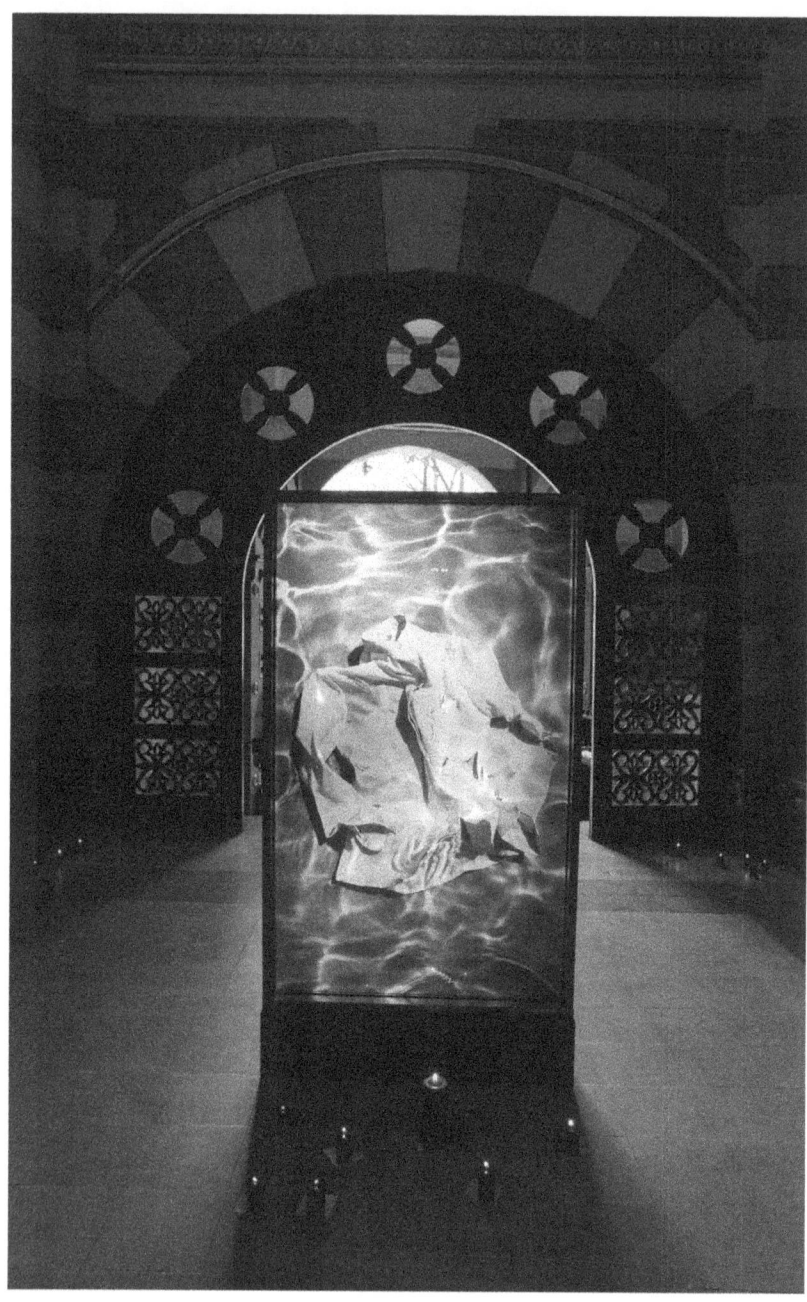

FIGURE 4.3. Installation of *Río Abajo*, Parroquia Nuestra Señora de las Nieves in Bogotá, 2014. Here the image of the shirt of a disappeared person seems to float. Relatives treated the image as a shrine of sorts, laying candles at its base. Source: Erika Diettes, with permission.

de la Luz, a monthly march organized by the victims' organizations to pray for peace while carrying candles through the streets, she realized that the images were being used precisely as focal points in the process of memorialization. Relatives ended the march at the images, placing their candles around them and spending time with them, remembering and praying. Sensing that the relatives found comfort through this relation to the image, she explicitly facilitated this role, installing each piece in its individually demarcated space with votive candles at its foot. Indeed, Diettes ended up making more pieces for the *Río Abajo* collection than she had thought possible at the outset, some 150, as ever more people asked to lend clothes and objects for the project.

Throughout this time, Diettes was deeply aware that the process of creating and showing the artworks had the potential to create a finality that was potentially painful for the families, not least because simply giving her the clothes was a tacit acceptance of the death. To keep the clothes stored at home was an indication that their hope that the relative might still return one day, and would need to wear his or her clothes once more, had not diminished. So—and even though Diettes always returned the pieces to the families—the artworks became for many the first public memorials to lives now considered lost. And in the absence of the possibility of a grave, they became charged with profound emotive force.

Relicarios (2010–17), a work that Diettes made over several years, was in many ways a continuation of the *Río Abajo* project. Again working with relatives, she was given treasured objects from them, a collection of personal belongings or mementos—a list of them would include ordinary, quotidian items such as a comb, a razor, shoes, a toothbrush, keys, a sports trophy, tools, toys, a tape measure, rosary beads, as well as photographs, among others—that, through the act of collecting, presenting, and curating, Diettes makes extraordinary. Diettes presented each object or set of objects in a cuboid form by setting them within rubber tripolymer, a soft, gel-like resin. The objects are held there, but seem to float within the gel (fig. 4.4). This preserves the item, and invites inspection of it, lending it the aura of a scientific specimen. Indeed, Diettes has said that her original inspiration for the presentation was amber, which "might have an insect preserved within it for millennia," a metaphor, for her, of Colombia's grieving over so many years of conflict, decade after decade, generation after generation.[52]

But it is not a scientific or forensic gaze requested here, one that seeks causality, since the "remainders" of a life cannot answer in that mode, nor do they seek to do so. Rather, Diettes has produced an archive of sorts, with each *Relicario* prompting the visitor to spend time with an individual's possessions.

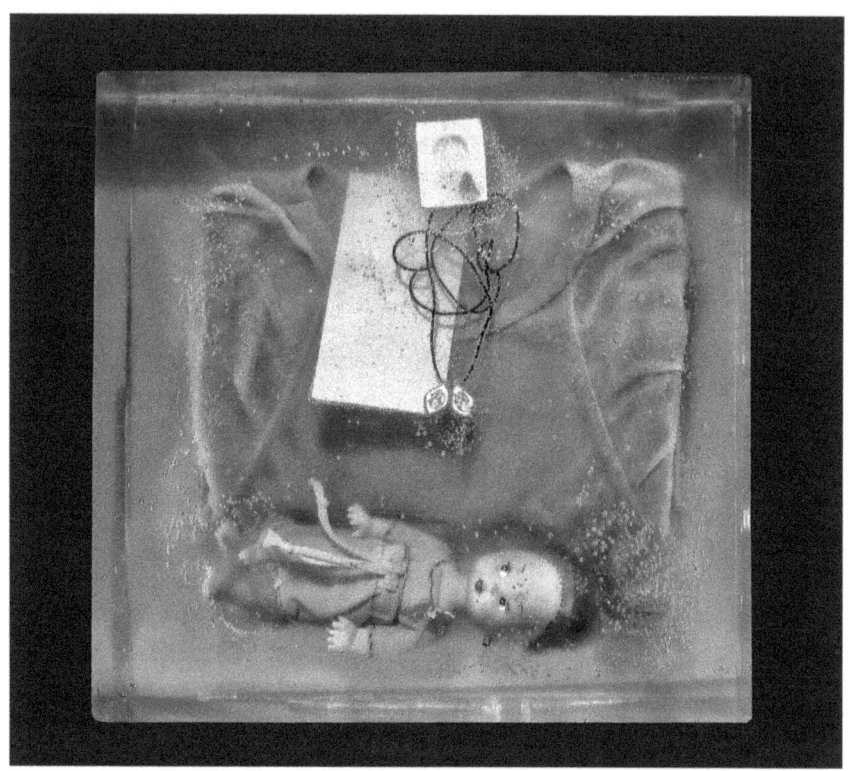

FIGURE 4.4. From the series *Relicarios*. Mixed media in rubber tripolymer, 2010–17. Source: Erika Diettes, with permission.

The object or objects may be mere fragments of a shattered life, but they are given value precisely by becoming part of this archive. Each item has been selected by the relatives for its ability to summon the deceased, and its participation in the exhibition intensifies that ability to conjure him or her up because it is asked, implicitly, to "stand for" that person. So while the number of pieces laid out in careful rows suggests an ordering and equivalence, like the repeated "NN" of the anonymous graves where graveyard keepers tried to abide by the administrative rules by recording the bodies lain to rest there, the idiosyncratic nature of the objects always suggests the specificity of one life, one case, fighting against generalizations. Any knowledge garnered, like any knowledge that might arise from contemplation of the clothes in *Río Abajo*, cannot be aggregated.

Displayed low on the floor, the *Relicarios* appear like small graves in a cemetery. This, especially for the many cases where there is an absence of a

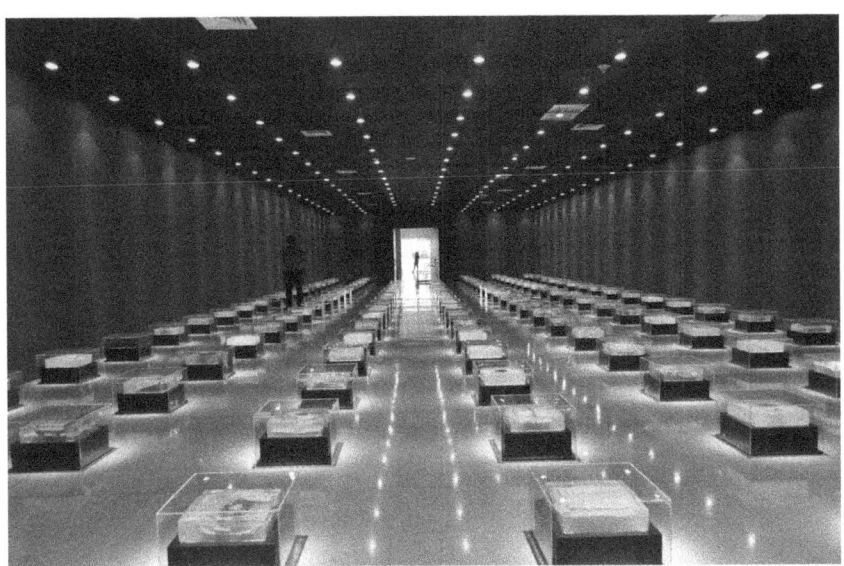

FIGURE 4.5. *Relicarios* installation at Museo de Antioquia in Medellín, 2016. Photo: Eliana Medina B. From the archive of the artist. Source: Erika Diettes, with permission.

real grave, adds poignancy to the installation, while the use of low lighting requests respect and quiet. Spotlights illuminating each cuboid lend drama and accentuate the transparency of the material and draw one to the detail of this beautiful work (fig. 4.5). Visitors need to adopt the respectful bodily posture of the mourner, as one must walk along narrow paths in order to look at them, cast one's eyes down to see the objects in each, and kneel beside them to see details, the chosen objects and personal possessions made poignant by their collection here. In one, for example, is a photographic portrait of a young girl, wearing sneakers with one leg crossed over the other, her long hair worn loose. On top of the photograph, Diettes has placed the girl's comb, a pink plastic wide-toothed comb, so that we glimpse her image through the lines of its teeth. The object is as resonant as the photograph here, something the girl would have had in her hands every day, now passing from the hands of the grieving mother to Diettes to include here. In her two-volume work, *Memento mori,* that documents the process of making the series, Diettes includes a photograph of the mother clutching the comb.[53]

Diettes senses the problems of making these stories into yet more images of tragedy in which the losses and experiences become interchangeable and the art becomes the opportunity to merely repeat an attitude of hopelessness in the face of the incomprehensibility of the armed conflict Colombia has suffered. Perhaps due to these concerns, Diettes was adamant that she wanted the relatives to be the first visitors to the initial exhibition at the Museum of Antioquia in Medellín. It was less that she wanted their approval, although she delights in the response that relatives have given her to the work and to the high-quality photographic images of each *Relicario* that she has given as a gift to the relatives, and more that she wanted to gather their experiences of the art-making process, to allow them to reflect on it and provide her with feedback. It was also fundamentally important for Diettes that the relatives were given time to meet and to listen to each other. The exhibition's opening was exclusively for the relatives and was followed by a three-day workshop, led by Diettes, for over three hundred relatives who traveled, some very long distances, to take part. On the first day the relatives discussed their experiences of giving the items and being part of the exhibition. It was overwhelmingly positive. One woman, for example, wrote of the comfort she found in seeing her *Relicario* in the museum: "I found the *Relicario* of my son and my husband. I felt happy to see them together and I was able to put my arms around them. I said a silent prayer and told them 'I haven't abandoned you. Look, my loves, where you are! In a museum as you deserve'... I felt satisfied that I had done my duty to give them so dignified and atmospheric a space. May they rest in peace."[54] Her sentiments suggest that the dignity and atmosphere of the museum restores her sense of fulfilling her role in relation to their memory, a role of nonabandonment, and that the museum setting also affords a status that reflects and extends a concern within the wider community. As de Duve has argued, speaking about the photographs of prisoners at S-21 in Cambodia, giving the name "art" has this potential: "Baptizing them, in the second person—'You are art'—is just one way, the clumsiest, certainly, of making sure that the people in the photos are restored to their humanity; and this, not their so-called art status, is what matters."[55] The museum requests not just looking, but *regard* for the work, and by extension, the people from whose stories the art arose. The second day gave them space to tell each other their stories, including listening to stories from people whose relatives had been members of an opposing armed group.[56] Diettes had explicitly wished for the work to allow this sharing of grief across different groups of the armed conflict, in order, as she explained, to listen to the victims of the "grieving country" as a whole; using art as a point of connection, a facilitating site, *Relicarios* brought together those who were victims of guerrillas, paramilitaries, and the scandalous "*falsos positivos*," those murdered by the Colombian army in order to boost their numbers of armed actors apprehended. Given the lack of such opportunities for the society to really listen to the victims through any official institutional channel, Diettes understands the importance of a space of listening and sharing such stories across and beyond the distinctions that conflict imposes.

What these activities and gestures underscore is that Diettes's art is not an attempt to "represent" the armed conflict or the violence perpetrated. Much as María del Rosario Acosta López has argued in her discussions of Colombian artists Oscar Muñoz, Doris Salcedo, and Juan Manuel Echavarría, Diettes's art is able to open up encounters with Colombia's past, but it does not seek to return us experientially to that past.[57] Nor indeed does Diettes wish to preserve memory eternally in the present. Instead, as Acosta López suggests, her art holds the possibility of allowing reflection on the present, working with the fragility of memory to offer society the chance to glimpse not only the absences that color the present, the memories that may yet not survive, but also to approach the sense in which the present is always hanging in the balance, on the point of disappearing—that is, "to accompany the past in its fading [as it disappears]."[58] While Diettes's intervention is first and foremost for the victims, relatives, and survivors of that violence, therefore, it is not an attempt to represent or "commemorate" their stories. She remains on and embraces art's register, which is to say that, by presenting something overtly—both merely and powerfully—aesthetic, Diettes seeks to reciprocate the gift of people's participation, to respond to their stories, with her beautiful and sensitive installations, while simultaneously acknowledging the limitations of the aesthetic register, inviting discussion around what art can *and cannot* offer. The families' continuing vulnerabilities, their emotional needs, are not only traumatic but also bound up with the *social* devastation that conflict has wrought, as well as the unanswered legal questions, the economic hardships, and the unresolved political situation. These are issues that art cannot ameliorate but that the art exhibition—as a specific form of social gathering—can provide an occasion to articulate and consider. Certainly with the workshops preceding *Relicarios*, discussion saw the relatives reflect on such issues as they expanded on the initial focus on the art-making process, its value, its affective qualities, and its role within the process of understanding what has happened in Colombia. The artwork's proposition emerges here that, beyond art's acknowledgment of the victims, and beyond the empathy we may feel for their sorrow while contemplating the artworks, there is an aching need at the heart of Colombia's attempt to establish the conditions for peace. That need is to be understood as an embodied and urgent one. Of course, the artwork cannot assume the place of the requisite political infrastructure, but the construction of such spaces and conversations models the possibility of peaceful coexistence in the only ways that it is able, that is, through its forms of acknowledgment, its exemplary care, and its aesthetic sensibilities.

Tender Forgetting: The *Oratorio for the Disappeared*

Over the course of 2020–22, amid the challenges of the COVID-19 pandemic, Diettes began a new project, one whose course I was lucky to follow through a series of conversations held with her over Zoom. Her ruminations on the process of making artworks with and for those touched by the conflict confirmed Diettes's approach as one that maintains a role for art that looks toward the horizon of peace routed through an ethics of care. Indeed, her new project arose in part through the observation that when *Relicarios* was exhibited at the museum in Medellín, it was the relatives of the disappeared who stayed the longest. For these relatives, Diettes wished to be able to offer them an established place in the world that recognized their specific agony, with the hope that giving such a place would also offer them a moment's respite. She explains: "When you are working with the victims, when you are listening to them, you wish for them to have just one minute pain free. You know, just one second."[59] The vision of the Oratorio came to her the morning after *Relicarios* exhibition opened. It will be a small chapel-like building on the mountainside in rural Antioquia, a simple rectangular building like a child might draw, with a high-pitched roof, set among lavender and dark leaved plants that will mark out the hillside of this hamlet as a special site, interrupting, as it will, the colors of the landscape (fig. 4.6). Inside this structure there will be photographs that Diettes has made in conversation with the relatives, images that feature objects the latter have chosen, printed onto Murano glass and arranged like so many stained-glass windows.

Unlike *Relicarios*, these images are not intended to represent the disappeared as such. Rather, they represent the relationship between the disappeared and those grieving them. Diettes explains, "These objects actually represent not the absence . . . but the story of the ongoing conversation that is eternal for the one who is grieving [*doliente*] the mourner of the disappeared."[60] Although still very much in process, the images Diettes has shared with me show objects that reflect these relationships. In one, champagne flutes represent the missing son whose mother still longs for him to return, refusing to allow anyone to toast her on her birthday because in his absence, the gesture is hollow. In another, a bowl represents the pain of a

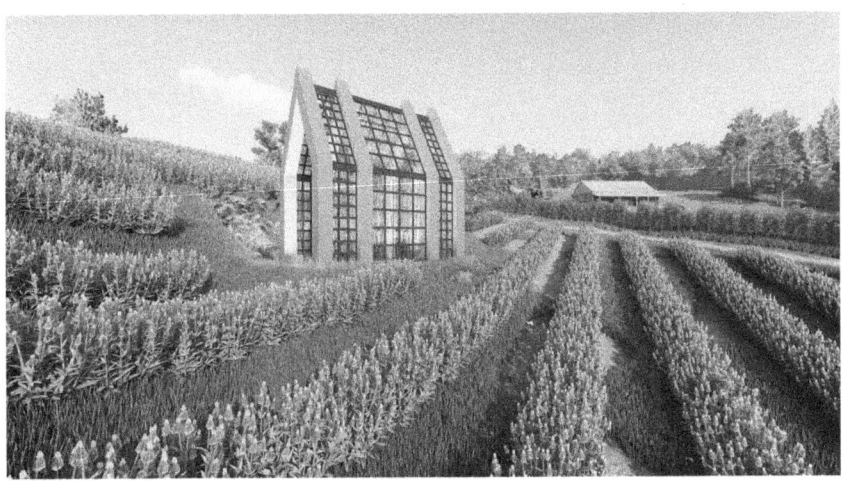

FIGURE 4.6. Architect's visualization of the Oratorio chapel on the hillside surrounded by rows of lavender. Rendering by Alejandro Vélez Restrepo. Source: Erika Diettes, with permission.

mother who still serves meals for her disappeared son, years after his disappearance, alongside drawings and letters from his young children who—she wishes to reassure him—are doing well in school and life (figs. 4.7 and 4.8). They are, as Diettes explains, images that reflect ongoing "conversations" with the disappeared. A third shows a photograph of a young man holding a baby, his photograph layered upon the *Relicario* image Diettes had previously created for his family, a layering of images that has a poignancy insofar as its repetition emphasizes the fact of the image as remnant (fig. 4.9). Once they have been printed onto the Murano glass panels, the glass chosen by Diettes for its beautiful opaque swirls of white that mean the image is more clearly visible in some parts than others, they will hang inside the Oratorio, creating a space that Diettes imagines as principally for the relatives and friends of the disappeared. Before the pandemic, Diettes invited a group of these relatives to the site to talk and share some time together, to do yoga, and to speak with her and some experienced therapists whom Diettes has met through her own work and through the "Transformative Memory" project that brings together academics, therapists, and artists in different parts of the world, headed by Pilar Riaño-Alcalá.[61] The workshop confirmed for her, she says, that the images should be shown without the stories alongside them. The Oratorio does a different sort of work from a documentary, she explains; it is not a museum or site of information, nor is its purpose to show the pain of disappearance to

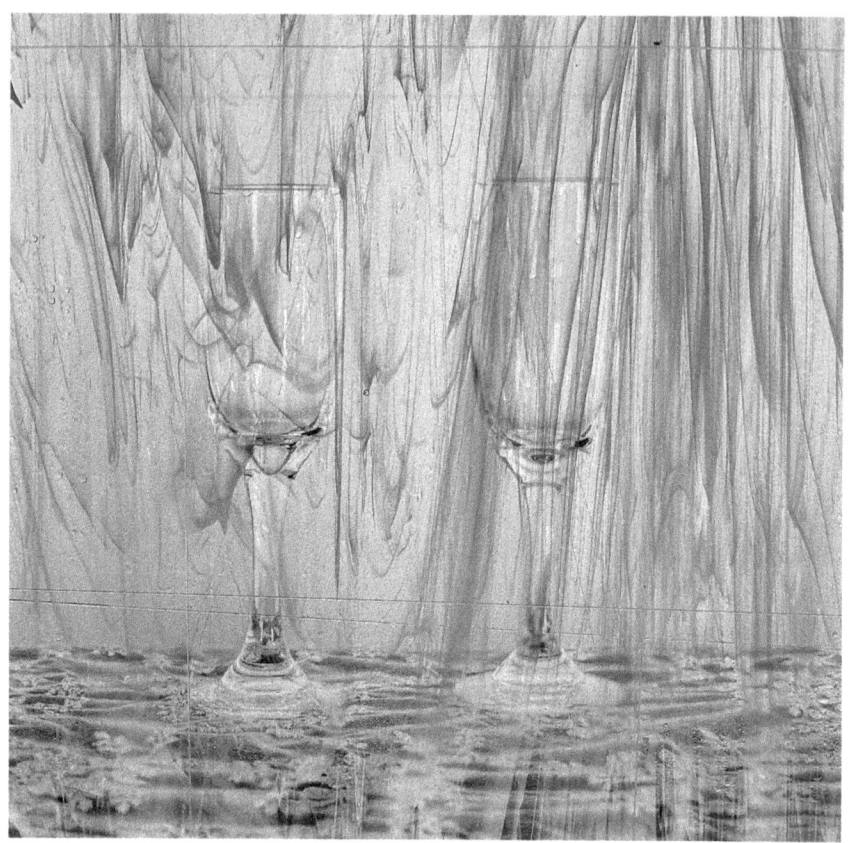

FIGURE 4.7. Murano glass panel with printed image. Source: Erika Diettes, with permission.

others, but it is to give the relatives a material place, a manifestation of the re-lationship whose loss they have suffered. Diettes will also include images that she has made with relatives elsewhere, including a series of works she has made with relatives of the disappeared in Tucumán, Argentina, where she was invited to meet them and to visit the exhumation site at Pozo de Vargas, a deep well where, decades after the end of the dictatorship, bodies of more than seventy of the disappeared were discovered. In one, she explained, "a daughter and a niece of a disappeared man brought the banners that they had taken on marches, a shawl of their father's, a *mate* [cup for drinking mate], and a little tin [*relicario*] with the hair of his child in it. She didn't really know her father, so her relationship with him was the experience of looking for him. Her image of her father is only as one of the disappeared" (fig. 4.10).[62]

FIGURE 4.8. Murano glass panel with printed image. Source: Erika Diettes, with permission.

In the Oratorio, Diettes does not seek to "explain" the image to others, and perhaps one cannot ever hope to do so—not only because the experience enfolded within each of these images is so personal, but because the image works as *all* images do, through the senses; this is their "seduction," as Nancy put it.[63] And indeed, Nancy's arguments suggests that all images are an "intensity of a concentration of world . . . outside language . . . the assembling of a sense without signification."[64] If these photographs are the concentration of the relationship of the *doliente* with the disappeared relative, they are extreme instances of the argument that Nancy makes whereby the image, any image, becomes an intimacy through the concentration that "suspends the course of the world and of meaning."[65] The image has—or *is*—an intensity. And it is an intensity, he argues, that "never stops tightening and condensing into itself."[66]

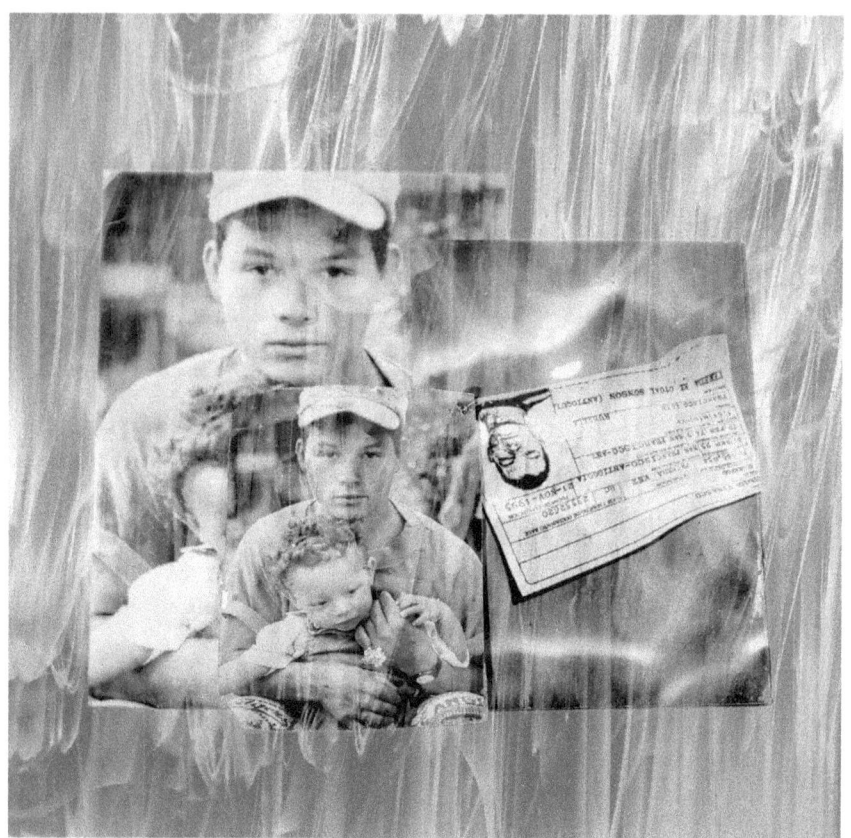

FIGURE 4.9. Murano glass panel with printed image. Source: Erika Diettes, with permission.

This intensity is a form of withdrawal of the image, separating itself from other presences in the world, and it is also, by the same token, what gives a *force* to artworks insofar as they have a form and are inserted into the world, as I have argued above. Diettes's hope is to allow, or to offer, that force to the relatives of the disappeared. Since the horror of disappearance leaves relatives in a state of limbo where life goes on without their loved one, but without them knowing if they are dead or alive, perhaps, just perhaps, Diettes wonders, the image and the space of the Oratorio will allow a certain exteriorization of that pain, and even allow a "release" of some sort, a "letting go." "Nobody deserves," she says, "to live in suffering endlessly."[67] Where so much memory politics insists on "a mantra of 'remember, remember, remember,'" where forgetting is associated with authoritarian denial, Diettes dares to

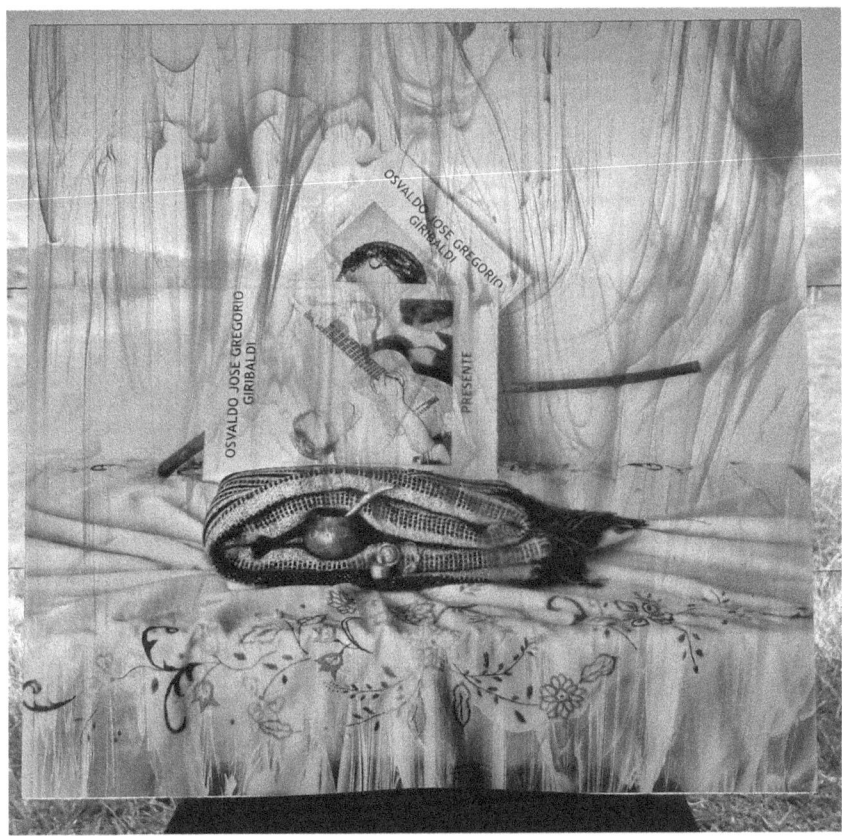

FIGURE 4.10. Murano glass panel with printed image. Source: Erika Diettes, with permission.

offer a site of memory that is premised on a notion that forgetting can also be a form of (self-)care, a healing. Diettes is explicit that she wishes to create a sacred place where the relatives can visit and have their pain recognized within a beautiful work of art. Alongside the intention to offer a place where they might come to mark that loss is the wish to create the conditions of possibility for them to feel they can leave that pain behind, allowing those ongoing conversations and the vulnerability that they sustain to pause and even eventually to cease. Together we came to term this a "tender forgetting," a gentle process that as Diettes says, is a hope that the relatives might achieve a state where they are beyond "the intensity of sorrow and achieve a softness, a softer memory," allowing them to remember their loved one with less pain and more joy, even delight.[68]

To repeat, art cannot do the work of justice systems and processes, but where no justice has been forthcoming, remembering has a necessary role in relation to these processes. This artwork's purpose revolves around the gesture of inserting a form into the world, a gift to those who have suffered profoundly in the conflict, that requests and thematizes the importance of giving time. Created through her ethic of care and accompaniment, the Oratorio offers its explicitly aesthetic response to the stories Diettes has heard. Of course she is aware that her own Catholic background may seep into her ideas of sacredness in relation to the site, and into language that she uses to explain it. Nancy, too, in the pages I have been quoting, refers his arguments concerning the intimacy of the image to Catholic "sacred intimacy" that would have a "fragment of matter" be "taken in and absorbed."[69] Yet the overt gift that the Oratorio will be—"everything, 100 percent of this project, is for the relatives," Diettes told me—makes its status as an artwork unusual; it does not aim to enact a form of communion with the spectator.[70] Indeed, the relationship that it courts with the spectator is partial in the sense that it seeks out certain spectators over others. The images on the glass focus on the relationship between the teller and their loved one; with the objects photographed chosen by the relative, not by Diettes, the Oratorio seeks to use its "force" to give recognition to and to honor those who remain behind. Eschewing the roles of the museum or memorial, it is a work that attempts a complicated affirmation, one that affirms the suffering while seeking to offer a consolation that will use the "withdrawal" that the image is, its very distinction as an image—and moreover, as an image that "belongs" and "calls" to a particular person or persons—to allow a threshold to appear. Diettes's hope is that that threshold might be one that allows a separation, that allows the intensity of the image to "hold" some of the truth of what it enfolds across its threshold.

Sometimes Nancy writes of the withdrawal, the gathering into itself that the image does, and that it *is*, in a more violent language, as the image "tearing" itself, or being torn, away.[71] That this tearing could be violent, and that as such the image might be received violently, is not in dispute here; there are no guarantees with the reception of an image. But interestingly, this withdrawal is also thematized by the Oratorio itself. I refer here to the "withdrawal" that will result from the location and design of the chapel, as the sun will stream through the glass and gradually the images will fade, leaving only the swirling marks of the glass. Diettes is keenly aware of this process, and is intrigued to see how the ink of the images "responds" to the sun in this way, how their "intra-action," without her hand, will see the different-colored inks fade at different paces, and how from within the Oratorio, the landscape glimpsed beyond the images will gradually be further revealed.[72] This fading will mimic the "withdrawal" of which Nancy writes, and also the "tender forgetting" for which Diettes hopes, insofar as maybe, at a future time, when the images have all but disappeared, the families will feel that they are also at a different point in their grief and their lives. The fading is a marking of time, or an "unmarking" if you will, and the "reappearance" of the landscape beyond the images will imply the reconnection of the relative-spectator with the landscape, the country, and its beauty. The gradual fading will leave them with the landscape Diettes explicitly hopes to offer comfort, to support and inspire them into living their lives. It is as if through the presence and literal withdrawal of the image, she wishes to (re)place these very special spectators "on the ground." Although this work has an "archival impulse," the phrase that Foster employed some time ago now to characterize a direction of contemporary artistic practice, then, the Oratorio is an anti-archive.[73] It gathers in order to dissipate. And although she is hesitant about saying it—knowing it could be misconstrued, and sound, in her words, "esoteric"—Diettes hopes that the spirit of the disappeared person will also be allowed to settle, to rest in peace. "Poetically at least," she comments, rather than continually seeking to bring them back, rather than understanding memory as a continual battle, "it seems right to let their spirits rest."[74]

To Have Regard

This chapter has explored Erika Diettes's artwork to date as a mode of wrestling with the force of art, exploring its possibilities and negotiating its complicities. To make art about the armed conflict in Colombia and its impact on those it touches cannot be understood in the same terms as interventions that are fueled by a desire to gather all the evidence, like an archive, nor to document, like a truth and reconciliation process, nor to judge, like a trial. Artworks need not be comprehensive or present explicit evaluations of the materials. Indeed, artworks are even able, somewhat paradoxically, to be less "visible," certainly less "legible." One can say, following Nancy once more, that the "evidence" or truth of artworks is never obvious or self-evident; art keeps secrets, it holds back an essential reserve.[75] Indeed, Diettes's artworks convey an intensity in large part because we sense that we are only glimpsing truths and realities. We are at the limit of what can be said in *Sudarios*, where there are both "no words"—no adequate words—*and* many more "in reserve." Likewise, we sense a lifetime of memories lies behind the images in *Río Abajo*, as they do the tiny selection of objects in *Relicarios* or the photographs to be hung in the Oratorio. These artworks do not "present evidence" of the impact of violence, but rather—as Nancy says of film—present the fact that *there is evidence*, that, to put it differently, there are survivors, there are accounts, there are remnants of their existences now ruined, displaced, cut short.[76] If Diettes explicitly demurs from narrating or presenting the stories of that violence, the art she makes nevertheless speaks to the suffering caused by the violence of the armed conflict, and its ripple effects—the impacts on the relatives and communities—on the aesthetic register. Through her careful making of the images, the siting and the staging of the installations, Diettes requests that we "have regard" for those whose lives have been indelibly marked by the armed conflict, that we "take a look," where "a look" suggests more than merely "seeing": not what is simply seen when we glance at the work but what becomes evident when one truly has regard for the stories emerging there.[77] Of course, to foster such an encounter, to negotiate the dangers that loom large in such art-making, Diettes has had to consider her decisions at every turn. The "cuts" and framings that allow any artwork to appear as such, that provide the focus and in that sense also choose the distance from which we the spectators consider and "weigh up" the work, will, through those same decisions and gestures, risk cutting into and cutting away. Without complacency, I have suggested that these risks inform the modes of care that Diettes has taken over her role in the making of these artworks. The resultant artworks are mobile forms that both gather and, in their different ways, dissipate. All are about processes rather than pronouncements or truth. They are—as Nancy wrote of Abbas Kiarostami, for many years a teacher—"concerned with something we should learn," but instead of presenting those things for contemplation, the work "set[s] in motion a movement of interest and an *education* in the precise sense where the word means 'to bring out.'"[78]

PART III

Argentina

5

A CRITICAL ECOLOGY OF PRACTICES

Forums and Their Arts of Dramatization

I would call civilized practice a practice able to exhibit its own, never innocent, divergence, the pragmatic space it creates, the specific way its practitioners world and word their world as Haraway would say. The way a practice diverges does not characterize its difference from others but the way it has its own world mattering, the values which commit its practitioners, what they take into account and how. —ISABELLE STENGERS, "The Challenge of Ontological Politics"

Implicit throughout *Promises Beyond Memory* is the premise that no one site has a monopoly on the keeping or telling of stories about violence, since they appear and circulate across multiple spaces. They do not begin with or *belong* to the archive, of course, and nor are they "arrested" there. Even if an archive collects and holds the stories, they may escape the archive, as is its desire in fact, circulating elsewhere and creating new gatherings around themselves. Indeed, for the promise of memory to be more than wishful thinking, these stories need to reappear, to be more than "archival," in order to pose their provocations for those in the present. Taking examples from my research in Argentina, this chapter explores how, as these stories move through differ-ent sites, or what I will term here forums, they are articulated, curated, and constrained differently. In the terms employed in chapter 3, their survivance is achieved differently as they are "breathed back to life" in distinct ways. Drawing on the thought of Isabelle Stengers, this chapter focuses on the distinct proce-dures and particularities that reign within the diverse sites in which stories are told. I will suggest that since the forums have these distinctions—articulating concerns and operating under specific rules or principles that pertain to, and even constitute, their milieus—different sorts of truths about the violence of the last dictatorship emerge. The focus is on how—the problematizations, the propositions, and the processes by which—these truths emerge, for as Stengers puts it in her discussion of William James's pragmatism, each forum affirms that there is something to think *and* that there is a way to think it.[1]

Establishing truths about the past, Stengers contends, making them ac-cepted as such, requires situated practices with more or less elaborate "arts of dramatization," technics of persuasion, and gatherings open to being so persuaded. For example, the truths that are articulated at the site of law are arrived at differently, and so are distinct, from those that arise in museums or art galleries. This is not simply to repeat the argument that truths are con-structed and multiple, entwined with the power relations that sustain them. Nor is the argument that truth-telling is difficult because of the clandestine nature of the violence perpetrated during the last military dictatorship in Ar-gentina, or the various ways in which the state attempted to cover up its ac-tions. Rather, by focusing on the processes, on how stories from the past are *made* to offer themselves up for consideration, my attention is on how they are conjured and constrained by the specificities of the forum in which they appear. It is worth noting at the outset that constraint is not necessarily to be given a negative connotation here, since it is through their specific constraints that the different sites are able to put propositions "to the test," as it were. Indeed, for Stengers, truths *must* be subjected to the procedures particular to their site of emergence, and this needs to happen in front of audiences attuned to the proceedings. To convince an audience of a truth, Stengers ar-gues, an artifice or device of some kind is required, asked to "testify" to the existence of a phenomenon, as happens with the presentation of scientific fact.[2] This artifice, it is worth noting, does not make the truths artificial, just as truths may be conjured up and passed along through storytelling, without being fictive in the sense of being made up.[3] Truths emerge only insofar as their relevance and veracity can be satisfactorily proven and sustained *by the procedures and mechanisms appropriate* to the site of their appearance.

Drawing on her own background as a chemist, Stengers's example is the art of dramatization entailed in the staging of a chemistry experiment. The chemist must assemble the apparatus and the type of circumstances in which the chemical actants display their capabilities, producing the results she seeks to demonstrate. Crucially, to be verified, propositions—or what she terms "candidates for truth"—must be made to strongly advocate *on their own behalf* in some sense. Thus, while a facilitator may be involved, she ultimately appears passively, drawing out the "propensity of things," which is to say, their ability to convincingly account or attest of their own accord.[4] It is crucial that the experiment simultaneously demonstrates that the result is independent, that the chemist herself had no part in causing the outcome.[5] Otherwise, audiences will remain unconvinced or suspicious. "This is the very meaning of the event that constitutes the experimental intervention," writes Stengers, "the invention of the power to confer on things the power of conferring on the experimenter the power to speak in their name."[6] It is crucial that this independence, achieved differently in different forums, is affirmed before any proposition would be affirmed as "truth."

In relation to the truths at stake here—those concerning the violent history and legacy of the dictatorship period in Argentina—the suggestion is that there are various forums where the past is animated and made present. Of course, legal forums have been a privileged site at which the past is put under scrutiny. It has long been argued that establishing the truth about the past requires the theatrical animation of evidence, as was implied by the description of the perpetrator trial as a "theatre of justice," in Shoshana Felman's highly influential work—and as Carlos Nino and Mark Osiel explored in reflecting on Argentina's 1985 trial of the military junta.[7] At the site of law, one can see the sense in which evidence is not "self-evident," but requires the forum and its procedures to confer upon it the status of truth. Someone presents, reflects, or performs in order to facilitate the animation of evidence, requesting the assent of those within the court. But law is not alone in this, and there are other forums with their own apparatus and procedures, that also gather those with the requisite expertise, and put their concerns and propositions about the truth of the past to the test, as it were, in front of interested audiences.[8] Not only lawyers, then, but also psychologists, forensic anthropologists, architects, archivists, academics, curators, and artists partake in the process of establishing truth. Obviously, these are practitioners who work differently, operating within distinct milieus whose attentions diverge. By these divergent practices, they constitute their own "ecologies" within which their arts are guided. It follows that they will have distinct modes of dramatization, imposing different constraints as they process what comes before their forum in order to seek specific forms of satisfaction. In contrast to a mode of argument, common within sociolegal literature, that values nonlegal sites of cultural production but tends to maintain an implicit deference to law, seeing the nonlegal realms of art and cultural practices only insofar as they constitute arenas in which legal decision is either celebrated or challenged, I suggest that Stengers's notion of ecologies of practice aids the appreciation of the specificities of practices in different forums. Indeed, a central argument here is that debates around the role of visual art, museums, Spaces of Memory, and archives might be framed less deferentially than has tended to be the case. Such activities and interventions are not supplementary or "remainder" sites, to be considered only where formal justice processes have failed, stalled, or ended, but as sites that have their own orientations and truth-telling capacities beyond law. That is, they explore different propositions and employ different processes to allow truths about the violent past to emerge and be endorsed.

Considered alongside each other, we can also appreciate how the distinct truths produced by the forums may "travel" beyond their initial milieu. In addition to the figures who adopt the expert or "demonstrator" roles, Stengers describes a further figure, that of the diplomat, the one who moves between forums, who seeks agreement or connection, and who typically intervenes in a situation without asserting or defending an "opinion" but in order to facilitate those connections.[9] Experts appear because their practice is considered relevant to the procedures of the forum, even if they are not sure how it will be taken into account; the diplomat, however, comes more humbly, asking for hesitation, and providing voice to those whose "mode of existence and whose identity are threatened by a decision."[10] The diplomat is the one who must repeatedly check back and forth, artfully presenting possible scenarios in order to bring other potential relevancies into consideration. These figures help one understand how the forums, including the criminal law court, necessarily entertain propositions from outside their parameters, deciding upon their relevance and impact, as they explore the concerns before them.

Law's Art of Dramatization

As the above implies, the attempt to produce truth and to speak "justly" in relation to the past is not confined to legal arenas, but the legal trial remains the most familiar of these forums. Moreover, we have become accustomed to considering it an arena where (legal) truths are produced performatively insofar as the trial requires the presentation of candidates for truth—that is, forms of evidence—and operates via the ability of the apparatus of law to produce the requisite problematizations of the scenario. The case has to be conjured up in the minds of the juries or—as in the cases dealing with past violence in Argentina—the minds of the judges. Of course, the consequent attribution of responsibility—law's "decisionist imperative" that relies upon a reduction of all accounts of a past event and the possibility of reaching a curtailment of discussion and dialogue—guides and colors the direction of the proceedings.[11] The arc of the criminal trial from indictment to judgment is a constraint insofar as all activity within its purview takes place under the parameters of the charge and possible verdicts; hence the constant challenges to what is *relevant* to the proceedings. Moreover, while the desire for legal truth is certainly entwined with the desire for an affirmation of historical truth in contemporary Argentina, and the performative dimensions of the trials to affirm an account of "what happened" escapes no one, each trial is constrained by the necessity to put *individuals* on trial, and the necessity to reach a conclusion about guilt just *once*.[12] Unlike academic historical interpretations of the past—and unlike artistic responses—trials are generally understood, as a prosecutor in the Milošević trial put it, as "one chance" to interpret the evidence correctly.[13]

The trials for human rights violations committed during the last dictatorship in Argentina face the problems that all "belated" or post-transitional justice processes face, not least that, if the rationale of the criminal trial is to punish the living for their actions, they are up against time.[14] The age of the defendants is a challenge for the possibility of holding the trials, and interrupts the primary intention of the court to gather those responsible; likewise, many witnesses are passing away. "Time favors death and is against us," Pablo Camuña, a federal prosecutor in Tucumán, told me in an interview conducted in 2015.[15] He continued: "The biggest problem has been, and is the case today more than ever before, that people are dying. The accused are dying, but principally the witnesses are dying, and the victims."[16] If prosecutors have convictions in their sights, and the verdict is the outcome toward and for which they work—their moment of satisfaction—the longer they have to wait for that outcome, the greater the risk that the perpetrators will "escape justice" and they will be disappointed in their task. Ultimately, says Camuña, "the passing of time is . . . on the side of the perpetrators."[17]

For Camuña, this pressure of time relates to the performative aspects of the trial. Indeed, the sense that the trial needs to employ dramatic techniques—the "predilection for drama" that pervades the prosecution, according to

Lawrence Douglas, and that so infuriated Hannah Arendt—was confirmed by him.[18] If one can include the immense potential of the living voice of the survivor, the prosecution's work proceeds more easily, Camuña comments. To lose the witnesses is to endanger the possibility of conviction, not only because the living witnesses hold the facts and the details that begin to break down the silence that the perpetrators have attempted to build around these crimes—by acting clandestinely, by destroying evidence, and of course, by disappearing people—but also because they are the most electrifying part of the trial. Camuña is explicit; they are *theatrical.* "Because the trials also have to have theatrical aspects to them," he says, "the reconstruction [of the scenes of violence] has to be as close as possible." To bring the judges, in his words, emotionally "back in time"—as close to really having been there, to having really witnessed these events—this is Camuña's aim. The best way to do this, he suggests, is to have the live witnesses present their stories in court—to consciously stage their testimony "unmediated," as it were—because their presence and words enable the judges to see and feel what the witnesses went through: "The empathy that a live witness generates is immensely . . . power-ful . . . and the judges . . . end up putting themselves in the position of the victims or their families."[19]

Interestingly, Camuña insists that the urgency to prosecute before the witnesses pass away is because the prosecution's chances of gaining a con-viction diminish when someone attempts to "play the role" and speak for the victim. A lawyer reading a statement on behalf of a survivor about their ex-perience, for example, cannot do that same affective work since, as Camuña cautions, "You will never get the same impact . . . nor the richness of the live witness."[20] As these comments imply, the prosecutors need to present their case and to "stage" the evidence; this art of dramatization is not for the sake of drama but so that, through careful preparation and persuasive presentation, the (legal) truth arises.[21] While Shoshana Felman's influential notion of a "theatre of justice" enables one to grasp the performative dimension of such trials, it is too quick a conflation of the legal forum with theater. The trial is not equivalent to theater, but a complex technical apparatus in which the lawyers—like the figure of the "modest witness" in Stengers's example of the chemistry demonstration—conduct events in order to facilitate the passage of an *independent* truth. To truly persuade the audience in a criminal trial, they—the judges or jury—must not only attribute guilt but simultaneously be persuaded that the impression of guilt is not a mere effect of the trial itself.

Beyond the witness statements, the court receives other forms of evi-dence, other arts of dramatization. Particularly striking is the use of visual

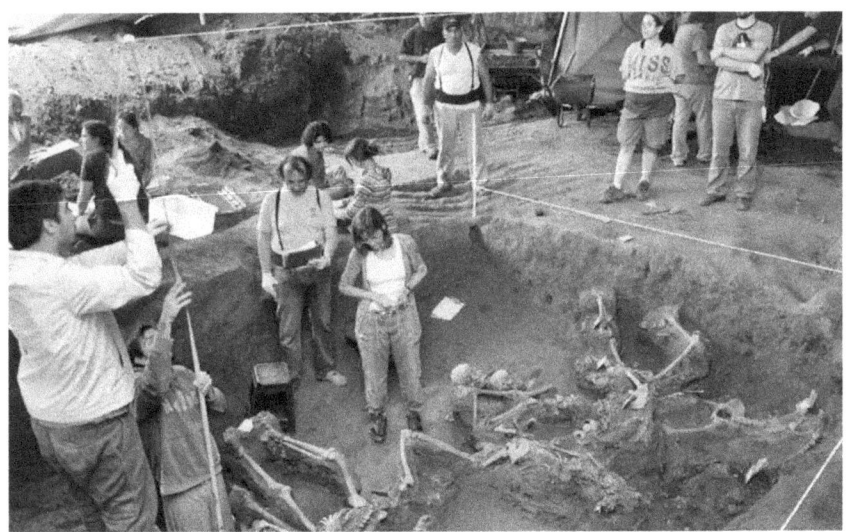

FIGURE 5.1. The EAAF team at the site of a communal grave, ex–Arsenal Miguel de Azcuénaga in Tucumán, December 2011. Source: Centro de Información Judicial. https://www.cij.gov.ar/nota-8393-Hallan-una-fosa-comun-de-inhumacion-en-un -centro-clandestino-de-detencion-en-la-provincia-de-Tucuman.html#.

evidence, including photographs, to mobilize the affective potentialities of the court. The photographs of human remains at the ex–clandestine center for detention, torture, and extermination (ex-CCDTYE) Arsenal Miguel de Azcuénaga in Tucumán being uncovered by the Argentine Forensic Anthropology team (Equipo Argentino de Antropología Forense, EAAF) in 2011 had an enormous impact in the *megacausa* that prosecuted those responsible for crimes at the site.[22] Camuña recalls the shock of the photographs of the team working at the graves when they were shown in the court (fig. 5.1): "[In] our megacausa, which lasted for more than a year, one of the most shocking images in the trial were those of the photos of the common grave where thirteen bodies were recovered."[23]

The EAAF team, now world famous for their endeavors to identify victims from bones and through their DNA-matching processes, have been involved in criminal prosecutions ever since their founder Clyde Snow was invited to go to Argentina in 1984 at the request of La Comisión Nacional sobre la Desaparición de Personas (CONADEP) and human rights organizations to help with exhuming and identifying human skeletal remains, and presented the findings at the junta trials in 1985.[24] Photographs are an integral part of their work.[25] The ones shown in the trial in Tucumán show the team at work, carefully uncovering, measuring, surveying, labeling, and documenting the grave.

While any photograph shown within a court of law is intended to operate as evidence and asks that the court understand it in an indexical manner, as a mode of documentation, what is also crucial is that, as Elizabeth Edwards once put it, the photograph projects the past into the present through an "affective tone." Filling the frame with the human remains of the disappeared, left in the awkward positions where they were thrown, these photographs operate, unavoidably, via the "theatricality of framing" and a resultant intensity.[26] There is both a containment of the court's attention and a heightening of affect.[27]

Faced with these affective possibilities and the "multidirectional" potential of photography, the prosecutor enrolls the figure of the "translator" or expert to help tether their meaning. The forensic anthropology team continues to contribute to the images' presentation, in Tucumán as elsewhere, usually via written reports for the court or—although less usual in Argentina—through presentations where they interpret what is being seen for the court.[28] In either case, the forensic anthropologists offer their expertise as a mode of translation from the silence of the skeletal remains and from the procedures of scientific practice into those of law, in order, in the words of current president of the EAAF Luis Fondebrider, to "complement" the testimony of survivors and "help the judges form a more complete picture."[29] At its heart, forensic work is an attempt to reconstruct what we can know of the final moments of this person's life, despite all that has happened between then and this moment of the skeleton's reappearance.[30] While over the years, the science involved has evolved—with the discovery of DNA, crucially, so that the skills and procedures the forensic anthropology team employ have altered—it is the application of scientific procedure that grounds the veracity of their evidence; it is the rigor of method and the "fit" of the explanation to the material evidence that convinces the scientific community. Building on that status as scientist, the forensic expert is able to model him- or herself as merely the "translator" of what the remains "say."

In presenting their evidence to the court, the forensic experts do not repeat but must *reconfigure* the technical work of the laboratory in such a way that their conclusions can be persuasive in the legal forum.[31] As Snow himself once suggested, this may be through a storytelling that articulates the bones' own narratives: "To be effective as an expert witness, you have to learn that in a way you're translating the skeletons themselves. The bones are the ones telling the story."[32] Moreover, an objective and neutral manner of presentation can be "rather cold." Interestingly, he recalls that in presenting his evidence to the 1985 junta trials, many aesthetic issues came into play.[33] Rather than present an overview through the presentation of statistics, they chose to select just a few of the many cases, in order better to convey the stories. They chose the case of Liliana Pereyra, not only because she was herself a "beautiful girl" but also because she was pregnant at the time of her disappearance. The bones established that they belonged to a young woman who had given birth, while photographs from the several stages of the reconstruction of the face from the skull using forensic techniques were projected on to a screen in order to take the court through that process, ending with "the last slide of this beautiful young woman."[34] The judges, Snow reports, were moved by this presentation, and people "told me later that many of the newsmen up in the balconies were crying."[35] Here Snow confirms that while the forensic evidence carries the weight of having passed through the scientific forum, so that the team is convinced of its truth, the law court is a different challenge, one where the scientific procedure is not repeated but where the resultant conclusions pass through a further "art of dramatization."

In trials such as the Tucumán *megacausa*, which relate to specific sites where multiple crimes occurred, the judges will usually make at least one visit to the site. On these visits, the architecture and the space are also asked to "testify," as it were. Again, human guides are usually on hand. Camuña recalls: "We made the whole tribunal go to where the bodies had been buried. This had a huge impact and enabled the presentation of much evidence, [especially since] over fifty people were able to speak about the place, describing it, talking about how it was, how it functioned, [showing] maps, etc. Going to the actual place—and especially to the common graves—has a great impact on the judges' perceptions of the trial. It also galvanizes us [the lawyers]."[36]

Sometimes the judges call upon the expertise of academic researchers to help synthesize the data about the sites. A young academic based in Tucumán explained how she used testimonies, architectural remains, and satellite photographs, inter alia, in her investigations of the former clandestine center for detention, torture, and extermination, Arsenal Miguel de Azcuénaga. Maria del Pilar Gómez Sánchez is part of an interdisciplinary research team tasked with the exploration of the site. Taking a cue from the testimonies of survivors, they employed archeological exploration—guided in part by the EAAF—and satellite photography. Through their interdisciplinary apparatus, they were able to piece together an account of how the site had operated in the past, especially by locating "infra-structural" evidence to confirm the survivors' recollections. They uncovered, for example, electrical cables where the survivors said there were lighted paths, and then employed satellite photographs taken in the 1970s to show that there were alternative access routes into the site that confirmed the recollections of survivors. This evidence—built up from the ruins, rubble, and records of the site and presented as computer-generated reconstructions—was important for the trial in Tucumán, since, as Gómez Sánchez put it, "archaeological evidence is one of the strongest, as it gives material evidence," lending further weight to the prosecution's case.[37]

A similar argument was articulated by architect and member of the archive Memoria Abierta, Gonzalo Conte, who has also participated in the trials, including the huge second ESMA *megacausa* in 2011, presenting computer-generated models of ex-CCDTYES and "audiovisual judicial records."[38] In our interview, Conte explained that speaking as a professional architect about the computer models that he has created of ex-CCDTYES, especially those that have since been demolished or altered in some way, helps to constrain and focus the imagination of those gathered in the court, so that the visions they construct of the places that are being described do not diverge from each other.

The digital audiovisual judicial records incorporate survivors' accounts of their experiences with facts about those buildings and brief videos of the spaces as they now appear. Commissioned to aid the judges conducting the trials, sometimes the survivors also appear in the embedded videos to offer their memories of the space. As the survivors walk through the clandestine centers, they point out different aspects of the site, provoked by the physical space to tell snippets of their stories on camera. Conte presents the record in court, allowing the survivors' testimonies to be understood alongside the presentation of the physical spaces in which the crimes took place, and allowing the "eye of the camera" to confirm the physical coordinates and appearance of the place, as well as to record chance encounters inevitably caught by a camera as it wanders through these often forlorn buildings. Sometimes, Conte suggests, it captures the pathos of the objects that still lie around, such as in one case, parts of syringes recalling the anesthetic that was forcibly injected into prisoners.

Faced with such emotive material, the ability of the architect to speak "scientifically," in his or her capacity as a professional, and to offer facts as "concrete, irrefutable," is important for the legal process, argued Conte, not least because it eases the task of the judges in relation to the weight of the decision they have to make: "When you explain [the evidence that relates to the layout of the buildings], with a lot of sincerity, the same as when [the survivor] speaks about his own torture, in that moment the judge begins to say, 'Ah, we need more of this, we need evidence, we need facts like this.' Because [with this evidence] it is easier for the judge to condemn [the defendant] for life."[39] For Conte, to appear as an expert is also preferable because his own story, the fact that his own brother was disappeared, becomes irrelevant to his role in the court; that story goes unmentioned.

Thus the trial coordinates different practices—with their attendant technics, forms of expertise, their spatializing and dramatizing procedures—into a network of partial connections articulated together at the site of law in order to produce legal truth. Much like Stengers's notion of an "ecology of practices," the different practices may have different interests and be only partially connected, but the event of the trial brings them into the same space. There they receive attention only insofar as they articulate evidence deemed both admissible, according to legal procedure, and relevant for the purpose of the trial. In a sense all the facts that nonlegal experts bring to the court become "mere" propositions in the legal realm. While the facts in question may have been validated elsewhere, in other forums, here they must be re-presented within the case being made by the prosecution or defense. As Thomas Keenan has argued: "Evidence is what is used to persuade. . . . It is not the matter of fact. Evidence does not convict, nor does it decide, nor does it settle or conclude or determine. . . . It is not an answer but a question: it asks for a decision, for a reading or an interpretation, it asks to be told what it says."[40] As bringers of propositions, the experts cannot *determine* how these facts come to matter for the court, but they offer them at its request, seeking to connect with the court's decision-making process.

The specificity of the legal forum and its distinction from the work of other forums was illustrated by way of a sort of counterexample articulated in the fascinating interview I conducted with psychologist Laura Sobredo. Sobredo had worked with survivors of the clandestine detention centers who were asked to deliver testimonies in court, including in the 2011 ESMA *mega-causa* mentioned above. She explained to me that while the justice process requires the survivors' accounts, her own principles of professional practice, built around promoting healing and psychological health, were repeatedly put under pressure in the courtroom. She states: "An effective justice process is impossible without these witnesses. But for us [psychologists] it is extremely difficult to ask [the survivors] to do something that is painful once again."[41] Sobredo felt the difference between the law court as a forum for telling and that of therapeutic clinical psychology acutely. In therapeutic practices, for example, one is able to allow people to talk at their own pace, even to fall away into silence. Silence is given space, she commented, understood as signaling the difficulties of articulating the past, and even as perhaps the most important moment in the telling of such stories, therapeutically speaking. But in the court, the "apparatus" and the principles that guide the work diverge from those of a therapeutic setting, and to give such space and time is not tolerated. Nevertheless, working alongside the important organization Centro de Estudios Legales y Sociales (CELS), Sobredo's role was to support those subpoenaed by the court. For this reason, Sobredo explicitly fashioned herself like Stengers's diplomat, moving between the needs of the court and its limitations as a place to talk about personal experiences, advising the witnesses how to negotiate between forums.[42]

With this diplomatic attitude, acutely aware that both she and the victims were shifting between forums, Sobredo explained that she would sometimes encourage her clients—where she sensed it appropriate—to use the court for their own journeys. For example, as a way to bring some aspect of their story of their own choosing into a public forum, even something deemed irrelevant from the perspective of the court might be worth sharing. Using the court not as a law court but simply as a public forum, the survivor might convey what these events mean to them, personally, and share details that continue to haunt them. To ignore the forum's concerns, as it were, and to assert instead their own concerns in this way is to "own" that moment in proceedings and help avoid the risk of feeling oneself becoming objectified once again.[43] For example, Sobredo encouraged one survivor to mention that for a long time, after having been released, she held her cup with two hands; she had been handcuffed during her imprisonment so that reaching and drinking with her wrists close together had become automatic. Sobredo suggests that these details may not be legally relevant to the trial but they enable the witness to feel that something of his or her particular story was shared. Moreover, these "irrelevant" memories might also forge a connection with the judges. Sobredo remarked: "In these trials the judges, the prosecutors, and sometimes the members of the public have listened to some terrible things, many, many, many times. And then appears a person who was intimately involved in those experiences and the judges, who have listened to so much, will [nevertheless] always remember this man who told them about a brief moment."[44] In other words, Sobredo suggests that a function of these legally irrelevant details offered by witnesses may intensify the evidence, animating it through their singular narrative account.[45]

Sobredo is a threshold figure in this way, careful about the boundaries between her own professional principles and obligations, as well as the specificities and limitations of the legal process. As a diplomat, she recognizes that the court has its own specificity and role, and does not seek to challenge that, but she also negotiates within its processes. In order to maintain her own ethos of care toward her clients, guided by her fundamental principles of care, she operates within the constraints of the law court while understanding its purpose as only one forum within which these stories are told.

Beyond Law: Art, Museum, Archive

Outside the courts, the art of dramatization of Argentina's violent past takes place in many other public forums, including the memorial museums, "Spaces of Memory," contemporary art spaces, and archives that lie at the heart of this research.[46] Among those I have visited in Argentina are those in Buenos Aires—the ex-ESMA and El Parque de la Memoria—in Rosario, where the first Museo de la Memoria was established and in Córdoba, the D2 and the Archivo Provincial de la Memoria, Espacio para la Memoria La Perla." On the one hand, such spaces are often implicitly considered less important than legal trials for establishing the truth about the past, as there is an understandable tendency to defer to the authority of law. On the other, among humanities scholars, they tend to be celebrated as alternative spaces, contesting and supplementing the restricted nature of legal truths. They are praised, inter alia, for their ability to shelter that which would otherwise be abandoned and lost from historical narratives, with visual and performance arts in particular elevated as uniquely able to produce evocative, affective spaces capable of transmitting something of the subjective experience of past violence.

While not disagreeing with such sentiments exactly, my argument here adopts a less deferential tone. Rather than understanding such spaces as supplements or alternatives to the legal, they can be approached more boldly, as alternative forums deploying their own arts of dramatization and offering their own "candidates for truth." It is important, in other words, to draw out the specificities of their contributions and particular capabilities to contribute to the "ecology of practices" in which the past is invited to appear. For these reveal that such spaces are differently delimited and even advantageous over law and legal forums, having a role to play in the elliptical "passing on" the past, long after legal trials have ceased. I will discuss three brief examples in order to try to begin to tease out the different principles and concerns at stake.

PAyS (Presente, Ahora y Siempre), the Temporary Exhibition
Space of El Parque de la Memoria, Buenos Aires

Art spaces have a certain freedom. Indeed, this freedom is arguably what, in our era, makes art recognizable as such, since the aesthetic experience has been constituted around an embodiment of such freedom. It is a freedom that, in approaching art, we encounter but, as Jacques Rancière argues, "we cannot possess."[47] By definition artists are able to choose what and how to put things in relation, at least those of contemporary times, and perhaps especially, as Andreas Huyssen has argued, within contemporary memory art that radicalizes the boundary-crossings of modernisms, frequently using installation that spatializes its form and draws audiences into the work.[48] Here, the "small" stories—those that would be unheard or heard as irrelevant in the courtroom—can become central, intensified through artistic attention, incorporated within unexpected montages, without the same strictures of relevance and clarity that bind a law court. In other words, artworks exhibit a sense of care for the encounters they create, and for how they position the spectator, but they are not tethered in the same way as legal presentations of evidence. It would be a mistake, however, to infer that, as a consequence, truths about the past are not proposed, and constituted, for wider acceptance here.

Albertina Carri's exhibition *Operación Fracasco y Sonido Recobrado* (Futile Operation and Recollected Sound) at Presente, Ahora y Siempre (PAyS) in November 2015, used letters from her mother, who was detained before being disappeared, recorded by an actor and played as an audio score, while onto the floor of the gallery were projected images of the fungus which she found growing on the film stock of militant films from the 1960s and 1970s, appearing here as enlarged, unrecognizable images, mysteriously beautiful (fig. 5.2). The collection of things put in relation—the disappearing images of the militant films, the pain of a mother separated from her children, the materiality of the letters and the film stock, the encroaching life of fungus—are clearly not presented as evidence such as that requested by law; nor are they random. The provocation of facing a multiplicity of objects and sensations is part of the experience of thought, affect, and visuality conveyed to the visitor of many a contemporary art exhibition. As Rancière has argued, such work purposely underdetermines how the collection of things will make meaning in relation to each other, presenting the viewer with a kind of enigma. While the spectator of artworks has always had their own kind of freedom— whether to be interested or not, of course, but also beyond this, how to "use"

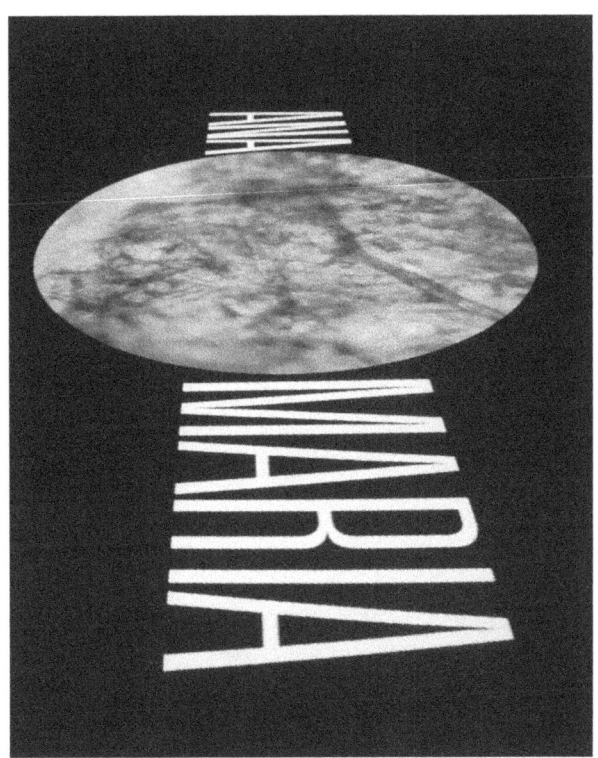

FIGURE 5.2. Albertina
Carri's exhibition
*Operación Fracasco
y Sonido Recobrado*
(Futile Operation and
Recollected Sound)
at PAyS, El Parque
de la Memoria, 2015.
Source: Vikki Bell.

or "behave" when confronted with these unexpected or unpredictable assemblages that neither describe nor explain an event—these works explicitly intensify the spectator position as the one to whom that enigma is posed.[49] Indeed, as in her celebrated film *Los Rubios*, part of Carri's message seems to insist that interpretations are contingently gathered from many elements, becoming indistinguishable from fictional creations, especially where issues to do with human recall and human desire are in the mix. As Jordana Blejmar has written, *Los Rubios* "explores the limits of the documentary form—and of the mediums that would supposedly deliver the truthful version of its object, namely testimonies, photographs and letters—and ultimately concludes that it is impossible to faithfully represent (the absence of) her parents, Ana María Caruso and Roberto Carri, using traditional documentary resources."[50]

If, in this exhibition as well as through her earlier work, Carri seeks to problematize memory in this way, this does not imply the absence of truth or "mere" fictionality but rather insists upon a necessary partiality to the truths that emerge. Her artworks decline the invitation to occupy the role of witness associated with law courts—that is, telling "what happened," "what

I remember," "what they looked like." Likewise, the artist has resigned the position of the translator, for she does not request that a certain message or meaning be conveyed. She is instead more akin to Stengers's diplomat, a "creature of speculation," insofar as she brings offerings and suggestions without herself insisting on one interpretation.[51] While she has certainly made a selection, and includes them precisely because she considers their relations to be potentially both relevant and provocative within the specific space of PAyS, the multiplicity simultaneously suggests a different sensibility, one that offers alternative values formed from a sensitivity to the fact that accounting for the past is not a natural process insofar as it will always require an apparatus of sorts. Carri repeatedly draws attention to the material support that memory requires: the materiality of the film; the paper of the letters; all of the decisions about "staging," editing, and showing the work. These aspects also necessarily imply a vulnerability and fragility. Even those aspects of the past that are captured on film, audio or written down, not to mention those that survive intangibly in human memory or bodies, hold no guarantees that they will manage to appear and manage to convey a story in the future.[52] Art exhibitions that deal with remnant-objects, as Boris Groys has argued, rely upon a *curation* that seeks to "cure" their powerlessness, to rescue the object's inability to show itself by itself, by rendering the object into an aesthetic image that we can sense and bring sense to.[53] Such propositions are likewise Carri's "propositions" or "candidates" for truth.

Museo de la Memoria, Rosario

How does a museum of memory differ from an art space such as PAyS? How do the propositions for memory posed there differ from the legal truths that arise from prosecutions? According to Paul Williams, memorial museums "concretize and distill" events, providing a place for events that may otherwise only exist disparately, in personal memories or in books, films, websites, and so on, becoming "surrogate homes for debates that would otherwise be placeless."[54] Whereas Carri's exhibition described above, for example, gathers its elements in order to produce an affective intensity for the spectator, the gathering that happens at a museum tends to be tethered by the institution's sense of social purpose. Such museum spaces—including the important Museo de la Memoria in Rosario, which is to date the only institution dealing with the last dictatorship in Argentina set up solely as a museum—are rarely simply about storage; in fostering debates, giving space to new articulations around the past, and thereby implicitly refusing to be "historical," they seek to enfold the past within the present and future. In line with a more wide-spread "new museum ethics," the focus is not so much on the preservation of objects and collections, therefore, as it is on the potential of the museum to "do good with museum resources."[55] However this injunction is understood, memorial museums are more often than not entwined with a future-oriented concern. Rosario's Museo de la Memoria, like the Museo Casa de la Memoria in Medellín discussed in chapter 3, has certainly taken the view that its role is not merely to narrate the past or to present objects from it, but also to promote an ethos of continual engagement—of both the local community and the tourists who visit—with the past's "lessons."[56] This pedagogic role for memorial museums dealing with what Roger Simon termed "difficult knowledge" becomes concerned, as Simon puts it, "with the question of how exhibitions might be presented so as to serve a transitive function that could open up an indeterminate reconsideration of the force of history in social life so that exhibitions that trace the lives of those who have lived and died in times and places other than our own may yet have some force that enjoins our capacities and felt responsibilities."[57]

Yet the question of how this potential is afforded the opportunity to unfold relies upon how the space is curated and what direction the museum desires. In an interview I conducted with her in 2015, the then-director of the Rosario museum, Viviana Nardoni, herself an ex–political prisoner, explained her own philosophy, tying her understanding of what "doing good" might mean to a perceived need for national education in democratic values: "We need to educate young people in the democratic way, so we are working in that path. We need to convince people that democracy is the only way to be a strong nation, to be a healthy society, and to have a strong future. It is difficult to teach about that and the examples of history help."[58] This goal, somewhat loftier than tends to be articulated in art spaces, reflects a sense of purpose whose concerns flow beyond the experience offered within the walls of the institution itself.

In order to meet such aims, the museum must attend to the theoretical principles and community obligations that are relevant to secure support for the museum's endeavors. Not least, the museum is obliged to be concerned with the experience of the visitor; this is a constraint, both practically and conceptually, and is in turn guided by how the directorate imagines the visitors and the museum's role in relation to them. As we have seen, Nardoni emphasizes the importance of the museum's pedagogic role, knowing that the museum is a resource for the city's schools, positing it within "post-memorial" endeavors at least insofar as it seeks to convey the past to those who did not experience it. While this is a pedagogical commitment to the next generation and a political commitment to democracy, Nardoni understands the museum as approaching these through the intimacy it offers with those who lived through the dictatorship. It is as if the museum wishes to impress on its visitors a sense of the bewilderment felt by those caught up in the period as a prelude to seeking this political commitment. Nardoni comments: "It is so difficult for young people to understand the difference between the freedom that democracy offers you and those moments [for example] when you knew that they had taken your brother and that no one, absolutely no one, would help you find where he was."[59] While the artist may use similar methods of engagement, even the same materials, as the museum, therefore, there is, at the Rosario museum at least, the desire to ensure that any shock or wonder that is provoked in the visitor reaches a positive resolution.

Yet there is also the need for the visitors to feel free to move around the space as they choose, to feel engaged on their own terms, and not to feel overwhelmed with detail or through shocking encounters with the past. Many visitors are tourists to Argentina, moreover, and so are likely to be undereducated in relation to the events of the dictatorship period. To this end, Nardoni explains that the museum's exhibits involve not only the intimacy of first-person accounts of the period of the dictatorship, but also more oblique and, as she implies, more easily digestible responses to the past. The involvement of contemporary—and especially local—artists with the museum is based on the notion that their works convey the importance of the recent past through various nondidactic modes of engagement. As well as the display of selected video interviews with key protagonists in the struggle against the dictatorship, a library with many relevant publications, and more permanent installations and artworks, the museum also incorporates a temporary exhibition space curated—at the time of my visit in 2015—by the locally based, internationally renowned artist Graciela Sacco. The nonlinear, somewhat fragmentary approach to the work of the museum, in which the visitor can move around exploring the exhibits in any order and with no singular narrative of history offered, had been the agreed task at the outset for this museum, also articulated as such by the previous director Rubén Chababo.[60] Whether it is antimonumental is a matter of debate, for although there is a sense in which the installations and one's experience of them can and should be open to change, the injunction to remember is the raison d'être of the space.

As an example, an installation by Norberto Puzzolo entitled *Evidencias* offers brief, poignant details of the disappeared, with its focus on the children who were victims of the dictatorship. It uses the space—the sunken

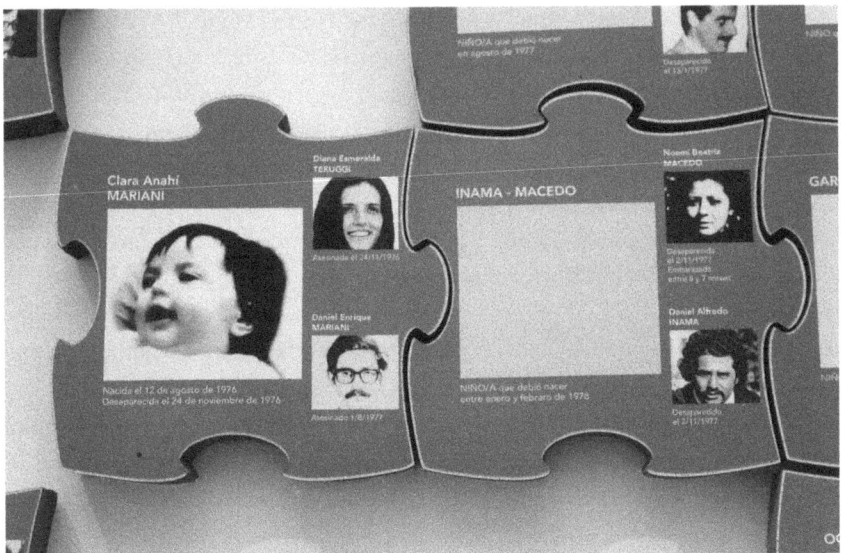

FIGURE 5.3. Norberto Puzzolo's *Evidencias* at the Museo de la Memoria. Photographed in 2015. Source: Vikki Bell.

court in the atrium—to invite the viewer down the steps to read the information displayed on shapes of a jigsaw puzzle. On one of the two opposing walls, the names and photographic portraits of all the children murdered or disappeared during the dictatorship are displayed on large blocks cut into the shapes of a jigsaw puzzle, together with the names and smaller portraits of their parents. If there are no existing images of the children or parents, or if they were one of the many born in captivity, there is a blank where the portrait would be (fig. 5.3). The "evidence" of the installation is not legal, nor do the facts relate to the crimes committed exactly, but the piece focuses instead on the bare details of these families affected, simply presented, alongside the unknowns, incorporated as questions within a wider "puzzle."

On the opposite wall, in another puzzle display, there are photographic portraits of the children who have been found. Every year, through the efforts of the Abuelas de Plaza de Mayo, more of these children are discovered, having questioned their identities and come forward to have their identities investigated. Many of those found were illegally adopted into military families but, through the truth-telling apparatus of the DNA test and the data banks established by the Abuelas, have had their identities "restored" as adults. Each year the museum stages a ceremony in which the piece pertaining to those so "found" is removed from one side of the court, a contemporary photograph added to it, and she or he joins those on the facing wall, a ceremony in which the museum involves the community and the relatives if they so wish. This participation is not therefore the same as "participatory art"—there is no requirement that the visitor participate, but there is a sense that this is an exhibit that has and will continue to change since facts about the dictatorship's actions continue to be uncovered. Unlike the legal trial, then, the gaps in information are part of the museum's message, which together with the lack of pressure of time that operates on the court, mean that the exhibit can reflect the lengthy gradual coming to light of information on the identities and whereabouts of the disappeared.

While the museum holds sacrosanct its attempt to convey something of the experience of those who struggled against and who suffered losses under the dictatorship, it continually reconsiders its decisions about what is appropriate to its space and role. There are boundaries to what it deems admissible. Indeed, Nardoni cautions that it is not the role or responsibility of the museum to "tell *all*." The video interviews with survivors, clips of which are shown on the walls of the museum and which visitors can hear through headphones, come from the audiovisual holdings of the archival organization Memoria Abierta, whose work I will return to below. These offer, according to Nardoni, the value of personal memories; but the museum will not, she explains, allow the personal memories of the repressors: "We want the people to know the protagonists of this story, the protagonists who were pursued by the dictatorship. We are not going to put the testimonies of the perpetrators (*represores*). There are a few images . . . and you will see a brief video of when Videla says that the disappeared don't exist and are simply 'elsewhere'. . . . But in general you will not find that here; this has also been a political decision. The words of those who committed genocide? No."[61]

Memorial museums have always had to engage in these debates about the parameters of inclusion, discussions which apply understandings of relevance and appropriateness. As I have written elsewhere, these are highly ethical questions, including also debates around such fundamental issues as who belongs to the category "the disappeared" itself.[62] Moreover, for Nardoni, some experiences are important for the courtroom, but she is adamant they should not be incorporated into the museal script. This distinction between the two forums she articulates in terms of a local decision about the museum's role, illustrating how the museum feels itself obliged to impose these parameters: "[We tell] what we decide to tell. And what we don't tell. There are some issues we don't explain unless we are in the court. . . . We prefer to tell the political history: about the prisoners of the dictatorship government, about the missing people, but not about the torture. How we were tortured and how other people were tortured. That was a choice—a decision—we made a long time ago. We only talk about these issues in court."[63]

The Memoria Abierta Archive

Finally, there is the archive. The work of the organization Memoria Abierta, mentioned above, is the example here. Memoria Abierta's work was initially based around the building of an archive, or as I explained in the introduction, a network of archives. Although at the time of its inception during the years of the Amnesty laws, "no one was interested in archives," comments Celina Flores, coordinator of the archive, it has grown to become an important resource, and now its value is better understood: "Our conviction [at the outset] was that civil society had the right and responsibility of preserving, looking after and providing access to the archives of the past." Since prosecutions for the crimes of the dictatorship were impossible, and knowledge of what had happened had not been fully gathered by CONADEP, the initiative was as a response to the inadequacies of the state. As Verónica Torras, the current director, phrased it: "[Memoria Abierta] was a sign that civil society was taking charge of memory work. Who else was going to do it when the government at the time was raising questions instead about 'reconciliation?'"[64]

Here, I want to focus on one key aspect of their archive-building, the making of video testimonies with survivors, because these offer another intriguing example of the staging of truth-telling outside the courts, but one where the different considerations at stake share little with legal procedures beyond the fact that the interviews are called *"testimonios"* by the group.[65] Claudia Bacci, who worked for Memoria Abierta for several years, explains that what distinguishes the project is its "sociological" focus, by which she means that these are not legal interviews searching for facts and evidence with a legal trial in mind. Nor are they personal life story interviews. Rather, the constraint that the group has placed upon this key aspect of their endeavors is the focus on collecting and conserving experiences from a delimited period in history, the dictatorship period, guided in general terms by "the objective and focus of the archive [rather than an attempt to record] the story of a complete life."[66] Nevertheless, as sociologist and oral history expert Alejandra Oberti, who has worked with the Oral Archive since 2005, commented, the full experience and unique quality of each individual account is respected and its integrity maintained.[67]

Bacci explains the process of conducting the interviews—of which there are now over 800 stored in the archives at their building on the ex-ESMA site where the group now has its offices—as one requiring careful preparation and sensitivity. First, the interviewers from Memoria Abierta meet with the interviewee in order to discuss the shape of the interview together, for the interviewee to raise her own doubts or share any foreseen difficulties about the content or process, and to explain the technology the recording will require. This first meeting is therefore to reassure the interviewee, to establish trust, as well as to "establish which story they want to talk about, [and for them] to understand what the archive's interests are. . . . If they don't talk easily, we may pose questions. But the sense of the questions is solely to help develop their story."[68] While the interests of the archive place a constraint on what is deemed of interest, Memoria Abierta operates under the principle that the story belongs to the storyteller: "The story is not ours. It is theirs."[69] The rule of the interview recording is consequently "do not interfere"; therefore, the initial meeting is also crucial so that the interviewee understands something of what will occur in practical terms while being assured that although there needs be such a protocol—the scene setting of the interview—the story remains his or hers for the telling.

Given all that this "noninterventionist" scene of the interview requires, that is, the practical assemblage—the lighting, the camera operator, who usually stands behind a large camera, the props the interviewees occasionally bring to help tell the story (photographs, letters, or other personal items), the interviewers, and of course the interviewee him- or herself—it might be tempting to consider the art of dramatization here as akin to filmmaking. However, the principles of this work suggest otherwise, not least because in addition to the "no scripting" principle there is no editing. If an interviewee is very distressed or needs to stop, the filming will pause, but otherwise in almost all circumstances the interview is filmed and archived in an unedited format. Indeed, the editing of the interviews to focus just on the most dramatic moments, such as the moment of their kidnapping, for example, is anathema to their purpose, Oberti commented, since the team cares for the "whole story."[70] It is *not* an exercise in drama, Bacci insists, but rather in what she calls "open listening": "[The] testimonies are not simply about recording the past but . . . they are about how to hear, how to listen."[71] When asked if the archive could be understood as a gift to the future, that its lack of constraints on telling was a way to try to give as much as possible to the future, perhaps even to anticipate that some aspects of the past that we presently do not consider of interest may become so in the future, Bacci agrees, emphasizing this concept of open listening: "Yes, if to anticipate [in that way] has to do with an open listening, to be open to listening to things with respect."[72]

This process and archival materials, therefore, may be dramatic, without seeking to dramatize in the same way that often happens in films or in a court, where people speak with the intention of holding attention or convincing others of the truth of their words. Instead, as Memoria Abierta member Gonzalo Conte reflected, the recording of testimonies operates by the golden rule of Memoria Abierta: to allow a person "his or her own truth," to allow them the space and time to articulate their accounts. While it may be that something dramatic occurs within the interview—even stunning those listening into silence as they glimpse something very profound that arises unexpectedly, and often intensely—the direction and intensity of its impact is deferred, left to a future unknown scenario in which the interview might be replayed.[73] In other words, the archive seeks to gift as much as possible of these protagonists' accounts of the last dictatorship period in Argentina to the future, even with the anticipation that some aspects of these stories that we do not presently consider of interest may become so. Indeed, Oberti has commented that this was the case in relation to understanding the sexual violence that many women experienced when they were kidnapped. "This aspect . . . had been little discussed in the public scene, and was often overlooked . . . nobody wanted to know."[74] But when the team decided to write about this aspect of the dictatorship's practices, revisiting the interviews with women who had been detained in the 1970s, Oberti realized that testimonies on sexual violence were present from the very first interviews.[75] An archive such as Memoria Abierta does not constitute an argument for truth in the sense that animates historical debate or legal trials. Nor does it intend to intrigue, delight, or educate the visitor as the art space or museum might. Instead, its proposition remains a speculative one insofar as the archive necessarily declines to articulate the parameters of the intervention that its contents might make, or the consequence that might ensue.

Conclusions

What I have attempted to describe in this chapter are some of the divergent ways in which forums deploy "arts of dramatization," which is to say, the ways they stage questions about the violence of the last dictatorship period in Argentina in order to propose, display, explore, preserve, confirm, and sometimes refute "candidates for truth." As we have seen, the various modes of staging the past conjure it up in distinct ways, placing different constraints on how it can appear, using different material assemblages in order to allow it to emerge, probing it according to different values and pursuing its details and contours under different principles, obligations, and constraints. While each of these forums is concerned with true accounts of the past, how and what emerges necessarily differs. What counts as evidence, what is understood as "successful," what is dismissed as irrelevant, are all dependent upon the concerns of the forum, so that such its practices are not only "situated" but also necessarily partial forms of world-making. That said, because they exist within an "ecology of practices," to use Stengers's term, these forums are not sealed off from each other, but exist in a web of often highly interdependent connections, wherein personnel, practices, audiences, and resultant "truths" travel. One example of this traveling is the use of Memoria Abierta's interviews in displays at the Museum of Memory in Rosario, where the visitor can sit and listen to the testimonies through headphones. Another is to be explored in chapter 6, where as part of the exhibitions in the ex-ESMA Space of Memory in Buenos Aires there is an explicit "borrowing" of the gravitas of legal truths, seeing this notorious building filled with audiovisual displays that inter alia show clips from the trials—both the 1985 trial of the junta and the 2011 ESMA *megacausa*—projected onto its walls.

This notion of an ecology of practices includes, of course, academia itself as a further site of proposal, dramatization, and challenge, employing devices such as those utilized here—interviews, observations, forms of "putting in relation," and arguments about relevance—to gather and persuade its audiences. This is not to imagine academia as a superior or "meta" place of gathering. Instead, it is to again acknowledge the porous interdependence of these sites, spaces, and forums. Nor is this ecology akin to a division of labor that will facilitate a collectively produced broader truth—named History, no doubt—to emerge in time. The dream of such future harmony is too hasty a conclusion, one that surrenders in the face of the injunction to provide a model for future peace. But to acknowledge the various modes of animated engagement across different gatherings is also to acknowledge the role of the diplomats—or perhaps better, to think less of persons than of diplomatic propositions—that do travel between these forums, challenging parameters and practices, whether quietly or boldly, or else beguiling audiences with stories from "elsewhere," prompting reflexive thought wherever highly delimited modes of addressing the past and their implicit exclusions articulate themselves.

6

RISKING IMAGES, AFTER ALL

Art at the Espacio Memoria y Derechos Humanos,
Ex-ESMA, Argentina

By definition trauma cannot be represented. But it can be approached, moved and transformed. This is not cure; it is *poesis*: making. —GRISELDA POLLOCK, *After-Affects/*
After-Images

December 2006. On my first research trip to Argentina, on the very first
day in fact, I visited the infamous ex–clandestine detention center in Buenos
Aires known by its acronym ESMA, a former navy training school that was
used as one of several hundred camps of detention, torture, and extermination across the country during the last dictatorship's so-called National
Reorganization Process.[1] An estimated five thousand people passed through
the center. Most were kidnapped, imprisoned, tortured, and murdered; only
a few hundred survived. At the time of that first visit, the navy's ownership
of the estate and all its buildings had relatively recently been rescinded, and
in 2004 it had become a Site of Memory (named the Espacio Memoria y Derechos Humanos, ex-ESMA). The site was closed to the general public, so one
had to have an educational reason to gain entrance, and make an appointment

in advance. On a guided tour, we wandered through the neglected buildings that stood in the huge estate before arriving at the gloomy spaces of the Casino building, which stood empty amid intense debates about the best course of action for its future. This was the building to which the kidnapped were brought after being kidnapped. Here they were tortured, forced to work, and imprisoned under the eaves of the roof, and from here they were "transferred," the euphemism for being murdered, often by being drugged and thrown from a plane into the Río de la Plata.[2] The space was emptied of furniture and no information or signs guided us, so that we had only our young guide's words and the building's own prompts, as we were invited to imagine these horrors.[3]

For many, the preservation of the building as it was, empty and forlorn, was an appropriate response to its history, reflecting concerns about the difficulties of achieving adequate modes of representing what had occurred in the space, and the dangers of failure at the site. The debates were both highly emotional and highly intellectual; they drew on psychoanalytic and philosophical texts as much as personal narratives, such as Jean-François Lyotard's warning that extreme events may be effectively forgotten when represented, if one naively thinks one can save memory by mere acts of inscription.[4] Giving form to memory reduces and contains what exceeds the possibility of representation, the argument runs; so while there is an impulse to historicize and analyze—common to both historicism and psychoanalysis—that stems from a resistance to the "formless mass" in order to "lend it form, a place in space, a moment in the temporal succession," the overwhelming challenges such historical events pose bring an incomprehensibility so profound and intense that humankind cannot process it.[5] To attempt to inscribe memory risks a paradoxical failure, therefore. Past traumatic events cannot be synthesized; no form will be able to contain them, since trauma by definition exceeds and escapes representation and narration. Nevertheless, for Lyotard, as for many voices in those debates in Argentina, there remains an injunction to try to represent, and to preserve memory. He writes: "One must, certainly, inscribe in words, in images. One cannot escape the necessity of representing. It would be a sin to believe oneself safe and sound."[6] The challenges of past events *should* continue to reverberate in consciousness, and viscerally too, despite the failure that awaits their representation. Hence the tragic nature of memorializing initiatives.

Since that first visit, however, there have been many changes, and I have made several return visits. The whole ESMA site has now been established as the Espacio Memoria y Derechos Humanos (ex-ESMA) and the Casino building has been established as a monument of historical importance and Site of Memory, which welcomes not only the educational visits of schools and researchers but also the casual visitor with no appointments necessary. The site as a whole is often bustling with events, including those at the Haroldo Conti Cultural Center that stands at the far end of the site from the Casino building, and many personnel now work here in the various human rights organizations—including the Madres de Plazo de Mayo, the Abuelas, the HIJOS—who have relocated here, as well as the archives of Memoria Abierta and the Archive of National Memory that houses the important CONADEP papers.[7] Moreover, the profound suspicion of images that had been in evidence—a suspicion that has been characterized as tending toward the "iconoclastic" policing of images—has retreated, or been quelled under the force of other arguments or concerns.[8] In short, the risk of representation has been taken. And certainly, the site is full of images, visual interventions, and installations.

This chapter focuses on the appearance of images at the site, a "reversal" that I suggest is not a resignation in the face of the difficulties of representation. Rather, I will argue that images do not seek to represent in the sense that that term is usually understood, but instead prompt and require forms of working, and working through, that are modes of making, of "poesis" in Griselda Pollock's sense.[9] Such poesis mobilizes what Seamus Deane once called the "consolation of form" while wrestling with the formlessness of terror.[10] Indeed, a visit to the site potentially entails encounters with several different modes of intervention, requesting that one embark upon a continual and profound oscillation between form and formlessness, an oscillation that is cognizant of the difficulties of the task of bringing images to the ex-ESMA. As an attempt to answer the complexities at stake, the oscillation operates as a prompt for certain forms of labor, which are necessary on the part of both those who choose to intervene at the site and those who visit. This chapter discusses different types of images that have appeared: the use of photo-portraits of the disappeared at the site, which were the first images to appear there; the display of other photographs that address issues of complicity, both during the dictatorship and more recently; the interesting decision to show footage of the witness statements at the trials for the crimes committed at the ESMA within the Casino building where those very crimes took place, and the most recent use of contemporary art photography. In the last section, a more recent intervention at the site is discussed, the challenging performance piece staged within the Casino building by the first international artist to be allowed to make a new work in response to the site, the Polish performance artist Wojtek Ziemilski.

Formlessness and Failure in the Aftermath

In his discussion, Lyotard refers to the analogous problematic of the Kantian sublime whereby the sublime overwhelms the imagination, and the latter fails in its task to represent it sensibly. Even to locate the sublime within time, the simplest task of synthesis that the imagination usually achieves by placing "a kind of frame, a threshold, a border or framework over the manifold," over the flux of things, becomes impossible. The sublime disrupts or exceeds that framing: "it has no moment."[11] There is nonetheless "a sublime feeling"—the mixture of pleasure and pain as Kant describes it, of attraction and repulsion, a trembling, a spasm—that indicates that "an 'excess' has touched the mind, more than it is able to handle. That is why the sublime has no consideration for form, why it is an 'unform.'"[12] By definition therefore, no form—including works of visual representation—will succeed in being able to capture the sublime. Yet interestingly, while the sublime cannot be given form, Kant did suggest that it leaves its trace, albeit one the imagination cannot capture; the trace that the sublime leaves is an unrealized "terror" without form. Lyotard writes that the imagination is "unable to collect the absolute (in largeness, in intensity) in order to represent it. . . . But something, at least, remains there, ignored by imagination, spread in the mind as both pleasure and pain—something Burke called terror, precisely, terror of a 'there is nothing' which threatens without making itself known, which does not 'realize' itself."[13]

This discussion is helpful to understand why, when Lyotard hints at what modes of representing might be able to wrestle with this "something" and to negotiate the paradox of the immemorial, he gestures toward an art that "does not say the unsayable, but says that it cannot say it."[14] He argues that art cannot "bear witness" to the profound trauma, but it can bear witness to "this aporia of art and to its pain."[15] So, while the overwhelming nature of trauma, like the sublime, simply cannot be captured within a representation that attempts to depict it, the unrealized form of it will travel across time and space such that it can—it will—be felt traversing the body. Any sincere attempt to grapple with these affective traces not only will have to acknowledge their necessary failure—as Judith Butler articulated it, "there is something unrepresentable that we nevertheless seek to represent, and *that paradox must be retained in the representation we give*"—but will also, as Lyotard implies, have to acknowledge the "formlessness," the transient, affective quality of such traces.[16] With this in mind, I will now turn to the first of the modes of "representation" that have appeared in the ex-ESMA.

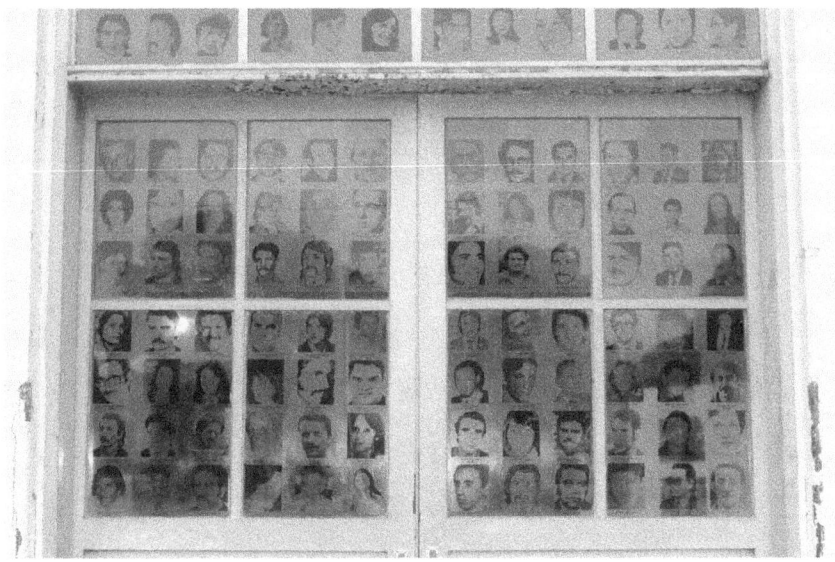

FIGURE 6.1. Faces of the disappeared looking out, ex-ESMA. Source: Vikki Bell.

Without even entering any of the buildings at the ex-ESMA, one will now encounter images as one walks through the grounds of the large estate. Simple portrait photographs, mostly, call from walls and noticeboards, or look out through windows. At one window, for example, black-and-white portraits, made transparent, create a mottled effect from a distance, an effect that resolves into a series of faces only when one approaches closer. Such photographs of the faces of the disappeared are "after-images," to use Griselda Pollock's term, insofar as they are repurposed images from a life "before," traces of a life interrupted (fig. 6.1). Ana Longoni has argued that the use of such photographs—mostly in the form of monochrome formal portraits from passports, school photographs, or other formal documents— "reaffirmed the existence of a biography that predated these subjects' kidnapping," quoting also Nelly Richard, who has argued that it is the tension between the "past carelessness of the face" and the present in which we see the photograph, that "generates the desperate *punctum* that makes these photographs from the album of the disappeared so moving."[17]

Clearly these are not images "of" the violence, and their collective showing—now ubiquitous and familiar—is arguably not an attempt to *represent* the trauma that the cruelty of disappearance wrought on those left without their loved ones. It is, however, a mode of wrestling with the aftermath of that period of violence, in which there was and remains an injunction to respond. Lined up in this fashion, as they have been in many demonstrations and sites since the very first marches of the Madres de Plaza de Mayo, the faces indicate the extent and indiscriminate nature of the state's campaign of violence. The images need and act alongside each other, as a measure of the scale of the violence and of its interruption of ordinary lives in which these photographs might otherwise have been consigned to identity documents or be destined only for family photograph albums. It is the work of the curation of the images—whether they are held or pinned onto bodies, or neatly pasted onto the window as they are here—that makes the images "artful," and makes them an attempt to give an account of what the State violence "meant."[18] And this curation is also a meditation on what "looking" in the aftermath is about. For such images, I would argue, always also underscore their own inadequacies and the ultimate transience of the aesthetic response.

According to Jean-Luc Nancy, all images "present" their objects as subjects, as the image "takes the object out of itself," and turns it "toward the outside."[19] In order to come to presence in the image, he argues, the object must assemble and gather itself, which also requires a withdrawal. This necessary withdrawal means the image is always marked by division and a tearing away, such that the resultant image will simultaneously present and dispute "the presence of the thing."[20] Photographs of the disappeared are particularly, doubly, intense in this respect. The image makes evident a (past) presence, an existence, but it presents a life we know to be (now) only a memory. Qualitatively, the encounter with the portrait photographs works in an intensely subjunctive mood; a "what if?" underscores the loss of the life of a unique individual. That is, such images prompt an attempt to imagine the arc of a life lived differently, while immediately challenging that endeavor, so that the form that imagination attempts dissipates. The task of looking is requested and defeated, therefore, since we cannot know the answer to that little question. In this way the images provoke an acknowledgment of impossibility. They are fragile; they appear, they question, and once again, they withdraw. Thus the imagination is engaged, but forms slip in and out of formlessness, requesting more, but arriving at resignation. While I would wish to concur with Didi-Huberman's influential argument, that turned the use of imagination into an ethical injunction, which is to say that *because* there is no adequate or complete representation, we *must* imagine, what is of interest here is a sense that that failure is enfolded into the process of attempting an aesthetic encounter.[21] The oscillation is integral to its provocation.

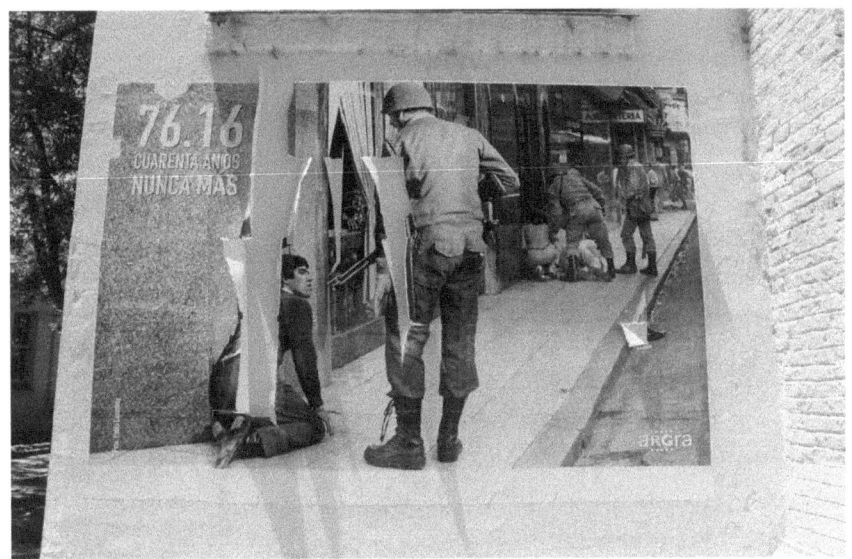

FIGURE 6.2. Photograph by Pablo Lasansky posted on a wall at the ex-ESMA.
Source: Vikki Bell.

Not all the photographs that present themselves as you walk through this
extensive site are focused on the biographies of the *desaparecidos* or murdered of the dictatorship period; other strategies also appear, including images that provoke otherwise, including around questions of complicity and
complacency, both historical and in contemporary times. One example is a
large poster-sized reproduction of a famous photograph by Pablo Lasansky. It
shows a soldier pointing his gun at a young man who kneels on the pavement
staring at the barrel of the gun, while in the background a similar scenario
has two soldiers forcing a couple more people onto the ground (fig. 6.2). The
original photograph was taken on March 28, 1982, during a union-organized
demonstration in central Buenos Aires. It is one of the photographs that is
often said to illustrate how everyday life continued during the dictatorship,
as through the window immediately behind the crouched man one can see
the checked shirt and hand of someone at their table in a café. Here at the
ex-ESMA, the photograph has been pasted onto the side of an exterior wall as
part of a "40 years since the coup" display. It is not a permanent exhibitit—it
is in fact peeling away from the wall the day I see it—but it is indicative of
the use of journalistic photographs as modes of remembering, or teaching

those who were not there, that this was a regime that practiced its repression openly in the streets and during daylight hours. This image seems, perhaps, "merely" documentary, with no accompanying text to explain its presence, relying instead upon its already widespread reproduction to make it and its "message" comprehensible since it has been repeatedly employed to "show" complicity, to suggest that "*no sabíamos*," the excuse that "we didn't know," is questionable. The image differs from those discussed above insofar as it starts to pursue an analysis that does not attempt to represent the atrocities of the dictatorship, nor does it deploy images of "victims" but concerns instead the construction of political subjectivities at that time, raising the issue of the civic complicities that were required to sustain the dictatorship's hold.

Further large-scale photographs pasted onto the walls are the work of the collective GAC (Grupo de Arte Callejero), a group of artists/activists who have long used urban streets as their stage and their canvas.[22] These are again portraits, but interestingly also include images of the more recently disappeared, including Jorge Julio López, who disappeared after giving testimony in a trial of the former police director of investigations, Miguel Etchecolatz, in 2006.[23] The GAC replaces these images every so often, and has also included a portrait of Santiago Maldonado, who went missing in August 2017, last seen alive at a demonstration supporting the claims to ancestral land rights of the Mapuche communities in Patagonia against the Italian fashion chain Benetton; his body was later found in the river (fig. 6.3).[24] Maldonado's disappearance and death has been widely protested. Elsewhere, a series of boards tells the story of Walter Bulacio, who was a victim of police brutality in 1991 at the age of seventeen. Nowadays the disappearance of young men taken into police custody has become an integral part of the work of GAC and its protests. These inclusions, as provocations that extend the viewer's task beyond the memorialization of those disappeared in the 1976–83 period, work in tandem with the portrait photographs of the disappeared of the dictatorship period. Their inclusion and curation across the whole estate poses questions about categorization and periodization, about who is to be included in the category of "the disappeared" or "victims," and how the period of state violence should be dated.

These images prompt the work of reflection in a different mode, therefore, reaching less for modes of identification or imaginative explorations premised on the "what if?" as discussed above, and more insistently focusing attention on the need for vigilance in relation to the state's role, as well as the need for civic responsibility in contemporary times. The labor requested

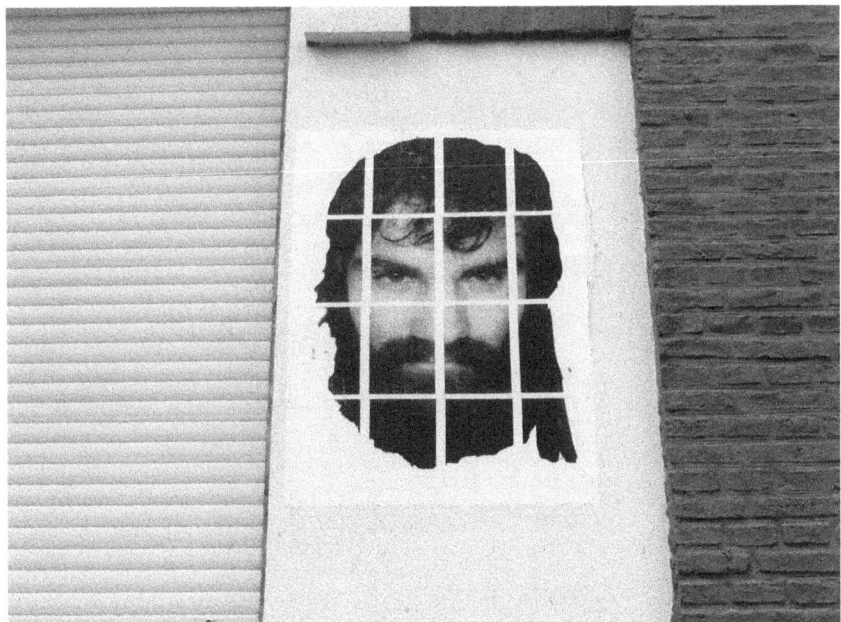

FIGURE 6.3. Face of Santiago Maldonado on a wall at the ex-ESMA. Source: Erica Teichert.

of the visitor here is less the "heteropathic" mode of identification that the faces of the *desaparecidos* prompt and that circle around oscillations between identification and disidentification—Silverman describes this mode as one that can simultaneously sustain both the sense that "I could have been you" and the fact that "I wasn't you"—moving instead to raise the related but distinct question of a shared responsibility to monitor and protest state abuses.[25] These are not "escapes" into memory, therefore, but demands to remain attentive to complicity in current political times.

Legal Speech Repurposed: Trials in the Ex-ESMA

By the time of my visit in March 2015, the Casino building itself had been curated as a site to tell the history of what occurred here, through a variety of different strategies adopted in its different spaces. This was already a distinct change from only a few years earlier, since as I noted in the introduction, it was around this building that the argument to keep the space empty had been most intense. One intriguing curatorial decision was to include within this key building the use of footage from the trials of crimes committed

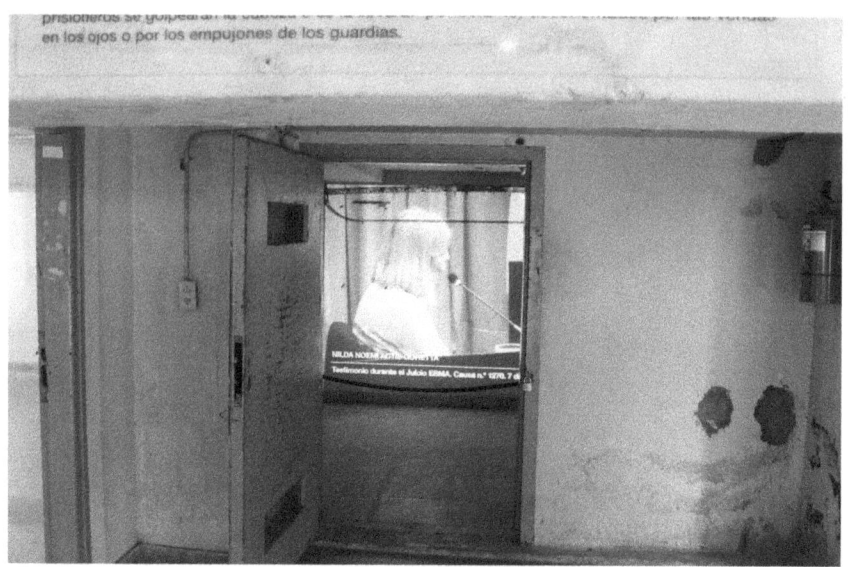

FIGURE 6.4. Footage of Nilda Noemi Actis Goretta, speaking at the 2011 ESMA *megacausa*, projected in a cell in the basement of the Casino building. Source: Vikki Bell.

there, from both the famous 1985 Juicio a las Juntas, which put the military leaders on trial, and from the more recent, long-awaited ESMA *megacausa*.[26]

In a strange fold of time, survivors repeated their stories of kidnap, torture, forced labor, and detention inside the very walls where these events happened, as films of the survivors' evidence given at these trials are projected onto the walls. Throughout the building—from the cells in the basement, where the kidnapped were tortured, all the way up to the *Capucha* (the hood), the attic space under the eves at the top of the Casino building where they were held—snippets of the evidence are being projected onto the walls. For example, figure 6.4 shows Nilda Noemi Actis Goretta, about whose account at the 2011 trial I have written previously.[27] She is projected, larger than life-size, in profile, giving evidence about events of 1970s and this building where she was held. This is disconcerting, as one is asked to locate oneself in multiple moments. We are there with Nilda's account in the 1970s, at the trial in 2011, and here at the site of her terrifying account, in the ex-ESMA basement in 2015. It is a giddying mix.

Up in the *Capucha*, footage of Miriam Lewin giving her testimony to the judges in the famous 1985 trial is projected onto the wall of one of the small partitions called "*cuchas*" (kennels) where the kidnapped were held,

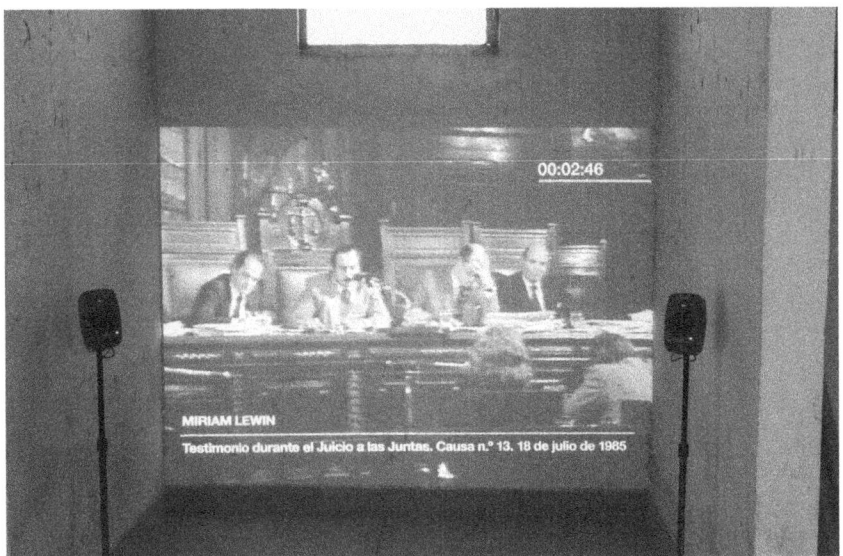

FIGURE 6.5. Footage of Miriam Lewin, speaking at the 1985 Juicio a las Juntas, projected onto the wall of the *Capucha* in the Casino building. Source: Vikki Bell.

hooded and shackled (fig. 6.5). Alongside her are projected excerpts from testimonies delivered at the 2011 ESMA *megacausa* by other survivors, such as Martín Gras, a lawyer, and Victor Basterra, now well known because it was he who managed to smuggle out the now well-known set of photographs that the *represores* took of the kidnapped (fig. 6.6).[28] These snippets are delivered in a peculiar storytelling mode, since the protagonists are not telling their stories for "us" but for the legal trial and the legal record, a fact that is reflected also in their form. These tellers rarely look at us. The camera in the trial was not the focus of the delivery, and as such it is ignored by the speakers, who are seen from behind in the 1985 trial, or from the side in the more recent trials, looking mostly down or toward the judges or lawyers. This is unchoreographed, salvaged footage that could easily have remained hidden away in the archives.

This repurposing of legal speech, which takes words spoken in the formal atmosphere of a court of law in front of the judges, and in front of the defendants, into an exhibition at the Casino building, may be understood as part of the "overflow" of the trial. Here, the survivor-witnesses become "guides," explaining the spaces in which we stand. Inter alia, the testimonies detail how the kidnapped were treated, how they interacted with each other,

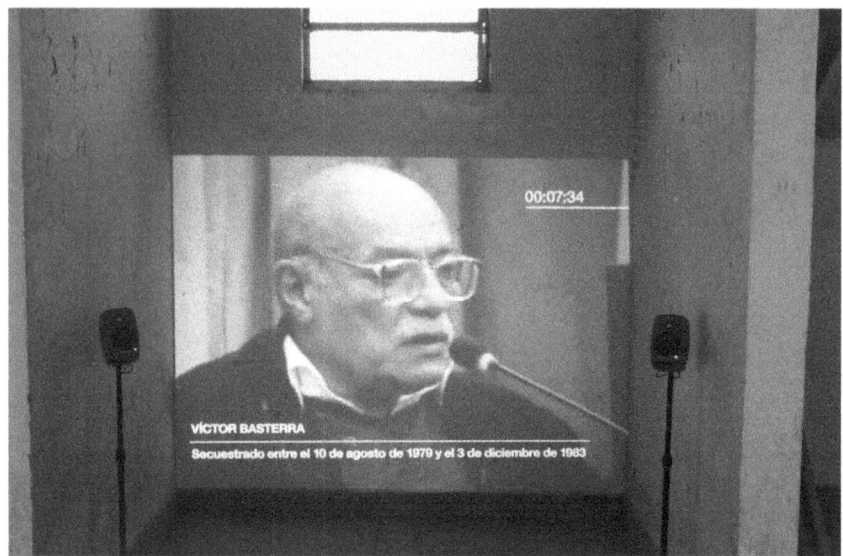

FIGURE 6.6. Footage of Victor Basterra, speaking at the ESMA *megacausa* 2009–11, projected onto the wall of the *Capucha* in the Casino building. Source: Vikki Bell

how they were forced to work, how they were "transferred," a euphemism for being murdered. The use of the footage conveys something of the "experience" of the past, although since it is delivered for the purposes of a legal case, it focuses mostly on events and procedures rather than emotions or reflections. But the decision to return these statements to this space is not, or not only, about passing on information; it is a curatorial decision. The use of the trial footage arresting because it reminds the visitors that this very space is also a crime scene; the building is not merely a "blank canvas" for the projections. Indeed, all the displays in the building have been designed so that the installations do not "touch" the walls, reinforcing the fact that these walls and these spaces are themselves material witnesses to the crimes committed there.[29] (On some of the walls in the *Capucha* there are protective sheets covering spots where the detainees scribbled or drew on the walls.)

Moreover, if the exhibit at the Casino building depends upon the dramatic nature of the trial and of the events recounted there and "borrows" that drama, it also "borrows" the gravitas of juridical truth. According to the communications and press officer for the site at that time, the witness testimonies were used precisely because they carry weight, having been given under oath in a court of law.[30]

Of course, the visitor is invited to engage with the exhibits in a very different mode of engagement and in a very different forum from that of a legal trial. While questions of justice are still in the air—How can a criminal trial "compensate" for these violences and losses? How can these actions be brought to language, these experiences conveyed, at all? Who will speak for those named but disappeared?—this is a different mode of *juris-diction*, of speaking about what justice is and how it can be achieved. The spectator is not constituted or enrolled in the process in the same way that a witness or juror is constituted in a trial. Perhaps we can use the language of obligation here, drawing on Isabelle Stengers's arguments, to say that in this forum, we are not *obliged* to judge or choose. We are asked neither to speak nor to affirm the truth of what is being said here, as we might be as judges or jurors in a trial. Released or removed from that task of judgment, we are asked instead to understand the "arts of dramatization" as part of the experience the installation proffers.[31] Its importance rests upon the possibility for questions raised by the trial's evidence to be considered in other ways. More akin to an encounter with an artwork, there is a request to exist with it, to suspend our lives in order to give time to the installation and its provocations.[32]

For this to happen, it has to be a space of reflection and rumination, not a simple repetition of already formulated positions.[33] Arguably, the work presented by the curator or artist remains "interested," so to speak, in the experience offered and its impact upon the spectator, but because an art forum has different concerns from a trial, there is also more freedom in *whether* to respond and *how* to do so.[34] This "freedom" in how to receive the footage is precisely what the exhibition risks, and what—ethically speaking—it shelters.[35]

With its distinct temporality, the exhibit requests that our concern shift to a logic or sequence different from that of the trial. Indeed, the organized and systematic nature of the repression is documented here not in order to convict, but in order to provide a life for these stories *beyond* the court and trial process. In this space, its provocation turns on how the witnesses' testimonies are in the process of becoming stories, retold and replayed in order to be passed on. We are invited to help these images and accounts survive, I would suggest, to agree to give further movement and life to the events and stories that may otherwise become lost within the legal record or staid, condensed into the anonymous narratives of history books. It bespeaks a concern beyond the legal decision, therefore, one that asks how such accounts of the past may be further enfolded into contemporary ethical, even normative, worlds.[36]

Ambiguity and Aesthetic Sensibility

December 2016: At the Casino building, for the first time, an exhibition understood and named as "art"—as opposed to documentary images—is being shown; it is a temporary exhibition that gathers the work of twelve practicing contemporary Argentine photographers.[37] A select few images by each photographer are projected on the walls—again, nothing except the light actually touches the walls. The images do not hold an obvious, explicatory relationship to the events that occurred here—although several do, in fact, in their different ways, have stories entwined with them—and their unity as an exhibition is held together minimally, by their shared choice of monochrome, by their implicit trust in what the photo-image alone may do, with very few supplementary words to explain them.

At the far end of the basement, in the space formerly used for torture, and where the photographic apparatus was situated that took images of the kidnapped when they were brought into the ESMA, there is an interesting display. Juxtaposed to the semipermanent exhibition of the photographs that Basterra smuggled out of this building, mentioned above, is a selection of the work of photographer Marcelo Brodsky. Marcelo's brother Fernando was disappeared in 1976 and appears in one of the images Basterra grabbed. Around the images Basterra "saved," some text explains how these images were part of a routine, systematic documentation by the regime, and how Basterra saw the opportunity to grab the negatives, at great risk, as evidence. Submitted in due course to the 1985 trial of the junta, these images also circulated beyond the trial in Argentina and elsewhere. The one of Fernando was also shown, once again, by his mother at the ESMA *megacausa* of 2009–11, and has appeared as I have written elsewhere, in Marcelo's art exhibitions. Showing here in the Casino building, where it was taken, and alongside the other "Basterra" photographs, it is particularly affecting. Alongside the perspex panel on which these haunting images are reproduced, Marcelo Brodsky has projected a few more alternating images of his brother. They are personal "snapshots." One is the first image he ever took of his brother in their bedroom. A little out of focus but clearly "there," Fernando sits with his head tilted down as if in contemplation. Then a photograph of the two brothers together on the boat from Buenos Aires to Montevideo, the churning wake extending behind them. These few images offer a glimpse of the life that was being lived prior to Fernando's kidnapping; Marcelo has commented on the poignancy that the images take on, the blurred face of the first making his visage elusive, paradoxically "immemorial," one might say; the second, on a

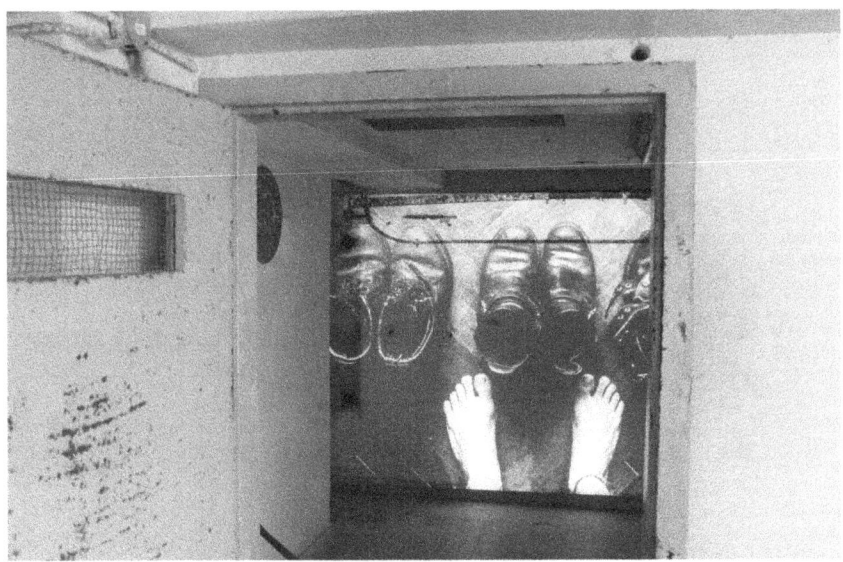

FIGURE 6.7. A photograph by Fernando Gutiérrez projected in a cell in the basement of the ex-ESMA. Source: Vikki Bell.

certain reading, uncannily foretelling his fate as he enjoys risking standing in front of the sign saying "Do Not Stand Here," as youth are wont to do.[38] Brodsky's projections reclaim this space for his brother, and for himself, rejecting the idea that the last image, taken in this basement of the Casino building and by those who killed Fernando, would stand as the only image for his life. Together, they perform an aesthetic demand to curate Fernando's image, to care for it, to create and circulate it as a work of art.

In the cell where the trial footage of Nilda Noemi Actis Goretta had been, there is now projected a photograph by Fernando Gutiérrez, an image of leather boots in pairs, neatly lined up, if a bit scuffed and wrinkled where they've been worn; a pair of bare feet, white and vulnerable, stands behind them (fig. 6.7). Unlike Actis's words, this image does not "speak" to what happened here. As visitors to the exhibition and situated as such in this space, we have only the option to engage in the imaginative and creative work of joining the image with the events that occurred here. Shoes are so evocative of loss, carrying, as they are apt to do, the idiosyncratic molding and marks of the particular human life to which they have been attached. They may recall the abandoned shoes elsewhere, such as those at Auschwitz, a history with all its comparisons to and distinction from the Argentine experience. But the defiance of the image is

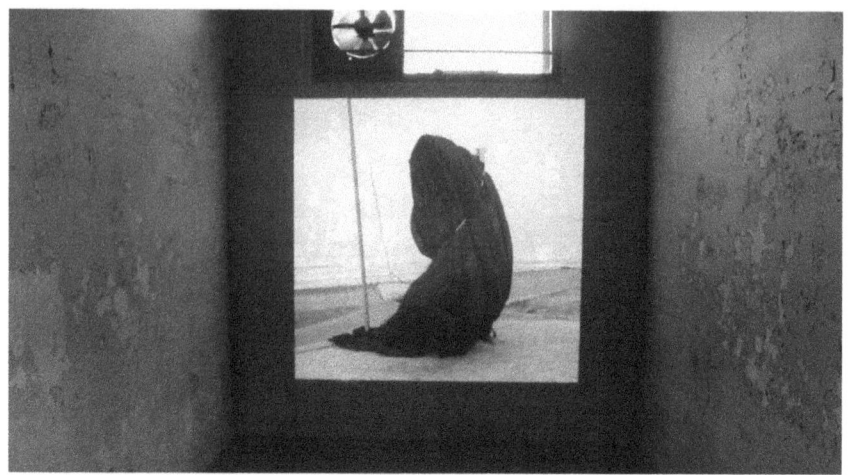

FIGURE 6.8. Juan Travnik's *Claromecó* (1995) projected onto the wall of the *Capucha* in the Casino building. Source: Vikki Bell.

less articulated; the image does not explicitly comment on the horrors that occurred in the space it now occupies. Its power is rather through its performative claiming of this space—of this very cell, its heavy door still attached—*for* creativity, *for* art, *for* its transformation into a space for art-viewing. Its accomplishment is in this turning of attentions from the illustrative to the explicitly illegible, the nondidactic world of contemporary image-making.

Arguably the exhibition as a whole makes this turn, distinguishing these images from the more conventionally museal ones that have appeared here. These images explicitly surrender a pedagogic role of instruction; their allusions to what happened are posed without verbal explanation, viscerally, obliquely.

In one of the *cuchas*, an image by Juan Travnik is projected (fig. 6.8). (I later learn that it is called simply after the place it was taken—Claromecó—and is dated 1995.) Some dark sacking seems to hang from a line, a rope tied around its middle. It is hanging there, improbably held by this makeshift setup, by the sea, with a small sailing boat in the distance on the sand; but it is the large dark, indeterminate form that dominates the image, and that leaves one to wonder whether there is a human form underneath these folds of cloth? We cannot know, but this unknowable form certainly takes on a brooding presence here, where human bodies were hooded and shackled.

The projection is on a loop that shows a few of Travnik's images in turn, all of which are similarly abstract but share an atmosphere of neglect and ruin. On the side of an abandoned wooden shack appears a ghostly imprint

of what appears to be a larger-than-life human form that had once been attached to its side. A white, possibly marble, statue of a woman, fallen to the
ground, still staring out along the horizontal. Something has happened in
each of these images or rather before each: a human form was left an imprint;
a statue has tumbled, or been pushed; and in "Claromecó," someone has tied
something up and left it hanging, for reasons we can only ponder.[39] These
images are unable to restrict us to one reading; they are beautiful, uncanny
images that provoke but refuse to confirm our interpretation, offering instead
an aesthetic experience that is intriguing, slowing down and unrailing the tak-
ing-in of "information" that museums tend to request. If there is an implicit
directive here, it is an unusual one insofar as the images ask the viewer to see
traces, which by definition are the remains or impressions of past events, but
to understand the connection between his images and this place where we encounter them as a *task*. They suggest that more research is required, not only to
understand what these images are of, but also why they appear here. Thus the
exhibition's intervention is not an appeal to empathy, identification, or notions
of civic responsibility, as many of the conversations around photography and
"post-trauma" have debated, but rather a meditation that begins from this conjuncture of images and place, to point toward a future in which there is more
work to be done. In Griselda Pollock's terms, it is a "post-traumatic art" that
suggests, "by a constant fidelity, by working towards a phrasing—not merely
linguistic, but gestural, sonic or graphic—a touching or encountering of some
affective elements capable of shifting us both subjectively and collectively that
do not arrive at containing the event in finite forms. The aesthetic performs a
shattering awakening into sensate thought and incites continual research for
ways to say what remains out of our cognitive reach."[40]

In Paula Luttringer's image, huge on the wall of the *Capucha*, an ant crawls
across a stone wall, from which a metal bar rises like a prison's barred window. Again, the image's relation to this space is approached obliquely, with
its attention on shadows and texture. Are we to feel repulsion or admiration
for the small insect, who goes about its industry regardless of human predicament? Only later, through tracing the artist's work, one comes to realize
that it is part of a series from the project *The Wailing of the Walls,* and this
particular image refers to the story of Ledda Barreiro, who was kidnapped in
1976 and says that when she was held—in the detention center known as La
Cueva—she remembers watching the ants, who were able to walk around in
the outside world then enter her cell: "Watching them I didn't feel so alone."[41]

Like the woman in Helen Zout's striking image (fig. 6.9), also projected in
the exhibition, we catch ourselves gazing, lost in thought, staring out onto

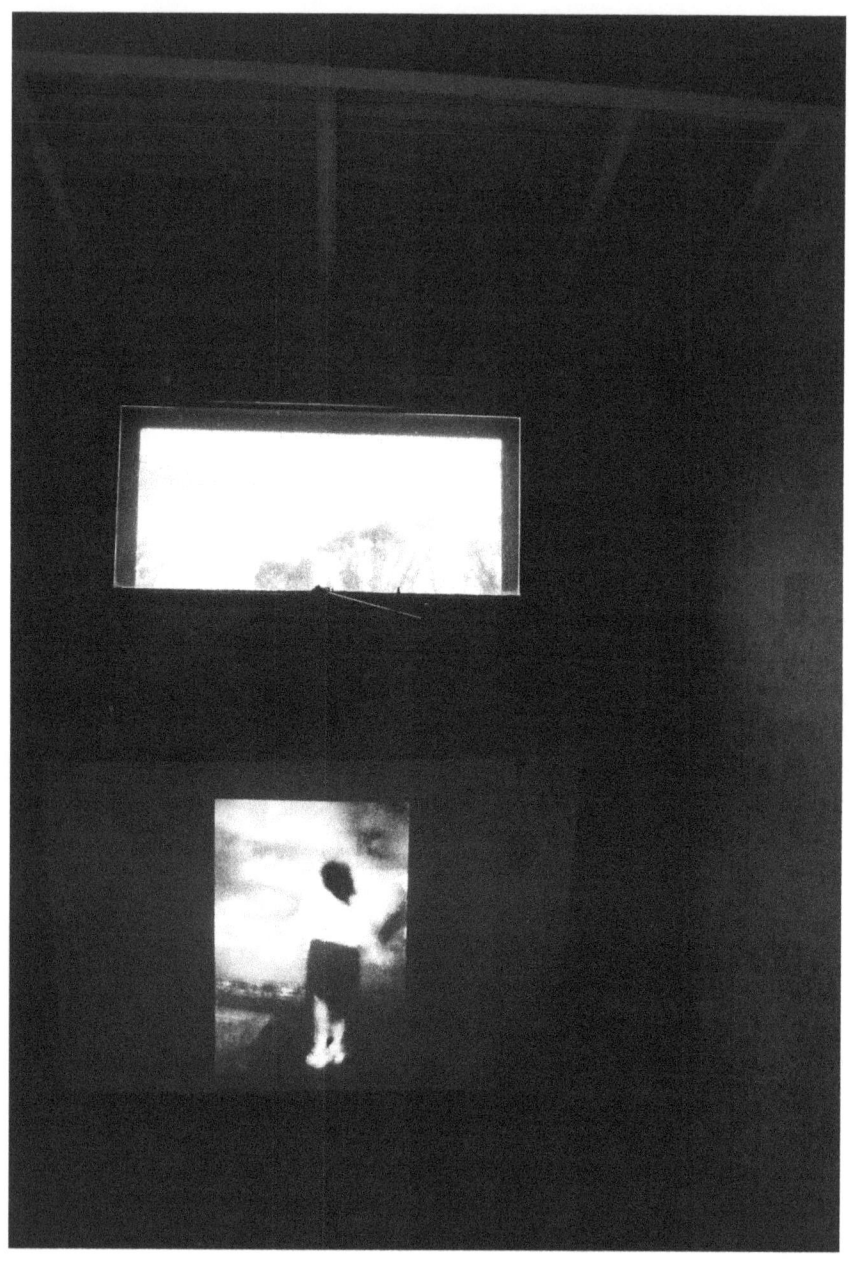

FIGURE 6.9. Helen Zout's photograph projected onto the wall of the *Capucha* in the Casino building. Source: Vikki Bell.

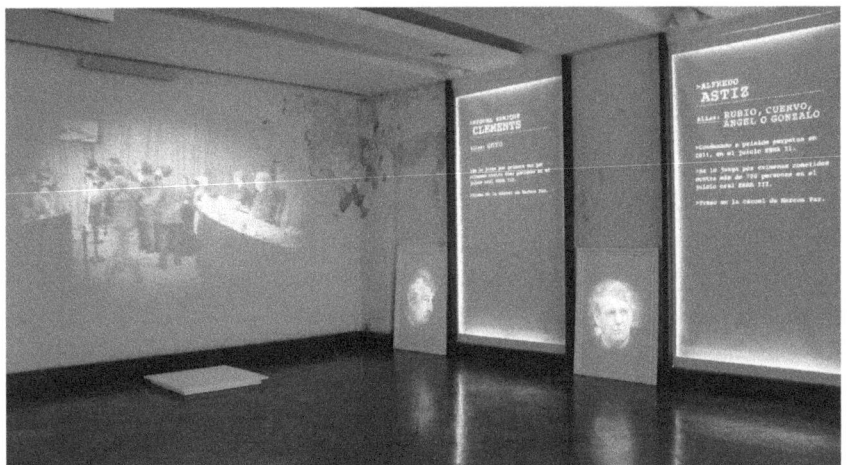

FIGURE 6.10. The *El Dorado* room showing the faces of *represores* in the Casino building. Source: Vikki Bell.

a landscape while wondering where and how to focus our attention, how to formulate our responses to the experience of the Casino building. Throughout the exhibition, dotted around the semipermanent museum's information and images, we are faced with these monochrome and more overtly "artistic" images that do not always resolve into recognizable forms, but that put us in touch with our aesthetic capacities and sensibilities. In itself this is arguably a mode of defiance, performing a response that turns on the fact that in the face and in the aftermath of atrocities people retain this aesthetic ability to judge images, and to be moved by them, whether they are survivors or visitors.[42] But we are also placed before our inability to really comprehend all, made to experience the unknowing that accompanies attempts to explain or contain such images, as it does the attempt to understand the suffering and the experience of being held here.

The contrast, after these tender and gentle provocations of the temporary exhibition's images, to the semipermanent exhibition in one of the last rooms, named *El Dorado*, could not be more stark. Having descended from the top of the building toward the exit, one enters the room devoted to those condemned for their part in the crimes committed here (fig. 6.10). The faces of the *represores* are projected onto the tomblike rectangular screens around the room, once at the age they were during the crimes, and again as they appeared in the courts. The details of their crimes and sentences (or deaths) are typed out onto the screens as if they were legal files. Against a soundscape of what sounds like slamming doors or even a judge's hammer, the words "Condemned" (or "Deceased" where relevant) are then stamped across their files, one by one. This is an important part of the story of what happened here, a performance of finality and a contrasting mode of providing an "account" of the past. Suffice it to say here that this "ending" contrasts with the tender work of the exhibition. By juxtaposing ambiguous images and allowing them to appear like surprises in the nooks and crannies of this very specific place, its curation gently insists that beyond these visual provocations, more thought, more research, is required. Such labor is never complete, and beyond any legal decision, it will necessarily continue into the future.

An Impossible Scene, or The Crying Perpetrator

The museum's then director Alejandra Naftal—an art historian by training and herself a survivor of the Vesubio detention center—introduced the idea of the "Five o'clock visits" on every last Saturday of the month as a way to continue bringing new voices and perspectives to the site. Over several years (2015–19), different thematic conversations took place as a wide variety of speakers offered their knowledge and experiences, reflecting on the space and its stories. Philosophers, artists, survivors, relatives, journalists, lawyers, international visitors, and more discussed issues such as modes of survival, gender and sexuality, and justice processes in Argentina and abroad in a series of well-attended events that held not only the promise of remembering what had happened in the ESMA but also that of creating fresh perspectives and even "new narratives about the past."[43]

November 2019. For the first time, a non-Argentine artist had been allowed to create an intervention, a performance work, to be shown inside the building.[44] Wojtek Ziemilski, a Polish performance artist and theater director, had spent several weeks at the museum and, working in collaboration with the well-known Argentine actor and director Rubén Szuchmacher, had produced an intervention that proved to be controversial, with some members of the board of the museum expressing their concerns about whether it should be allowed to be staged there at all, and some choosing not to attend.[45] Naftal introduced the event on the day as "a risk."[46] The controversy arose because of the approach and subject matter on which Ziemilski chose to focus the piece. Naftal had told Ziemilski that one of the difficult spaces in the museum—difficult in the sense of knowing what the museum should do with it—was the self-contained ground floor apartment that had been the domestic living quarters of Vice Admiral Rubén Chamorro, the director of the ESMA and its infamous Task Group 3.3.2 during the most violent years of its operations (1976–79). These rooms had not been successfully incorporated into the museum experience, Naftal felt, having been minimally curated with only a simple television set playing the witness statement given at the 1985 trial by a friend of Chamorro's daughter recalling that, at age eleven, she had been on a playdate there when through the window she saw a woman, hooded and handcuffed, being lifted out of a Ford Falcon car and carried into the building by two armed officers.[47] The idea of "private" life continuing in the midst of the torture and killing of the kidnapped no doubt provoked Ziemilski to consider what was said by those committing these crimes in the privacy of their own lives, behind closed doors. What were they thinking in private, what did they say, what did they feel? Moreover, as Néstor Fuentes, survivor of the ESMA, put it in the discussion after the performance, sometimes one wonders: "What are they like now? What is going through their minds now? Do any of them regret what they did?"[48]

Ziemilski's piece became a response to the space and a provocation to consider how one imagines the perpetrators' inner lives, and—more pointedly—how the fact of their guilt constrains, frustrates, or even curtails our imaginations. Artists have the possibility to be the "court jester," Ziemilski told me in an interview I conducted with him in 2021, to be the one "who's allowed to say things which normally you wouldn't allow somebody to say."[49] Adopting the posture of naivety, artists may open doors that have been closed off: "[They] go places where you don't want to go, places that are difficult. In terms of memory, places that we don't want to think about."[50]

On a large screen covering the wall of the apartment's main room, a film is projected. The title, *An Impossible Scene*, appears then fades to black as an older man appears, dressed in an unremarkable civilian black suit, shirt, and tie. Since he is well-known, the audience may well recognize the actor as Rubén Szuchmacher.[51] He stares straight out at the camera, at "us" in the museum, for a full awkward half-minute, his mouth slightly opening and closing again, his jaw tight, before he looks down despondently and his face falls. It is unclear whether he is going to smile or cry, but his half-grimace and a sharp intake of breath suggest the latter. His eyebrows raise and, righting himself and raising his head, he once again stares out at us, as if he wants to speak, as if he has resolved to do so. But once again he is overwhelmed, anxious and hesitant; he sniffles, his eyes casting up then back to us, and his struggle continues, with his mouth opening wide with words that don't arrive. Although there is no attempt to make Szuchmacher look like Chamorro, here, in the

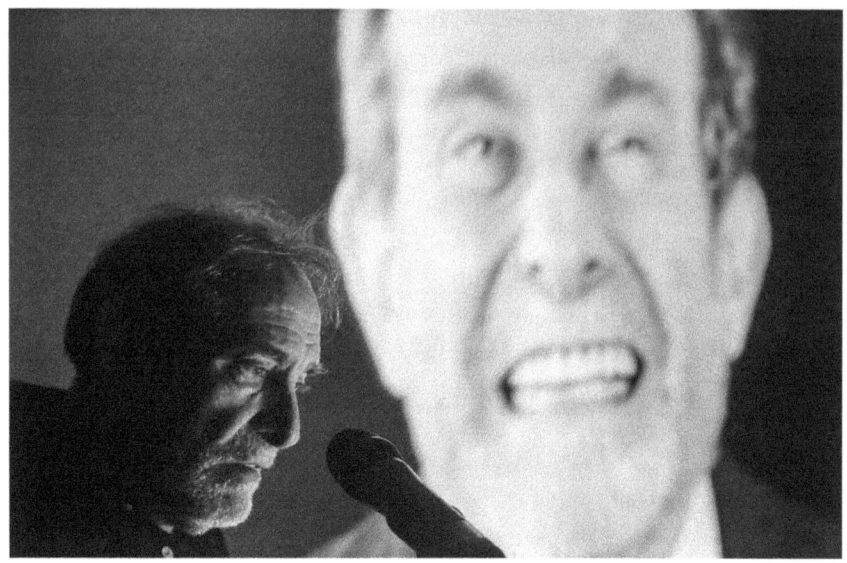

FIGURE 6.11. Wojtek Ziemilski's *An Impossible Scene*, with actor Rubén Szuchmacher, 2019. With permission of the artist.

latter's former living quarters, he is "in the air." After four and half minutes of watching this man struggle, one could be forgiven for losing patience with him, with this work.

Suddenly, there is another man in front of the audience, in the room, standing at a lectern. It is Szuchmacher himself, "doubling" his image (fig. 6.11). But at the lectern, much smaller than the face on the screen, he assumes the stance of a critic or a chorus, commenting on the film as it continues behind him. He is not narrating the action; instead, he is dismissive. "I have no idea what can pass between a perpetrator and his emotions."[52] Soon the impossibility in the title becomes clear as finally, after more anguish, coughing, sniffling, and staring, and five long minutes into the piece, a few clipped words emanate from the man's mouth: "Sorry, sorry sorry."[53]

Typically, the *represores* in Argentina have not apologized or shown remorse for their crimes against humanity. The attitude of those accused of crimes against humanity has always been steadfastly unapologetic and imperious, including during the famous 1985 trial of the junta and the more recent series of trials. Collectively, they have repeatedly asserted their justification in terms of a nationalist duty to rid Argentina of the violent subversion that was threatening to destroy the nation, refusing to show any remorse. In the 2011 ESMA trial, for example, Alfredo Astiz, one of the most notorious members of the Task Group 3.3.2—who was known as the "angel of death" and who, among other crimes, infiltrated the Madres de Plaza de Mayo pretending to be the brother of a disappeared man in order to kidnap and murder Azucena Villaflor and two other founding members—used the opportunity of the trial to deliver a speech in the manner of a condescending history professor, explaining how they were loyal subjects acting dutifully, and that history would be on their side.[54] His performance at the trial could not be in greater contrast to the perpetrator in Ziemilski's piece. One important exception was the dramatic 1995 confession of former officer Adolfo Scilingo, who, in a series of interviews with the journalist Verbitsky, gave an account of his participation in the "death flights" that, as mentioned earlier, killed the kidnapped by drugging them and throwing them, unconscious, into the waters of the Río de la Plata from small planes.[55] Scilingo did seem to express something approaching remorse, leading another *represor* Julio Simón to comment, "I'm no crybaby like that sorry Scilingo."[56] But, as Robben has argued, his confession was delivered in such a manner and context that it should be viewed as just as much a part of the repertoire of perpetrator agency as the more common denials and silences. Scilingo portrayed himself as the emotionally wrought victim of the immoral military, his confession accompanied by half-truths and lies, and when he fled to Spain he recanted to try to save himself from prosecution, an attempt that failed.[57]

He grimaces, squeezes his eyes tight, and gasps. He seems always about to cry, but no tears flow. Szuchmacher-as-critic continues to dismiss the image of the emotional perpetrator: "If a perpetrator cries, it is probably merely a physical discharge." And when the man raises his hands to cover his face, he rejects this display: "Crocodile tears. That's what I think when I think of a crying perpetrator." He is no doubt articulating the sentiments of many of the audience members in the room, including not only many of whom have fought for years to find answers to what happened to their loved ones; also in the room are members of the group Historias Desobedientes, who are children of the *represores* in Argentina who have publicly denounced and disowned their military fathers for their roles in the repression.[58] But hereafter, Szuchmacher-as-critic's response becomes more complex, as he questions why he is being asked to look at this performance: "The image of a crying perpetrator also upsets me. Because I feel manipulated."[59] The narrator then starts to switch back and forth with his statements, as if trying out different responses to the image behind him:

> I want him to cry.
> I don't want his tears.
> I want him to cry.
> I want him to feel guilty. He is guilty.
> Leave him to cry because he is guilty.
> I don't want his tears.[60]

After this seeming confusion, the script then "finds" the position and language that the human rights groups have predominantly adopted for decades: "I don't need his tears. *I need information and justice*."[61] The long struggle for truth and justice in Argentina has not ended with the guilty verdicts that the last fifteen years of trials have delivered; while the sentences may have brought some comfort and vindication to the relatives, still there is an absence of crucial information, which those responsible have continued to withhold. Many relatives have themselves passed away without ever knowing where the remains of their loved ones are.

Having found a line of argument, as it were, the script moves immediately back to the affective register:

> What should I do with his emotions?
> I can't look at this. I have to look away.
> He is not human.
> The man cries, and he is not human. I don't want him to cry.[62]

Here is the central question or paradox that this performance piece circles: how to resolve the issue of humans acting inhumanely, what Derrida referred to as the "suicidal" aspect of human rights violations. To reject these individuals, to consider them as lacking humanity, is to set up a division that avoids having to consider them or the tasks that would follow from such consideration.

By placing the critic within the piece, Ziemilski preempts a conversation that could well have taken place after the performance, as the narrator-critic articulates several of the responses that the audience, many of them with a personal relationship to the ex-ESMA, could have been expected to articulate. While on the film the man manages another feeble "sorry, sorry," the narrator-critic starts to lose his temper: "*I* was the one who cried."[63] And then he starts to articulate a list, a collectivity among whom he seems to situate himself: "*We* were the ones who cried. *Us*. Us mothers. Us fathers. Us sons. Us daughters. Us brothers. Us sisters. We did the weeping." In his anger now he shakes a finger at the screen. "What is this? I don't know. I don't know what I want from this. But certainly not this."[64] In my interview with him, Ziemilski explained that during his time in Argentina, he was made aware that the piece would be criticized: "[After skepticism and resistance was reported to me], I realized that I needed some sort of critical commentary to this work, inside the work, to build a level of empathy."[65] The narrator is angry, judging the attempts to apologize and the attempt to cry in terms that do not quite cohere, his logic faltering: "Is this supposed to be crying? He doesn't know how to cry. How can you declare yourself guilty if you don't know how to cry?"

Crucially, the commentary is contradictory, even incoherent, asking first "Can, frankly, someone who was a perpetrator cry?" Then trying the rephrasing "*Can't* someone who was a perpetrator cry?" The identification that the piece promotes between the audience and the narrator-critic, therefore, allows by the same token, for the difficult questions—the self-doubt—to arise, as was Ziemilski's intention. In our interview, he explained that the notion of the perpetrator as beyond humanity allows people to avoid consideration of the fellow human being "behind" their role in the repression. By having the commentary dismissing the performance of the perpetrator within the performance, the piece emphasized the role-playing, of a scripted performance. First, the appearance of the embodied actor in tension with the appearance of the film-image is clear, underscoring the latter as a fabrication: "It's curious that it should be [so] difficult to empathize with another human being. Of course, it's understandable, you know, [since] there is [an aspect of] that human being which is such a problem. But I thought that *the aliveness of Rubén made it possible to change the way of looking at the image*. And the fact that it's him, of course, that he is talking about his own image, and that his own image is so theatrical and . . . at the same time, it is so convincing."[66]

The uncomfortable question arises as to whether the *represores*, too, were "acting" in their activities, in their self-presentation as steadfast and committed out of nationalist loyalty to their murderous task: Who was, or is, the other person who existed beyond that role? Would he have cried? Ziemilski told me that he had met some of the "disobedient" children of the *represores* and had seen an interview with a woman who continues to visit her father in prison regularly although she is active in the Historias Desobedientes movement: "She was asked why she was still visiting her father and she said, 'well, he was a very good father', and I thought that was just like, I had tears in my eyes because, yeah, it's possible. There is a possibility of somebody being a good human being in one respect even though they were a terrible human being in another."[67]

But secondly, the narrator-critic is also himself revealed as scripted: "He's as much acting. He's literally reading a script, as is the person on the screen."[68] And that Rubén Szuchmacher can play *both*—the *represor* and the critic-narrator—likewise creates a situation in which the artificiality of the performance is key. The audience is released from the task of imagining the identity of the performance with the performer, as these become unmoored from each other in Brechtian fashion.[69] This could lead, as Ziemilski suggested, to a position of saying, "Well, there's no human being here, it's all fiction," whether that amounts to a position of comfort—"don't worry, it's all fiction"—or one of despair, even nihilism: There is no "doer," nothing is truly of value. The movements that Ziemilski's piece sets up, the movements of suspicion and doubt, questioning theater's role, the audience's role, even the role of critique, were not designed to lead the audience to one particular conclusion. It did not seek to "contain the event in finite form," as Pollock would put it, but to use theatrical space that could produce an affective encounter that might incite continual questioning. Not least, it raised the challenge of how we create figures that ease our comprehension, such that some questions are repeatedly diverted, even disallowed.[70] His piece is, I think, less an argument that we are all "trapped in bad scripts," in the sense that Diana Taylor argued some time ago that the Madres of Plaza de Mayo had become trapped in a certain scripting of their position, and more a provocation around how certain modes of imagining and enquiring about the past become occluded over time through habits of thinking.[71] Ziemilski played upon his position as an "outsider" here, since he brought his "anachronisms" and raised questions in ways that have not been common in Argentina, by veering, as it were, "off-script." If making the audience suffer the spectacle of the *represor* and his struggle with his own guilt led to the critique that this was a way of surreptitiously attempting to stage a scene of reconciliation more like South Africa's experience of the Truth and Reconciliation Committee, in a sense this was true.[72] Ziemilski's provocation was indeed precisely to put that anachronistic scene of guilty confession before this audience, raising the issue of what impact that "missing scene" might have had, or indeed, what impact that missing that scene *has* had. There is no implication that such a scene of confession of guilt should have been or should be sought in Argentina; rather, it is more that a series of questions arises around why envisaging it is both so improbable and so uncomfortable.[73]

Concluding Remarks: Moving Images

Griselda Pollock asks the following of what she terms "after-images": "Can aesthetic practices, the creation of after-images, bring about transformation—this does not imply cure or resolution—of the traces, the *after-affects*, of trauma, personal or historical . . . ?"[74] Her interest is in the encounters made possible by the appearance of the forms that art practice offers up into the world. Without over-claiming for what after-images can achieve, she seeks to explore how creative practices may involve the shaping of psychic economies that "enable encounters with traumatic moments that can be processed transitively, hence be shared, transported and passed into another bearer, be that the artwork or the willing partner who comes to meet it."[75] What is particularly relevant here is the focus Pollock puts on the *movements* at stake, the transformations that must occur between the events and the artist, the artwork and the one who encounters it, that are not only psychological but material, situated, precarious processes. She emphasizes the necessity that there be such a creative process: "I repeatedly stress the significance of form formation transformation in order to explore the mediation between after-affect and after-image, that moves from the psychic intimacy between aesthesis and trauma, structurally, to the role of art-working in touching and thus offering a novel, poetically generated form for the encounter with that which, by definition, is not yet in the grasp of representation."[76]

In this chapter I have suggested that the risk of images at the ex-ESMA, and especially in the Casino building itself, has been taken variously, with each attempt a negotiation of what an encounter with the site entails. From the images of faces of the disappeared and murdered, which appear in multiple ways, to the use of trial footage and then the mingling of art photography within the space, to Ziemilski's provocative performance piece, these approaches are multiple. Rather than seeking to judge these responses in terms of their "success," one can begin from the understanding that they are so many different modes of negotiating their own failure. While they are not all of a piece and adopt different modes of "giving form" to the formlessness, they are engagements with *making* that transform the past violence into multiple forms. They are not attempts to represent so much as to *move* the past, becoming so many different modes of request to tarry with their forms awhile. A visit to the site now involves a series of encounters with forms that appear—often unexpectedly—within its architectural landscape and dissipate once again, making the experience an oscillation between form and formlessness, between these visual provocations and imaginative flights.

CONCLUSION

The archive: if we want to know what this will have meant, we will only know in the times to come. Perhaps. —JACQUES DERRIDA, *Archive Fever*

During the decade that I have been writing these chapters, interest in the relationship between archives and conflict-affected countries has grown, such that scholars have begun speaking about "transitional" or "justice" archives as a way to group studies of archives from across the globe.[1] In their introduction to a special issue on this umbrella term, Julia Viebach, Dagmar Hovestädt, and Ulrike Lühe suggest that we must tell "archive stories" both in the sense of the story of their creation, how archives comes into existence—whether that occurs during or after the conflict—and in the sense of the uses of archives, with their main focus on their deployment in legal and quasi-legal processes of transitional justice.[2] *Promises Beyond Memory* shares much with this welcome endeavor. I too have sought to appreciate archives as complex achievements, illuminating their historical contexts and the roles of the people and organizations that created them, as well as to explore how they "hold" stories and documents until such time that they are, in Viebach and colleagues' term, "activated," or in Maria Elander and Rachel Hughes's term, "pressed" into service elsewhere.[3] Yet a different conceptual framework and different methodological commitments have guided my more sociological explorations of how such stories are conjured up from the traces of the past. Not least because I have wanted to follow the afterlives of documents, of photographs, of places, of the stories of victims, survivors, and relatives, as they circulate and (re)appear in a variety of spaces and forums, including law but also including those community or—for want of a better word— "cultural" spaces that, although not without a relationship to law, practice distinct modes of gathering.[4] Isabelle Stengers's suggestions that we can study the diverse "arts of dramatization" conducted within an "ecology of practices" prompted me to consider how evidence or "truth" is asked to appear variously and to "speak" differently, how it is cajoled through distinct apparatuses, and—as importantly—how as a consequence it is differently "heard." None of this is a simple process. We have seen, for example, how stories from the past are filtered for relevance to the space in which they appear, are interrupted by challenges and disagreements about their modes of presentation, or are creatively layered with anachronistic references to create new propositions for memory. If at the heart of *Promises Beyond Memory* has been the exploration of how people nevertheless negotiate these spaces to make present the violence that they have endured, to help themselves, or ask others to remember or to address it, the archive emerges as just one such site among several interconnected modes of inheriting and sharing such knowledge. Hence the double sense of the idea of "moving stories" with which I introduced this book, as affecting and as circulating into other spaces.

Opening with Chile and the remarkable story of Chacabuco, considering how one might "hear" its many layered stories, whether in the materiality of the site, the cinematic archive, or the words of the interview conducted with Caliche and Luis, questions of how one receives stories from the past have been woven throughout the book. Through what materials, via what modes of presentation, by what forms of attuning, do we create the conditions to receive these accounts? Attempting to read the story of Carmen Bueno Cifuentes through documents in her case file in the FUNVISOL archive in chapter 2, I argued that perhaps one could somehow "hear" the turmoil of the relatives and friends of this young woman through the weight of paper, the repeated unanswered letters and the trace of their attempts to construct a legal path to demand accountability and to locate her. Even in the very typeface, if you will, one "sees" that ordinary citizens were sensing their abandonment by their state as the democratic notion they had held of a People was being erased, at least in terms of those fundamental processes of legal redress, and so their imagined sovereignty was slipping away. That Carmen's—and her partner Jorge Müller Silva's—story still circulates, however, that her image circulated first during the Pinochet era through the efforts of the family's campaigns, and that it continues to do so through documentary film and museal engagement with their stories, inter alia, can be a source of optimism. These new materials and forums suggest a continuing solidarity, and continue to pose "propositions for memory," asking that not just the facts but the efforts for solidarity, for the People, persist. Is to say so a cruel optimism, in Berlant's sense? Probably. But the work of the Vicaría de la Solidaridad and its extraordinarily brave workers, who quite literally put their lives on the line to document the abuses happening around them, infuses the papers of the archive and inspires those who work in the museum as it does the young people who continue to recall the disappeared within their own contemporary campaigns. Likewise, chapter 3 appreciates the enormous collective effort that the Centro Nacional de Memoria Histórica made in Colombia to try to document the violence suffered throughout the country with their archival project. The initial response to the impossible task they were given, by force of law, to create an archive of all archives was strategic and creative. In order to respond to this command, their mode of "hearing" became sociological, based on influential participatory notions of research as espoused by Fals Borda. It was also of course necessarily selective, which was not without controversy. And further controversies about how the archives are to be housed have also arisen. Not least, the mothers who lost children as a result of the *"falso positivos"* scandal are concerned that their gift of their archives may be placed alongside those of the army who perpetrated those crimes, if the proposed museum enacts modes of equivalence they deem inappropriate. That forum, they argue, needs to foster modes of hearing that would pass on their stories in ways they recognize, especially as museums have a pedagogic role, guiding the next generations in their understanding of Colombia's complex conflict. There is hope insofar as the proposed script for the new museum, written by members of the Centro, seeks to articulate the complexity of the conflict through a thematic approach that creatively employs multiple modes of listening. Impacts of the conflict beyond the human, in the suffering of Colombia's rivers, for example, prompt multiple propositions for memory and beyond memory, real engagement and active response. While we await its completion, the space created by Medellín's Museo Casa de la Memoria provides an example of an attempt to explicitly refrain from reducing the complexity to one authoritative narrative account, and attends to the need for new forums and gatherings, providing various spaces within its walls for many voices to participate in the conversation. It was here that Rosalba de Jesús Usma Patiño from the Madres de la Candelaria made her poetic and visual intervention, using the new museum as a backdrop for her story as she held up the photographs of her children printed onto white squares of cloth in order to tell her story about the ongoing impact of violence on families, sharing her own devastating experience with the people assembled there.

Through speaking with Erika Diettes and observing her at work, I was offered the precious opportunity to see how a professional artist, someone who has herself lived through Colombia's years of violent conflict, responds to the stories of devastation around her. The "freedom" of art that she enjoys, responding in her own choice of medium, with her own points of emphasis and aesthetic judgments, allows Diettes to articulate a response that obeys her own proclivities and its own temporality, unhurried by the formal constraints of, say, a legal trial. That said, the need to respond not in general but specifically to the survivors and relatives, to gift them something that in some more expansive, nonlegal sense "does justice" to their plight and to repay their generosity in engaging with the art process, infuses the work. In the art space, the artist not only makes her own subtle propositions, requesting the attention and thoughtfulness of the visitor, but is also engaged in her negotiation of the potential force of art that is never fully under her control. She negotiates but cannot remove all the risks of repeating the violence, of aestheticizing the violence, of disempowering those whose stories appear in public, and so on. She must accept those risks, and does so in order to suggest, to respond to those who have allowed her to be close to their suffering, to offer them an experience, if only for a moment, in which they might sense the artworks as a comfort—even giving them access to a proposition of memory that performs an anti-archival gesture of "tender forgetting"—while at the same time, as I argued in chapter 4, proposing that we, the spectators, must "have regard," a notion that implies also that we must seek to educate ourselves. Resonating with this last plea is Griselda Pollock's argument that "there is more research to be done," which guides the next chapter exploring the changing strategies and appearances of images at the site of the clandestine center for detention, torture, and extermination in Buenos Aires, the ex-ESMA. The various strategies and images that have appeared there are not of a piece, but have brought their propositions of memory in different forms in order to *move* the past into the present, as it were, holding it up like the crystal of chapter 1, for new aspects and imaginative responses to emerge. This we saw through the numerous interventions at the site, including the intriguing movement of the trial footage into the Casino building, the very space where the kidnapped were held.

Moving stories, in this sense, both "back" to the site at which these crimes occurred and "forward" into the Museum of Memory that now exists there, provides a compelling example by which to consider the distinct potentialities that pertain to the different forums in which the past appears. The ability of the artist to take the legal document and "breathe" it into a new life, as it were, is a creative exercise in "extending" the life of the footage and deploying it as a call for new audiences as well as, in Pollock's terms, for new research. The distinctions between law courts and artistic spaces are also at stake in the last chapter, where I suggested that they enact different criteria of relevance, and employ distinct arts of dramatization in order to convince their audiences of the truth of their propositions. Recall how Carri's fungus- and mold-damaged film, for example, while holding negligible value in a legal case, can become the focus of her affecting artwork. Thus, there are multiple sites at which the past is conjured up and reappears to demand attention, but the modes by which that occurs and how it is received will be various. Not that the distinctions between these forums should be too tightly drawn. For not only are there moments in which one space can morph into another—as with the diplomat psychologist's suggestion that a witness might use her appearance as a witness in the court for another, more psychologically affirming purpose—but these practices exist in an ecology such that they exist in mobile relation. The archive emerges as a nodal point within these various practices, playing as it does a perhaps understated role, sometimes awaiting moments in which it is asked to service and feed into the other forums, sometimes poised to receive their traces of events that have happened beyond its boundaries, and sometimes working—as with Memoria Abierta— with an eye to a future, attempting to preempt its own role with its own initiatives. In these ways, such an archive is a work of anticipatory imagination, attempting to ready itself for its many potential but as yet unknown futures.

I wrote in the introduction that the archives were "wise, as it turns out," to seek to organize collected materials and shelter them for further consultation. As I finish this book, we are seeing in all three countries how the past remains publicly contested and can be rearticulated by powerful voices. In Argentina, the new right-wing presidency of 2023 has caused alarm for human rights organizations, with President Javier Milei and Vice President

Victoria Villarruel overtly supportive of the last military dictatorship, calling its actions a campaign against terrorism in a discourse that constitutes a resurgence of the "two devils" thesis that one might have thought the country had moved beyond. In 2006 Villarruel was involved in the establishment of the Center for Legal Studies on Terrorism and Its Victims, which has promoted the campaign for "Complete Memory," using the rhetoric of human rights to attempt to shift the memory of that period to those who were the victims of left-wing attacks.[5] "For forty years, the victims of terrorism have been disappeared from memory," she said at a rally in September 2023, deliberately mimicking and twisting the terms used by campaigns of the relatives of the disappeared. In her account, it is the military who have been mistreated by the Kirchners' pro-memory stance and policies that embraced the human rights groups and supported their ventures. Of the site where the archive Memoria Abierta is housed (the ex-ESMA), which I discuss in this book, Villarruel and the Complete Memory group have made no secret that their opinion is that the whole estate should be reclaimed for "the enjoyment of *all* the Argentine people," a pointed remark meant to suggest an opposing narrative to the human rights groups who have their offices there. At the same time, the application for UNESCO status for the Casino building at the site, the building where the detained and disappeared were held, and where the Museum of Memory is now located, was approved; acknowledging its "outstanding universal status," the UNESCO website appeals to a national purpose in a different sense, that is, as part of the struggle for nonrepetition—*Nunca Más*—for the Argentine people and for all peoples across the world.[6] In 2024, in another politically divisive move, Villarruel has overseen the appointment of an ex–military officer as the director of the Malvinas Museum, causing concern for those who always understood Cristina Kirchner's purpose in setting up the museum within the estate as bringing that conflict under the rubric of human rights. Instead, the concern is that the intention will be, in the words of one commentator, to distract by "cover[ing] the Dirty War with this supposed 'clean' war."[7]

In Chile, too, the heightened sociopolitical division that remains around how to remember the dictatorship and its legacy has been evident in recent years and months, with particular clarity since the Estallido Social, the social uprising that began in October 2019, and that arose, many argue, precisely due to the frustrations of long-standing social and economic inequality understood as the enduring consequence of the Pinochet era. The demonstrations, which saw thousands fill the capital's streets united in their anger and demands for change, were met with the widespread misuse of force, tear gas, and live ammunition by the *carabineros* (the Chilean police) as they responded to the daily protests.[8] Protesters highlighted the irony of this show of state violence and police impunity; it showed, they argued, the authoritarian residues that could no longer denied, and that they would no longer accept. "Today Like Yesterday, the Dictatorship Continues!" "Where are they? Truth and Justice" and "Chile has awoken!" the banners read.[9] Concerns became concentrated on the fact that Chile still lives with a constitution written by the Pinochet government, which ensconced a neoliberal economic model and imposes high legal thresholds and conditions for reform. Hopes were raised when the new government under socialist President Gabriel Boric was given the mandate of the people to establish a constitution convention to rewrite the Pinochet-era constitution, an opportunity understood by many to enshrine human rights and embark upon a new era for the country. Led by an indigenous woman, the gender-balanced and inclusive assembly's draft was progressive, reflecting an attempt to reset the political self-understanding of the country. It was, however, rejected by the countrywide referendum, necessitating a second draft, led this time by the conservative majority, which many on the left regarded as potentially even worse than the current constitution. When put to referendum in December 2023, this second proposal also failed. Tensions and fractures in the social body were in evidence on the fiftieth anniversary of the coup in September 2023, when what many had hoped would bring an opportunity to celebrate Chilean democracy became one to display these divisions. In this atmosphere of division, where the disproportionate use of force by the *carabineros* during the social uprising has not been adequately addressed, political disagreements around Pinochet's legacy remain fiercely divisive.[10] For its part, Boric's left-wing government has launched its program to support and cement the country's commitment to memory and to human rights, establishing, inter alia, the Plan Nacional de Búsqueda, a national plan to confirm the circumstances and locate the bodies of those disappeared or murdered. But concerns remain as to whether this government will survive the next elections to follow through with its progressive desires.

Meanwhile, hope was engendered by Colombia's election of left-wing President Petro in 2022 on campaign promises of progressive change including, inter alia, around education, reducing extractivism, infrastructural improvements, and of course ending the violence associated with still active groups such as the National Liberation Army (Ejército de Liberación Nacional, ELN) and the rival armed groups involved in illicit drugs and mining. While the 2016 Peace Agreement secured with the FARC decreased the number of people losing their lives to the conflict, the establishment of Estado Mayor Central (EMC-FARC) by former FARC members who rejected the agreement, meant their deployment of violence also reemerged.[11] Many regions of the country have been and remain affected by repeated instances of violent confrontations and targeted attacks. Especially shocking has been the targeting of social leaders—community activists and defenders—defending their communities and territories, and of ex-combatants who have withdrawn from conflict, murdered for their refusal to rearm.[12] As I write, the agreement to a ceasefire with the EMC-FARC is holding, but the ceasefire is only a temporary one of ten months, as is that which the government agreed with the ELN. And also as I write, news reports arrive of the murder of another social leader, Carmelina Yule Paví, an indigenous Nasa woman member of the Regional Indigenous Council of Cauca, by the EMC-FARC.[13] It is in this deeply troubling context that the transitional justice mechanisms proceed. The JEP—the Special Jurisdiction for Peace set up by the 2016 Agreement—continues to conduct its work, bringing indictments as well as facilitating the first "recognition of responsibility" events.[14] Moreover, Petro's attempts at the implementation of other aspects of the 2016 deal—significantly, the purchasing and "redistribution" of arable land—have proven difficult and have been met with sharp criticism for effectively rewarding those who had themselves some culpability in the violence.

It is difficult, given these challenging times, to maintain the optimism that I have expressed in this book about what an archive might do. Yet, while acknowledging all the reasons to fall into despair, I want to insist that there is a wisdom to these archives and the archival endeavor, one rooted in and accompanied by an understated optimism that the stories they hold have the potential to cross their boundaries, to find resonances and relationships with contemporary politically affirmative projects. To receive these stories and to work with them, to pass them on in the bobbing elliptical fashion I described in the introduction, is a way of moving them beyond mere remembrance, beyond memory, helping them not just to survive but to pose their questions of the present. My hope is that *Promises Beyond Memory* might act as a small part of that movement out of but in the spirit of the archive. Whether in artistic, legal, museal, or indeed academic projects, the moving of stories has the potential to open a critical imagination, as, turning them in the light, we allow the past to pose its questions within our present worlds.

Notes

INTRODUCTION

1 On affective frissons in archival research, especially those documenting past vio-lence, see Russell, "Affect in the Archive." The affective impact of archival "finds" is also beautifully discussed in Campt, *Image Matters*.

2 Potter, "Afterword," 382.

3 Berger, *Our Faces, My Heart*, 33.

4 Personal communication, January 2019.

5 The full name of the archive is Fundación de Documentación y Archivo de la Vicaría de la Solidaridad, FUNVISOL.

6 Bernasconi, *Resistance to Political Violence*.

7 The notion of "missed appointments" is one I borrow from Kaja Silverman; see *Flesh of My Flesh*. I have written Silverman's notion in my previous book, *Art of Post-Dictatorship*.

8 Sharpe, *In the Wake*.

9 My translation. Jacqueline Paulette Drouilly Yurich (FUNVISOL, SAD139) was kidnapped on October 30, 1974, from a friend's home in Santiago. She was twenty-five years old and three months pregnant. Her husband, Marcelo Salinas Eytel, was arrested the next day. They remain disappeared. See "Jacqueline Paulette Drouilly Yurich," accessed September 18, 2023, https://www.memoriaviva.com/English /victims/drouilly.html).

10 Berger, *Our Faces, My Heart*, 33.

11 Berger, *Our Faces, My Heart*, 31.

12 Fritsch, "Taking Turns." See also Derrida, *Rogues*.

13 Fritsch, "Taking Turns," 154. Fritsch argues that "accepting an inheritance means promising to restate it in a different context, to remain faithful to it in such a way as to inevitably change it." Fritsch, "Taking Turns," 159. See also Bell, *Art of Post-Dictatorship*, 59.

14 Hartman's "note on method" states that her book *Wayward Lives, Beautiful Exper-iments* "elaborates, augments, transposes and breaks open archival documents" in order to "yield a richer picture of the social upheaval that transformed black life in the twentieth century" in the United States. Hartman, *Wayward Lives*, xiv. See also Hartman, "Venus in Two Acts."

15 These are the meanings of the word *archive* with which Derrida begins his dis-cussion of *Archive Fever*, an oft-quoted warning that although the concept of the

archive "shelters itself from the memory of the name *arkhē*," it also shelters itself from that memory, which is to say, "it forgets it." Derrida, *Archive Fever*, 2.

16 Stoler, "On Archiving." Stoler is writing speculatively about how the Palestinian archive of the Ibrahim Abu-Lughod Institute of International Studies at Birzeit University might create an archive that invites ways of imagining and sustaining dissensus. I don't claim that these archives are archiving dissensus in all the possible senses that Stoler explores, but confine my claims to those I develop in following chapters.

17 In the same way that Hochberg describes many of the endeavors she analyzed in *Becoming Palestine*.

18 See Viebach, "Transitional Archives"; Rangelov and Teitel, "Justice Archive."

19 See my article "Documenting Dictatorship."

20 Ferraris, *Documentality*; Accatino and Collins, "Truth, Evidence, Truth"; Hau et al., "Registration and Documentation."

21 Hochberg, *Becoming Palestine*.

22 Appadurai, "Archive and Aspiration."

23 Appadurai, "Archive and Aspiration," 16.

24 See, for example, Alcalá and Uribe, "Constructing Memory Amidst War."

25 Derrida, *Beast and the Sovereign*, 131, emphasis added.

26 Grandmothers of Plaza de Mayo, Mothers of Plaza de Mayo—Linea Fundadora, Center of Legal and Social Studies, Permanent Assembly for Human Rights, Relatives of the Disappeared and Detained for Political Reasons and Service for Peace and Justice.

27 This is a suggestion I have made previously. See Bell, "Between Documentality and Imagination." As of September 2023, Argentina's Attorney General's Office reported 3,732 people charged, 1,159 convicted, and 178 acquitted of crimes against humanity. Human Rights Watch, World Report 2024, "Argentina: Events of 2023," https://www.hrw.org/world-report/2024/country-chapters/argentina.

28 De Baecque and Jousse, "Cinema and Its Ghosts," 39. Derrida says: "When I speak about my past, whether voluntarily or not, I select, I inscribe, and I exclude. I don't believe there are archives that only preserve; this is something I try to point out in a short book, *Archive Fever*. The archive is a violent initiative taken by some authority, some power; it takes power for the future, it pre-occupies the future: it confiscates the past, the present, and the future. Everyone knows there is no such thing as innocent archives."

29 A wealth of literature has added in the last decade or two to the discussion and critique of the archive, reflecting upon the power and inequities with which they are entwined, especially of course where these are state or police archives. A few of the numerous possible references that have been useful to thinking about researching archives critically and creatively are Azoulay, *Potential History*; Foucault, "Lives of Infamous Men"; Hartman, *Wayward Lives, Beautiful Experiments*; Stoler, *Along the Archival Grain*; Weld, *Paper Cadavers*; Hochberg, *Becoming Palestine*.

30 Naas, *End of the World*, 128.

31 Colombia is an unusual case, as many have commented, because it has attempted to implement transitional justice mechanisms despite the fact that it cannot be

said to be beyond conflict. See, for example, Garcia-Godos and Lid, "Transitional Justice and Victims' Rights." A package of peace agreements was finally reached at the end of 2016 between the government of President Juan Manuel Santos and the FARC-EP (Fuerzas Armadas Revolucionarias de Colombia—Ejército del Pueblo; the Revolutionary Armed Forces of Colombia—People's Army) meaning that more than five decades of conflict came to a fragile close. The public referendum on the agreement had been rejected by a small margin in October 2016, and it had needed to be revised before it was approved by parliament. It was a partial peace agreement, moreover, since other groups including the equally established ELN (Ejército de Liberación Nacional, the National Liberation Army) were not a part of that agreement, and the peace established has been continuously challenged and complicated. Voices of opposition to the peace process have not diminished, while social leaders and activities have been targeted and killed in alarming numbers, paramilitary groups have murdered former FARC-EP members, and violence associated with the illegal drugs trade continues. Some dissident members of the FARC re-formed in 2019, to which the state responded preemptively and necessitating more talks and peace negotiations. These have led to an agreement in 2023 to cease violence until June 2024, which as of March 2024 has held, again precariously.

32 Taylor, *Archive and the Repertoire*, 26.
33 Taylor, *Archive and the Repertoire*, 18.
34 Taylor, *Archive and the Repertoire*, 21, 31.
35 Taylor, *¡Presente!*
36 Derrida uses the phrase "house arrest" to refer to the domiciliation of archives. He argues that the notion of the archive itself "holds" the history of the term *arkheion* within it, that is, the place where documents are held, the home of those superior magistrates, the *archons*, who had the right also to interpret those documents. Derrida, *Archive Fever*, 2.
37 Taylor, *Archive and the Repertoire*, 19.
38 Taylor, *Archive and the Repertoire*, 21.
39 I have written about Stengers's thought elsewhere, however. See, for example, Bell, "On Isabelle Stengers' 'Cosmopolitics.'"
40 Stengers, "Speculative Philosophy and the Art of Dramatization."
41 I am thinking here of Mihaela Mihai's arguments that artworks—in her case literature and cinematic interventions—can be understood as forms of caring for the past, and for the future. Mihai, *Political Memory*.
42 Stengers, "Speculative Philosophy," 202.
43 Keenan, "Getting the Dead to Tell Me," 45.
44 Latour, "Why Has Critique Run Out of Steam?"
45 Stengers, "Introductory Notes." I am also drawing here on Stengers, "Cosmopolitical Proposal."
46 Foucault, "Lives of Infamous Men."
47 *The Battle of Chile* (dir. Patricio Guzmán, 1975).
48 As of March 2024, the museum remains unfinished, its construction halted due to a lack of funds.

49 Nancy, *Ground of the Image*.

50 Nancy, *Ground of the Image*, 107.

1. ENTWINED TELLINGS

Epigraphs: Orlando "Caliche" Valdés Barrientos, interview, Santiago, 2016; Berger, *Our Faces, My Heart*, 31.

This chapter is a lightly edited version of an article previously published in the cultural studies journal *Third Text*.

1 Hirst, "Geoglyphic Art." Hirst is citing Briones-M, "Geoglyphs of the North."

2 Ex-nitrate mine Chacabuco. Constructed 1922–24. Number of workers 1,700. Population 7,000. Annual production 180,000 T/M of nitrate. 1940 Stopped functioning as nitrate mine. Declared Historical Monument 1971.

3 Somewhat as Bergson's arguments about the co-emergence of perception and memory-images. The recollection is "created step by step with the perception itself," as he writes (indeed, his analogy is "as the shadow falls beside the body"). Bergson, *Key Writings*, 144.

4 Germany's development of a synthetic nitrate in the 1920s spelled the end of this industry, which suffered, as one of the captions in the theater's museum puts it, "a slow and inexorable death."

5 Caliche is the raw material required to produce saltpeter.

6 This is how the accompanying text for the display describes the workers at the mine.

7 As the accompanying text describes them.

8 Cavarero, "Narrative Against Destruction," 14.

9 The title is a quotation from Rosa Luxemburg, who in her very last words had the revolution "speak" to those who thought they had suppressed the uprising in Berlin in 1919 and restored "order." She wrote: "Your 'order' is built on sand. Tomorrow the revolution will 'rise up again, clashing its weapons,' and to your horror it will proclaim with trumpets blazing, 'I have been, I am, I will be!'" Luxemburg, "Order Prevails in Berlin."

10 For decades, Miguel Herberg's involvement in gaining the footage and conducting the interviews has been overlooked, as his voice was dubbed over in the film. The cameraman, Peter Hellmich, who worked with Herberg, is credited in the 1974 film.

11 My translation.

12 Martin-Jones, "Archival Landscapes."

13 Martin-Jones, "Archival Landscapes," 713.

14 Former prisoner Alberto Gamboa recalls the suicide of Oscar Vega González in his memoirs of Chacabuco. Gamboa, *Vida de perros*.

15 Despret, "Talking Before the Dead."

16 Gordillo, *Rubble*.

17 Benjamin, "Storyteller," 89, 90, 96.

18 Benjamin, "Storyteller," 91.

19 Benjamin, "Storyteller," 91.

20 Haraway, *Staying with the Trouble*, 34.

21 Caliche, interview, Santiago, May 2016.

22 Ben Lerner writes: "All of Berger's work—which includes poems, novels, drawings, paintings, and screenwriting—is to me a beautiful and bracing argument that political commitment requires maintaining a position of wonder. Sexual desire, the rhythms (or increasing arrhythmia) of the seasons, the mysterious gaze of an animal, the spark of camaraderie released by sharing a meal and story, the way certain art works transform an idiosyncratic way of seeing into a commons—such experiences promise us, albeit briefly, an alternative to a world in which money is the only measure of value. And, Berger's work suggests, they aren't forms of forgetfulness but of presentness, memory, recovery, because they place you in relation to, in community with, the dead." Lerner, "Postscript: John Berger."

23 Caliche, interview, Santiago, May 2016.

24 Many more were held over the course of the dictatorship—one estimate is 40,000.

25 Luis, interview, Santiago, May 2016.

26 Luis, interview, 2016.

27 Luis, interview, 2016.

28 Luis, interview, 2016.

29 Luis, interview, 2016.

30 Caliche, interview, 2016.

31 Luis, interview, 2016.

32 Luis, interview, 2016.

33 Cavarero, *Relating Narratives*, 3.

34 Caliche and Luis were taken from the national stadium to Chacabuco in a ship called the *Andalién*, a ship previously used for the transportation of *caliche*, into whose storage spaces the men were compressed, with nowhere to relieve themselves except a simple bucket. On the three-day journey, Caliche recalls, he was able to be mostly above deck, as he had been assigned the task of preparing vegetables for the meals. On the last day, he recalls, a warplane with mounted guns started to swoop down onto the ship, threatening them. It came and went, and several military personnel became sick with watching the plane while also negotiating the lilting movement of the ship. "An officer asked me," Caliche told us, "'Can you fire a machine gun?' And he passed over a gun to me in case we had to fire at the plane!" After a couple of dives, however, the warplane flew away: "They probably thought the better of it." Interview, May 2016. This unpredictable variation between the captors' cruelty and their seeming trust in the prisoners was to continue as a theme in their account of Chacabuco.

35 Luis, interview, 2016.

36 Caliche, interview, 2016.

37 Caliche, interview, 2016; Luis, interview, 2016.

38 Caliche, interview, 2016.

39 Luis, interview, Santiago, May 2016. Oscar Bonilla was one of the principal architects of the coup, first minister of the interior then minister of defense. He spoke out about torture he witnessed at the concentration camp Tejas Verdes, but died shortly afterward, in March 1975, in a helicopter accident under mysterious circumstances.

40 Caliche, interview, 2016.

41 Caliche, interview, 2016.

42 Luis, interview, 2016.

43 Luis, interview, 2016.

44 Caliche, interview, 2016.

45 Caliche, interview, 2016.

46 Caliche, interview, 2016.

47 The prisoners had announced a prize of a Chilean football team kit; in fact, they had packaged up a worthless photograph of the team torn from a newspaper. Dirección de Inteligencia Nacional (DINA) were Pinochet's secret police, given powers to detain anyone indefinitely during the state of emergency, and responsible for detainees' mistreatment, torture, sexual abuse, murder, and disappearance.

48 Caliche, interview, 2016.

49 Caliche, interview, 2016.

50 Caliche, interview, 2016.

51 There was music in the camp, as mentioned, including Ángel Parra, Violeta Parra's son. Luis tells us:

> He was very famous, nationally and internationally, because of his mother, Violeta. Ángel never sang for the *milicos*. Never did he sing. He formed the group El Chacabucano, and he composed the "Passion According to St John," which was also sung to [Cardinal] Silva Henríquez when he came to visit us. But Ángel, he only played the guitar. And he directed the band. He never sang. The only time he sang was when they announced that "[at] 6 P.M. Ángel Parra will be singing, Luis Ángel Parra," where they told him that he would be transferred to Santiago and then liberated into freedom. And what was the story? That Parra was going to be set free, it was the Festival de Vina, it was a music festival, folkloric, quite famous. And the idea of the junta was to present Ángel Parra in the festival of Vina . . . to showcase him. So there is an announcement that he is going to be transferred, given freedom, and that is the only time that Angel sang to us. He sang for us a song about his daughter and his son, and another one I don't remember.

Parra did not sing at the festival but managed to leave Chile and take up exile in France. Interview, 2016. Parra died in 2017.

52 Caliche explains that people would buy them because they knew they were made by the detainees. The prisoners would ask for things in return—tomatoes, lemons, and often raisins. The latter were no longer granted when the military realized that the prisoners were using them to make alcohol ("We had several excellent chemists amongst us!"). Nor were the military consistent in their support for the prisoners; every fortnight, with the personnel change, "we would lose our tools" as the guards would confiscate them. Interview, Santiago, May 2016.

53 Luis, interview, Santiago, May 2016.

54 Luis, interview, Santiago, May 2016.

55 I will return to this sense of belonging through citizenship, and the existential shock that was meted out to those who had "enjoyed" a sense of being a citizen by the military junta in the next chapter.

56 Luis, interview, Santiago, May 2016.

57 Luis, interview, Santiago, May 2016.

58 Becker, *Telling About Society*.

59 "Life stories never have an author," Adriana Cavarero writes, quoting Arendt. Cavarero, *Relating Narratives*, 36.

60 Cavarero takes a cue from Arendt, who argued that "who" someone is in their singularity retains a "curiously intangibility," and is a matter of biography; there is a uniqueness to each individual that philosophy cannot express, so instead strays to speak of "what" a person is or was. Arendt, *The Human Condition*.

2. PAPER AFTERLIVES

Epigraph to closing section: Roland Barthes, *Camera Lucida*, 65, emphasis added.

1 For more details on the history and practices of the Vicaría de la Solidaridad, see Bernasconi, *Resistance to Political Violence*. See also Bell, "Documenting Dictatorship." There is also a documentary on the organization entitled *Habeas Corpus*, directed by Claudia Barrill and Sebastián Moreno.

2 On the legal uses of the archive, see Hau et al., "Registration and Documentation." See also Accatino and Collins, "Truth, Evidence, Truth."

3 Bell, "Documenting Dictatorship."

4 It is not clear who created this little archive of photographs. It is thought that it was a project of a worker, but it is incomplete, and does not contain all of the photographs within the wider archive.

5 Carmen's file was one of several that I consulted before making the decision to focus on her story for the purposes of this chapter.

6 Foucault, "Lives of Infamous Men."

7 Santner, *Royal Remains*.

8 Derrida, *Archive Fever*, 17.

9 Weld, *Paper Cadavers*. See also Ruiz and Bernasconi, "Reports on Categorization and Classification," for a discussion of how the Vicaría classified and rendered these cases onto paper.

10 FUNVISOL, File SAD108, "Summary."

11 Santner, *Royal Remains*, 3. Here Santner is paraphrasing Lefort's argument.

12 Santner, *Royal Remains*, 3.

13 Santner, *Royal Remains*, 5.

14 They were "exposed and threatened on the threshold in which life and law, outside and inside, are becoming indistinguishable. It is literally not possible to say whether the one who has been banned is outside or inside the juridical order." Agamben, *Homo Sacer*, 28–29.

15 I have written before about this attempt to sustain one's position within scenes of torture and extreme "exposure" to the human/creature threshold in "Between Documentality," 149.

16 Santner, *Royal Remains*, 6.

17 A fact that indicates that the legal authorities knew full well about the existence of these centers and that people were held without charge within them.

18 FUNVISOL, File SAD108. My translation.

19 FUNVISOL, Document D.JUR 30-11-75, File SAD108. My translation.

20 This is confirmed by information from Villa Grimaldi. See also Gomez-Barris, *Where Memory Dwells*.

21 Agamben, *Homo Sacer*, 29.

22 FUNVISOL, Document D.JUR 30-11-75, File SAD108. My translation.

23 Santner, *Creaturely Life*, 28. Santner quotes Julia Lupton, who in her study of Caliban, writes that the "*creatura* is a thing always in the process of undergoing creation; the creature is actively passive or, better, passionate, perpetually becoming created, subject to transformations at the behest of the arbitrary commands of an Other." Santner, *Royal Remains*, 6.

24 Santner, *Creaturely Life*, 29. Santner continues to elaborate on Julia Lupton's arguments here.

25 FUNVISOL, File SAD108. My translation.

26 FUNVISOL, File SAD108. My translation.

27 FUNVISOL, newspaper clipping, File SAD108. My translation.

28 FUNVISOL, File SAD108. My translation.

29 FUNVISOL, Document DJ 57.11.76, File SAD108. My translation.

30 FUNVISOL, File SAD108. My translation.

31 FUNVISOL, File SAD108. My translation.

32 FUNVISOL, File SAD108. My translation.

33 Cuatro Álamos operated from a separate building within the grounds of Tres Álamos. Although in the latter many of the prisoners were officially recorded and could even receive visits, in the former they were held clandestinely and without record.

34 FUNVISOL, File SAD108. My translation.

35 FUNVISOL, File SAD204. My translation.

36 FUNVISOL, File SAD204. My translation.

37 FUNVISOL, File SAD204. My translation.

38 The case papers were filed with the military court in Santiago, where they joined the papers from other cases including those of a case brought by seventy families against the DINA General Manuel Contreras Sepúlveda and other security officials, a case that had been similarly stalled and declared itself "incompetent." The decision to stop the Jordán investigation completely was appealed by the families, showing once again their tenacity and faith in legal justice, but was again denied at both the Court of Appeal and the Supreme Court.

Several years later, in November 1989, the army asked that the law of amnesty (DL 2.191) be applied to the case since after ten years in process "no one had been deemed responsible"; this was agreed. Again, there was an appeal to the martial court, which was denied in January 1992, and a further complaint was filed to the Supreme Court. At the time that Carmen Bueno's summary in the FUNVISOL archive was written, at the end of 1992, that complaint had not received a response.

39 Weld, *Paper Cadavers*.

40 Ferraris, *Documentality*.

41 In Jorge Müller's file, his national identity card has been photocopied, for example.

42 Kantorowicz, *The King's Two Bodies*; Santner, *Royal Remains*, 33.

43 Santner, *Royal Remains*, 34.

44 This is the thesis developed by Ferraris, *Documentality*.

45 Santner, *Royal Remains*, 3.

46 Foucault, "Lecture of 17th March 1976."

47 Santner draws critically upon Esposito's thesis. Esposito, *Immunitas*.

48 FUNVISOL, CERT1225, File SAD204. My translation.

49 London-based painter Francis Bacon, born 1909, Dublin. Died 1992.

50 Santner, *Royal Remains*, 140.

51 Santner, *Royal Remains*, 140.

52 In *Royal Remains*, Santner draws, inter alia, on T. J. Clark's analysis of Jacques-Louis David's 1793 *Death of Marat*, through which Clark argues that the impossibility of Marat "standing for the People" simultaneously meant the technique of representation as such—as technique—had to be recognized. That modern art would always fail to "find its object" led to the "shame" that modern art, especially abstractionism, entails and reveals. Santner, *Royal Remains*, 89–94.

53 *A La Sombra del Sol* (dir. Pablo Perelman, 1974).

54 The building of the votive temple for the Virgin Mary—also known as the Basilica of Our Lady of Mount Carmel—at this site had been ordered in 1818 by Bernardo O'Higgins after the victory in the Battle of Maipú, the battle in which the Spanish were defeated and the independence of central parts of Chile was won. The earthquake of 1906 destroyed the temple and the building of a replacement had suffered various setbacks, lack of will and finance, so the 1974 inauguration had been a long time coming.

55 FUNVISOL, CERT6330, File SAD108. My translation.

56 The program was made by Sergio Trabucco, who kept the film safe thereafter. It was then shown again in 2014 on the fortieth anniversary of the couple's disappearance. "Cine de mujeres: Documentales → Año Santo Chileno," Cineteca Universidad de Chile, accessed January 19, 2021, http://cinetecavirtual.uchile.cl /cineteca/index.php/Detail/objects/2495.

57 Although he was singing along, Carmen and Jorge's participation in filming the event may not have been driven by religious faith, Di Lauro comments, but by the wish to be part of a professional team and perhaps, he adds, by "a general faith in human beings, in hope."

58 Santner, *Royal Remains*, 141.

59 Here Guzmán is talking to film critic José Carlos Avellar, in 1997, about both the first film he shot on returning to Chile, and the later films that became *The Battle of Chile*. "Patricio Guzmán on The Battle of Chile," 1997, YouTube, posted November 7, 2017, https://www.youtube.com/watch?v=CnTPJ6kmBos.

60 The film reels had to be smuggled out of the country to Sweden, and were only edited later, when Guzmán took the decision to make them into a trilogy of films. Released in 1975, *The Battle of Chile* was banned from being shown in Chile itself and was not shown there publicly until the mid-1990s. The films were dedicated

to Jorge's memory, who—by the time the first was released—had already been disappeared for a year.

61 Although Allende at times appears as if he occupied the status of a king in terms of the crowd's reaction to him, and several photographers—including Armindo Cardoso—created images of him that have become iconic, his rhetoric and that of his supporters was steadfastly on "popular unity."

62 "We also had a wide angle, which we hardly ever used, as the zoom was better suited to our mobility. We had three batteries. We had no stabilizer." Guzmán quoted in "Jorge Müller ACC, Imagen Latente de una generación," November 7, 2020, https://acc-chile.com/jorge-muller-imagen-latente-de-una-generacion. "One of the great virtues of the Éclair," he adds, "is that the chassis snaps into the camera body without the need to thread the film. Jorge always kept our spare chassis loaded because there were many breaks. We had a black bag and two portable lights that ran on very unstable, precarious and heavy batteries."

63 "Patricio Guzmán on The Battle of Chile," at 18:00. He also shows the image of Guzmán and Müller filming on top of the Moneda, and some images of the team sitting inside the Moneda. In one of these "backstage" photographs, Jorge is raising his hand into a fist of struggle and empowerment, holding his camera in the other hand. But he is smiling as if he is play-acting for the image.

64 The Battle of Chile, Part 1, at 10:00.

65 The Battle of Chile, Part 1, at 1:13:00.

66 Müller had also filmed Fidel Castro on his visit to the north of Chile, and filmed the 1971 funeral of Lucíano Cruz Aguayo, founder of the MIR, portions of which are shown in the film 29 de noviembre, by Carla Toro Rubio and Mauricio Villarroel Valenzuela, 2017. This latter film is discussed below.

67 The last part of the documentary Chile: Obstinate Memory (1997) follows the reaction of the audience to the eventual showing of the first films in Chile. See Gómez-Barris, Where Memory Dwells, for a nuanced analysis of this last part.

68 While the soldier whose shot actually killed Henrichsen remains unknown, Corporal Héctor Bustamente Gómez, who began the shooting at the journalists, prompting his men to also shoot, was identified. He died in 2007 awaiting trial for the murder after Henrichsen's children filed a wrongful killing suit in 2005.

69 Henrichsen's lack of fear at that moment is common, Guzmán comments, because when filming one can become so involved in the scene that one considers oneself somehow protected by the camera, looking at the scene from afar. It is a moment of forgetting as one becomes caught up in the scene as seen through the lens: "The action is so enthralling—and a battle is enthralling—that you forget everything else. You feel scared but something else . . . carries you, you're in the midst of it. It's unconscious. You feel scared afterwards. And before. Before something blows up you say, 'What's going to happen here?' After it explodes, well, you're already at the dance." "Patricio Guzmán on The Battle of Chile," at 13.05.

70 "The revolutionaries and the workers must immediately extend the seizure of factories and estates, increase defense preparations, promote popular power as local government, independent of the power of the state. The warrant officers and the police must disobey the orders of fascist officers [who wish for a coup] and

in that way all forms of resistance will be justified. Then it really will be true that the workers along with the soldiers, the sailors, the police, the warrant officers, and the loyal officers will have the right to build their own army—the army of the people!" *The Battle of Chile*, Part 2.

71 FUNVISOL, Informe Individual, File SAD108. My translation.

72 Quoted in Lazzara, "Militancy Then and Now."

73 Lazzara, "Militancy," 2.

74 Müller's parents quoted in Stone, "The Battle of Chile."

75 Guzmán, *Chile, Obstinate Memory*, Flores speaking at 34:00.

76 Guzmán, *Chile, Obstinate Memory*, at 35:00. Pablo Perelman shared a house with Jorge and Carmen during the year before their disappearance. It had been the home of Pablo's partner Paula Sánchez's mother, whose partner was Ángel Parra, the musician, who as mentioned in chapter 1, was imprisoned at Chacabuco before going into exile. Before his exile, Paula recalls, Jorge and Ángel would play guitars together for hours in that house. Ruiz, *119 de nosotros*, 415–16.

77 Carmen Rojas quoted in Gómez-Barris, *Where Memory Dwells*, 59.

78 Jamison, *Retazos de Vida*.

79 Jamison, *Retazos de Vida*.

80 Jamison, *Retazos de Vida*.

81 Santner, *Creaturely Life*, 16–17. Santner's argument elaborates on Walter Benjamin's idiosyncratic argument that natural history is constituted when an artifact loses its place within a historical form of life, that is, when that form of life decays, is exhausted, or passes away. The artifact becomes a relic of historical being, and life continues without need of it. See Benjamin, *Origin of German Tragic Drama*. I am suggesting here that the relatives refuse to allow the photograph to become an historical artifact in this way; rather, they insist that these symbolic forms retain their vitality.

82 This argument has been explored by Nelly Richard and Ana Longoni, among others. Richard, *Fracturas de la memoria*; Longoni, *Traiciones*; and more recently, Longoni, "Fotos reaparecidas."
    This is not to say that the "domestic" use of photographic images has not been retained alongside these public interventions. Ludmila Silva da Catela has studied how photographs also remain in the families of those who have suffered a disappearance, becoming sacred objects within their private rituals. They act in the homes as "reservoirs of affection," and support the relatives in their struggles, reaffirming them, giving them the energy to continue. See Silva da Catela, "Photography and Disappearance." In the documentary mentioned above, *Retazos de Vida*, in which Jorge's mother speaks about him, one sees behind her a photograph of Jorge on her desk; this is where photographs of loved ones "should" be. It is moving to read Carmen's sister's report that as her last request, their mother, Mariola Cifuentes, asked for Carmen's photograph to be placed in her coffin, which they did so that "they were both buried together." Ruiz, *119 de nosotros*.

83 Symbolic forms lose their vitality when they have been hollowed out and come to appear as enigmatic signifiers, "hieroglyphs." Santner, *Creaturely Life*, 17.

84 See Bell, "On Fernando's Photograph."

85 Mitchell, "What Do Pictures Want," 81.

86 Barthes, *Camera Lucida*, 96.

87 Mitchell, "What Do Pictures Want," 81.

88 The government's lack of response was what led the Episcopal Conference to declare that November that they believed the disappeared persons had been arrested by the government's security forces and that their whereabouts were not being investigated; regretfully, they stated, they had to conclude that many, if not all, had died under "unlawful circumstances." Later, in 1993, *¿Donde Están?* was updated as the "Red Books (Libros Rojos)" which documented the by then total of 984 cases of disappearance. See Bernasconi et al., *Resistance to Political Violence*, 59.

89 At Villa Grimaldi, too, a small wooden hut displays some photographs and artefacts belonging to the disappeared who were held there. Carmen's image appears here, with some objects that belonged to her, including her camera. An image of this display appears in Gómez-Barris, *Where Memory Dwells*, 67, so that although the text does not refer to Carmen's own story, her photograph also continues to circulate within academic forums.

90 Then-president Michelle Bachelet announced the commitment to building the museum in 2007, and she inaugurated it two months before her term as president ended, in January 2010. The fact that that year also saw the election of right-wing Sebástian Piñera and a return to the articulation of Pinochet-sympathetic politics underscores its intended role, and its necessity. For description and insightful analysis of the permanent displays held there see Andermann, "Showcasing Dictatorship."

91 Andermann, "Showcasing," 73–74.

92 Andermann, "Showcasing," 90.

93 The computer, located in front of the wall of photographs, also shows the viewer where to locate the images on the wall of portraits that extends up the double-height wall. When I did so, I found it poignant that also included on the wall is another disappeared man whose photograph I was shown by Marcela at the FUNVISOL archive in 2019: Carlos Alberto Carrasco Matus, known as Mauro. A young conscript to the army, he was a guard at Villa Grimaldi when the couple were held there. Mentioned in several of the witness reports held at FUNVISOL, including witnesses to Carmen's case, he was sympathetic to the detainees and was remembered by them for his little kindnesses. When his associations with them were discovered, however, he also was "disappeared."

94 The film *29 de noviembre* (2017) was directed by Gabriela Chandía Ruiz and produced by Francisca Cea Valencia, Carla Toro Rubio and Mauricio Villarroel Valenzuela. It is available via the museum in Santiago and also on YouTube: "29 de Noviembre - Largometraje documental," posted August 14, 2018, accessed March 2, 2021, https://www.youtube.com/watch?v=yK5etu88OdY.

95 Later in the film someone stitches the photographs back together again—again it is an anonymous sequence—in bright red stitches that remain visible after the "repair" is done. It is an attempt to show simultaneously the pain and the repair

work, the promise and the impossibility of its representation, a theme I will return to in chapter 6. Ruiz, *29 de noviembre*, at 56:00.

96 Quoted in Gómez-Barris, *Where Memory Dwells*, 59.

3. COLOMBIA'S PROPOSITIONS FOR MEMORY

1 CNMH, *¡Basta Ya!*

2 This challenge is one that I have faced myself when writing, with my colleagues, a chapter of our research report on archives of violence that focused on Colombia. Our attempt at the task can be found in Bell et al., *Archives of Violence*.

3 Uribe, "Dismembering."

4 Violence has stolen the temporal and spatial coordinates that enable fictive nations to cohere, hence the difficulty of narrating the nation as such. Uribe, "Dismembering," 79, citing Bhabha's influential work *Nation and Narration*. Colombians appear, Uribe argues, only as "beings filled with fear," a characterization that eclipses more nuanced approaches to understanding the country's experience of decades of violent events and their effects on the people who have lived through it. Uribe, "Dismembering," 81.

5 Pécaut, *La experiencia*. Pécaut also discussed these arguments in a 2018 lecture and in his early work. See Pécaut, "Considerations." Pécaut argued that the difficulties of narrating the violence into collective historical narratives has consequences at every level, including the subjective, especially for victims of violence. Writing at the end of the 1990s, Pécaut argued that a "mythic temporality" in which "the same violence has been here forever" means that a collective orientation and interpretation of the armed conflict has not arisen in Colombia. Each shock of a violent event fades without any stable public opinion or national narrative forming, leading to what he termed a "kaleidoscopic configuration of time" with no consistent framework for temporal orientation. Pécaut, "Considerations," 139–40, 143–46.

6 I use the phrase "pull the strings" because depictions of violence as personified are reminiscent of Benjamin's critical image of Marxist deployments of "historical materialism," where the concept is made to work like an automated chess-playing puppet, winning every game. But, Benjamin avers, this is an illusory trick that disguises the fact that it is theology that, like a "wizened old man," is hiding within and pulling its strings. In ways that are resonant for our discussion, Michael Löwy argues that for Benjamin the term *theology* here refers to two concepts— remembrance (*Eingedenken*) and messianic redemption (*Erlösung*)—that are essential components of the new "concept of history" that Benjamin promotes in "Theses on the Philosophy of History." Löwy, *Fire Alarm*.

7 Established by articles 50 and 51 of the law.

8 Suárez, interview, November 2, 2018. The victims were defined by Law 1448 as individuals or collectives who have suffered harm as a result of the internal armed conflict since January 1, 1985.

9 Articles 146–48 of Law 1448.

10 Article 147 of Law 1448.

11 Article 148 of Law 1448.

12 The new legal and institutional landscape established in 2016 is called the Comprehensive System of Truth, Justice, Reparation and Non-Repetition (SIVJRNR). The Agreement did not alter the independence of the Centro or tasks as given by the 2011 law, but it rearranged the transitional mechanisms so that the Centro is now obliged to work and cooperate with newly created institutions to complete its tasks. The three institutions of the system are the Special Jurisdiction for Peace (JEP), which is the judicial branch of the system; the Commission for the Clarification of the Truth, Coexistence and Non-Recurrence (CEV), which is the closest institution requiring the Centre's collaboration; and the Unit for the Search for Missing Persons, with its specific task to seek out the truth and if possible the location of those disappeared during the conflict.

13 Benjamin, "Theses on the Philosophy of History," 246.

14 Alcalá, "Constructing Memory Amidst War." See also Jaramillo Marín, *Pasados y presentes.*

15 They were supported financially by the Swiss government, initially, and were allowed to appoint an international advisory group to guide and support them.

16 Previous governmental attempts to consider giving amnesty to the paramilitaries had not been received well inside or outside Colombia. With this law, those who had not committed serious crimes were given amnesty but those who had were given these relatively short sentences.

17 Suárez, interview, November 2018.

18 Suárez, interview, November 2018.

19 Suárez, interview, November 2018.

20 Gonzalo Sánchez, interview, April 2020.

21 Martha Nubia Bello, speaking in the CNMH film *No Hubo Tiempo para la Tristeza* (dir. Jorge Mario Betancur, 2013), at 37:00. The film is also available on YouTube: "No hubo tiempo para la tristeza," posted November 27, 2013, https://www .youtube.com/watch?v=das2Pipwp2w.

22 Gonzalo Sánchez, interview, May 2020.

23 Both procedurally and ethically, the research methods adopted by the team reflected their disciplinary backgrounds, especially the sensibility and the participative legacy of Colombian sociologist Orlando Fals Borda. On Fals Borda's method, see Rappaport, *Cowards Don't Make History.*

24 Gonzalo Sánchez, interview, May 2020.

25 Suárez, interview, November 2018.

26 Luis Carlos Sánchez, interview, October 2018.

27 CNMH, *Trujillo.*

28 A survivor speaking at one of the Group's Memory Workshops, quoted in the report *Trujillo*, 232. My translation.

29 Luis Carlos Sánchez, interview, October 2018.

30 Alcalá, "Constructing Memory."

31 Gonzalo Sánchez, interview, May 2020.

32 Gonzalo Sánchez, interview, May 2020. That said, one of the consequences of the reports was in fact that prosecutions were reopened. This happened with the very first report into the Trujillo massacre, as it did with another of the early reports, that into the massacre of Sergovia, where state forces acted with the paramilitaries in a horrific attack on the Unión Patriótica, an opposition party founded in 1985. Thus the "memory work" of the investigations, although conceptually separate for the *Grupo* from the explicitly judicial work of the *Acuerdos*, did on occasions exert pressure on the judicial system because "they showed that the judicial system was negligent."

33 CNMH, *¡Basta Ya!*

34 CNMH, *¡Basta Ya!*, 325.

35 CNMH, *¡Basta Ya!*, 271.

36 CNMH, *¡Basta Ya!*, 24.

37 CNMH, *No Hubo Tiempo.*

38 CNMH, *No Hubo Tiempo.*

39 CNMH, *No Hubo Tiempo*, at 45:00.

40 CNMH, *No Hubo Tiempo*, at 46:00.

41 CNMH, *No Hubo Tiempo*, at 39:00.

42 CNMH, *No Hubo Tiempo*, at 38:00.

43 CNMH, *No Hubo Tiempo*, at 40:00.

44 CNMH, *No Hubo Tiempo*, at 40:00.

45 That is, they were to continue receiving the *Acuerdos de Verdad* through a network of several branches across the country, and continue investigations and reports. To date, the Centro has published over 150 reports.

46 Benjamin, "Theses on the Philosophy of History."

47 Derrida, *Beast and the Sovereign*, 131, emphasis added.

48 Derrida, *Beast and the Sovereign*, 131.

49 Derrida, *Beast and the Sovereign*, 131.

50 As Margot Guerrero, director of the Archive until 2018, pointed out in our interview, November 2018. Moreover, one of the first events of the Centro was to organize an international conference on human rights archives for which members of Argentina's Memoria Abierta visited the Centro to share their experiences, especially in relation to the oral archive, an important issue especially given the predominantly oral cultures of indigenous groups in Colombia, as noted by Paula Illa, group interview with CNMH archive workers, November 2018.

51 A point made by Miriam Loaiza, archive worker, group interview, November 2018.

52 Drawing to mind Saadawi's novel *Frankenstein.*

53 Miriam Loaiza, group interview, November 2018.

54 Miriam Loaiza, group interview, November 2018. With the help of a research grant, the community and the Centro were able to piece together and co-construct this archive, so that it could be preserved and held in their community capital, Valledupar. The Centro's work in helping to create an archive where none was believed to exist, guided by an ethic of what they term "accompaniment," thus brought a "new body" into existence.

55 Derrida, *Beast and the Sovereign*, 141.

56 For example, items from Fabiola Lalinde's archive—photographs, documents, objects—were shown at the National University of Colombia at Medellín, alongside artwork made by artist Erika Diettes, who has worked extensively with victims' relatives. See the YouTube documentary about the archive and exhibition, *Facultad de Ciencias Humanas y Económias*, Fabiola Lalinde, posted May 17, 2018, https://www.youtube.com/watch?v=Kel7nGjsMPQ.

Also, items donated by members of the community surrounding the horrific murder of the priest Tiberio Fernández in the massacre of Trujillo (Valle), including a book full of the community's drawings remembering him, were consulted for artistic works such as the play *El Deber de Fenster* (written by Humberto Dorado and Matías Maldonado). Group interview, November 2018.

57 In relation to the latter, the Centro supports both public and private efforts to provide the legal promise of comprehensive care to victims, the guarantee of human rights, and the application of international humanitarian law. In order to assist victims, the CNMH helps the entities in charge of the reparation processes provided by the state, and also helps with the formulation of new public policies. Often, data such as dates, personal details, and facts are requested by lawyers involved in reparation cases, and the archive is able to provide these. This is important also within the current framework of the implementation of the judicial processes of the 2016 peace agreement, as the archive is used by the Commission for the Clarification of the Truth, Coexistence and Non-Recurrence (CEV) and the Special Jurisdiction for Peace (JEP). In relation to this relationship, Margot Guerrero observes that all the information that arrives at the Centro archive, once it is ready for publication, can be passed to the JEP in order to provide information for the cases that this body is dealing with (interview, November 1, 2018). Initially, it was difficult to handle this aspect of the work because they had not always sought the appropriate permission from their respondents to disseminate it in this way, but as the archive has grown and processes improved, consent is routinely requested to allow for the publication and such uses of the information.

58 Dora Betancourt, group interview, 2018.

59 *El Espectador*, June 4, 2020. The so-called false positives (*falsos positivos*) were mostly poor young men who the military killed, set up mendaciously as guerrillas, and counted as "positives"—victories in the war against guerrilla groups—in order to receive governmental rewards for higher numbers of apprehensions, whether dead or alive.

60 Rubén Dario Avecedo was the director 2019–22.

61 *El Espectador*, June 4, 2020.

62 It continues to be expanded through the Centro's activities, including through continuing research projects, the new *Acuerdos* given under the 2016 Peace Agreement by ex-members of the FARC, and through the registration of objects and experiences that have been shared by communities or through activities associated with the itinerant exhibition *Voces para transformar a Colombia* that will be discussed below. All of the materials are copied, stored, and retrieved in digital form, with the originals returned to the donors. This is very important for the ethical and political stance of the Centro, as the physical items remain within

communities, which have their own memory practices and registration needs and processes. It is not a requirement that all of the communities and individuals whose archives are registered with it allow them to be so digitalized. In fact, in the case of the Arhuaco, the Centro did not copy and does not have access to that archive; it is kept in Valledupar for the community itself. Yet most of those working with the Centro do allow this digitalization, consenting to different levels of access.

63 The task was described in the Law as a pedagogic undertaking that would enrich and "strengthen collective memory" about the facts of recent history, through the design, creation, and administration of a museum of memory (Article 148).

64 Luis Carlos Sánchez, interview, October 2018.

65 Luis Carlos Sánchez, interview, October 2018.

66 Luis Carlos Sánchez, interview, October 2018.

67 See the Wilson Center website, www.wilsoncenter.org.

68 See Museo de Memoria de Colombia, www.museodememoria.gov.co.

69 Alcalá et al., *Guion conceptual*.

70 Alcalá et al., *Guion conceptual*, 21. It is quoting statistics gathered both by CNMH and elsewhere.

71 Alcalá et al., *Guion conceptual*, 22.

72 Alcalá et al., *Guion conceptual*, 13.

73 Alcalá et al., *Guion conceptual*, 18, 11.

74 Alcalá et al., *Guion conceptual*, 20. Here the document is quoting Aranguren, "Inmunización y militarización."

75 Alcalá et al., *Guion conceptual*, 22–23.

76 Alcalá et al., *Guion conceptual*, 28.

77 Alcalá et al., *Guion conceptual*, 31. Quoting from the Registry of Victims.

78 Alcalá et al., *Guion conceptual*, 32.

79 Alcalá et al., *Guion conceptual*, 35. Quoting Atuahene, "From Reparation to Restoration."

80 The statement mentions the following groups here: the ANUC (Asociación Nacional de Usarios Campesinos), the ATCC (Asociación de trabajadores Campesinos del Carare), Magdalena Medio, the ACIA (Asociación Campesina Integral del Atrato), and the ANMUCIC (Asociación Nacional de Mujeres Campesinas, Negras e Indígenas).

81 Alcalá et al., *Guion conceptual*, 25–26.

82 Alcalá et al., *Guion conceptual*, 33.

83 Alcalá et al., *Guion conceptual*, 27.

84 Alcalá et al., *Guion conceptual*, 40. "As a body and substance in movement, with currents, flows, twists, swirls," water will not only reflect the historical dynamics of the conflict, its transformations and interconnections, but also enable narrative and symbolic connections.

85 Alcalá et al., *Guion conceptual*, 39, quoting Jaramillo et al., *Colombia Antifibia*, and Krause, "Living Water."

86 Among other rivers that are for many areas and communities the only way to access their territories. Alcalá et al., *Guion conceptual*, 41.

87 Alcalá et al., *Guion conceptual*, 44–45.

88 Alcalá et al., *Guion conceptual*, 49.

89 Butler, *Parting Ways*, 103–4.

90 Butler, *Parting Ways*, 106.

91 Alcalá et al., *Guion conceptual*, 49.

92 Butler, *Parting Ways*, 109.

93 After the Bogotá launch (April 17–May 2, 2018, with 77,000 visitors) the exhibition traveled to Medellín (Fiesta del Libro y de la Cultura, September 7–16, 2018, with 23,000 visitors). In 2019 it was shown in Cali, at La Tertulia Museum, with 15,000 visitors and, as a smaller version, in Villavicencio for ten days (1,500 visitors) and in Cúcuta for a month (4,500 visitors). There was controversy over the exhibition in Cali. See González-Ayala, "Voices of Water and Violence."

94 Luis Carlos Sánchez, interview, October 2018.

95 Monica Álvarez, interview, November 2018.

96 Monica Álvarez, interview, November 2018.

97 Monica Álvarez, interview, November 2018.

98 González-Ayala, "Voices of Water," 185.

99 Thomas, "Museum as Method."

100 González-Ayala, "Voices of Water and Violence," 185.

101 Lleras et al., "Curatorship for Meaning Making," 547.

102 Luis Carlos Sánchez, interview, October, 2018.

103 Luis Carlos Sánchez, interview, October 2018.

104 *El Espectador*, June 2020. See Jurisdiccion Especial para La Paz, "Información de prensa," accessed October 18, 2025, https://www.jep.gov.co/Sala-de-Prensa.

105 Museo de Memoria, https://www.museodememoria.gov.co. Unfortunately, since I wrote this chapter, construction has now stalled and the building remains incomplete.

106 Cathalina Sánchez Escobar, interview, October 2019.

107 The mural, on the theme of reconciliation, was a collaboration between the Museum and Fundación Pintuco, and was a part of the new exhibition *La Voz de las manos: Prácticas que reconcilian*. Under the direction of artist Jomang, the collaboration included Elemento ilegal, Klan Guetto Popular, Fundación EPA, Fundación Trash Art, Taller Graffiti Art, and Colectivo Pirañas Crew. The Museo Casa de la Memoria opened in 2006. It was created from an initiative by the local government through its Victims Care Program.

108 Cathalina Sánchez Escobar, interview, October 2019.

109 Cathalina Sánchez Escobar, interview, October 2019.

110 Bal, *Double Exposures*.

111 Bal, *Double Exposures*, 217–20. She is drawing here upon Gregory Nagy's analysis of Herodotus's *Historiae* in his book *Pindar's Homer*.

112 Bal, *Double Exposures*, 2–3.

113 For example, see Arnold-de Simine, "Memory Museum and Museum Text."

114 Murders, massacres, kidnappings, antipersonnel mines, forced displacements, actions and contacts (threats), selective assassinations, forced disappearances.

115 *Museo Casa de la Memoria*, pamphlet guide, n.d., ca. 2016–19, my emphasis.

116 His story is also part of the exhibition, where quotations from people's stories offer multiple perspectives on the conflict. The stories are printed onto cards so that the visitors can sit and read them. A circular bench invites them to sit together, an invitation to dialogue.

117 Bautista was a social worker and social leader of the Paez/Nasa people who live on the Tacueyo reservation in Toribio, Cauca. She was shot on October 29, 2019, in an attack by alleged FARC dissidents. She had spoken out, including at the United Nations, about the shocking number of killings of indigenous people and social leaders and the plight of Indigenous women in particular.

118 See, for example, the work of anthropologist and former member of the CNMH, María Victoria Uribe, in several important articles on Colombia's experience of violence and its narration. Uribe, "Violence as a Symptom."

119 Butler, *Parting Ways*, 104.

120 Butler, *Parting Ways*, 106.

4. NEGOTIATING THE FORCE OF ART

1 Among the texts that I have found particularly useful to think and teach with in this area are: Azoulay, *Civic Contract of Photography*; Batchen et al., *Picturing Atrocity*; Didi-Huberman, *Images in Spite of All*; Guerin, *Image and the Witness*; Pollock, *After-Affects/After-Images*; Rothberg, *Implicated Subject*; Silverman, *Flesh of My Flesh*.

2 Stern, "Artist's Truth," 271.

3 Stern, "Artist's Truth," 259, quoting Müller-Doohm's *Adorno*, where Adorno's 1962 writing is discussed. Müller-Doohm, *Adorno*.

4 Stern, "Artist's Truth," 271.

5 Stern, "Artist's Truth." Further works about art in the context of the southern cone that confirm the importance of this debate include: Feld, *El pasado que miramos*; Giunta, *Political Body*; Huyssen, *Memory Art*; Jelin, *Escrituras, imágenes y escenarios*; Phu et al., *Cold War Camera*; Ramírez, *Cantos paralelos*.

6 Although I do not discuss it here, Diettes's first substantial work, *Silencios*, explored the lives of survivors of Auschwitz and other concentration camps who were now living in Colombia. See *Silencios*, on Diettes's website, https://www.erikadiettes.com/.

7 Nancy, *Ground of the Image*.

8 Diettes does speak of them in her talks and published interviews; see Diettes and Tucker," Conversations"; Diettes, "Stories Told from the Threshold."

9 Andreas Huyssen suggests this of Salcedo's 1997 work "Unland: The Orphan's Tunic," a piece that also has resonance with Diettes's work insofar as it responds to the story of a witness (in Salcedo's case a six-year-old girl who witnessed her mother's murder) through a meditation on her dress or tunic, that becomes in the installation piece—in Huyssen's words—precisely "a shroud." Huyssen, *Memory Art*, 36–40.

10 The project of the Historical Memory Group (later the Centro Nacional de Memoria Histórica, CNMH) provides an overview of the uses of different forms of violence by the armed agents in Colombia's conflict. Although massacres (defined in the research as the assassination of more than four people in situations of helplessness, and with the majority—58.9 percent—of the 1,982 mas-

sacres documented by the research carried out by paramilitary groups) have been perhaps the most spectacular of these forms, the other forms—including selective assassinations, forced disappearances, sexual violence, and destruction of property—also involve the intention to terrorize and subdue resistance of civilian populations. See especially chapter 1 of CNMH, *¡Basta Ya!*

11 Marks, *Touch*, 2–3.

12 Moten, *In the Break*, 200. Moten is making this argument in relation to the image of Emmett Till in his open casket, an image that "must be accompanied by listening and this, even though what is listened to—echo of a whistle or a phrase, moaning, mourning, desperate testimony and flight—is also unbearable." See also Campt, who writes beautifully on the "lyric of the archive" in *Image Matters*.

13 Personal communication, December 2019.

14 James, *A Pluralistic Universe.*

15 *The Quintet of the Astonished*, 15:20, dir. Bill Viola, perf. John Malpede, Weba Garretson, Tom Fitzpatrick, John Fleck, and Dan Gerrity, 2000; *Dolorosa*, 11:00, dir. Bill Viola, perf. Natasha Basley and Shishir Kurup, 2000.

16 Hansen, *New Philosophy*, 260.

17 What psychoanalyst Daniel Stern has called "vitality affects," as opposed to emotions. Hansen, *New Philosophy*, 260.

18 Hansen, *New Philosophy*, 266.

19 This figure is the estimate by the CNMH. From 1958–2012, over 80 percent of victims were civilians, the remainder being combatants. The numbers of civilians killed peaked in 2002–3. CNMH, *¡Basta Ya!*, 38.

20 Mihai, *Political Memory*, 62.

21 Erika Diettes, interview with author, 2019.

22 Azoulay, *Civil Contract of Photography*, 148.

23 Diéguez, "Erika Diettes: Imágenes en Duelo," 33.

24 Diettes keeps all the notes and messages she has received from them, expressing how much it means to them. It is important to Diettes that the women know when and where the exhibition is being shown, that they can visit it where possible, and that they can follow its reception.

25 Mihai, *Political Memory*, 61.

26 Huyssen, *Memory Art*, 40.

27 Diettes, interview with author, 2019.

28 Nancy, *Ground of the Image*, 105.

29 Nancy, *Ground of the Image*, 105.

30 Nancy, *Ground of the Image*, 106.

31 Nancy, *Fall of Sleep*, 15.

32 Nancy, *Ground of the Image*, 106.

33 Nancy, *Ground of the Image*, 107.

34 Levinas, "Useless Suffering." See my discussion in Bell, *Culture and Performance.*

35 Bal, *Louise Bourgeois' Spider.*

36 Nancy, *Ground of the Image*, 20–21; Bell, "Between Documentality and Imagination."

37 Diettes, *Memento Mori*, 148; the newspaper article was by Luz María Sierra, April 24, 2007.

38 Diettes, interview with author, 2019.

39 Diettes, interview with author, 2019.

40 Stoler, *On Archiving*, 46, 52.

41 Diettes, interview with author, 2019.

42 Diettes, quoted in Dieguez, "Erika Diettes: Imágenes en Duelo," 34.

43 Armed agents threw bodies of the disappeared into rivers, and forbade the communities to remove them. For example, this happened as part of the massacre at Trujillo in March and April 1990, but it was a practice that also occurred in other parts of the country; see CNMH, *¡Basta Ya!*, 67. Here as elsewhere, people were sometimes able to pull the bodies from the rivers, as also reported to GMH.

44 Derrida, "Force of Law," 258.

45 Derrida, "Force of Law."

46 Levi, *If This Is a Man*, emphasis added.

47 Perrin, "Breath from Nowhere." These references to the Holocaust are not anachronistic here, as they speak directly to problematics and points of reference traversing Diettes's ouevre, seen most explicitly in her earlier 2005 work *Silencios*, in which she made sensitive portraits of thirty survivors of Nazi concentration camps now living in Colombia. See Diettes's website, https://www.erikadiettes.com, accessed May 9, 2023.

48 Quoted in Diettes, *Memento Mori*, 25, emphasis added.

49 Showing the work at the different locations from which they had been lent—exhibiting it in over eighteen towns in Colombia—also meant that Diettes was obliged to make some smaller, A5-sized pieces so that they could be transported more easily.

50 In the documentary *Erika Diettes: Somos los vivos los que recordamos*, made for DW Fuerza Latina, Diettes realizes for the first time a connection between her decision to print the images on glass and her own personal history of the violence in Colombia. When her uncle—who worked for INPEC, the central agency for administering the prisons in Colombia—was assassinated in 1996, she saw the image of the broken car window through which he had been shot on television reportage and reproduced in the newspapers. Framed by the broken glass of the car window, his hat lay on the car seat, just as in Río Abajo, looking through the glass, we see items pertaining to the victims. It is another intense moment in which we understand the sense in which violence leaves images, indeed *creates* images, into which new image-making can withdraw. "Erika Diettes: 'Somos los vivos los que recordamos' I Fuerza Latina DW," YouTube, posted November 15, 2022, accessed July 2, 2023, https://www.youtube.com/watch?v=mXMOB-VyplU&t=350s.

51 Diettes, interview with author, 2019.

52 Diettes, *Memento Mori*, 26.

53 Diettes, *Memento Mori*, 139.

54 Diettes, quoting a mother, interview with author, 2019.

55 De Duve, "Art in the Face of Radical Evil," 23.

56 Aware of the sensitivities of such processes, Diettes had a team of ten psychologists available to talk to the relatives. Furthermore, the relatives continued to have free access to the museum for the exhibition's duration, and many returned each week to visit the *Relicarios*. The museum staff was instructed to allow the relatives

to make noise, to touch, to pray, and to generally have the freedom to do as they wished around the exhibition.

57 Acosta López, "Las fragilidades de la memoria."

58 Acosta López, "Las fragilidades de la memoria," 25.

59 Diettes, interview with author, July 2021.

60 Diettes, interview with author, July 2021. Huyssen argues that Salcedo's work is, similar to Diettes's, working to fill an absence in public and collective memory of the armed conflict, but without representing victims directly. In Salcedo's own words, her art is instead a memory work that operates "between the figure of the one that has died and the life disfigured by the death." See Huyssen, *Memory Art*, 57.

61 See "Transformative Memory" project website, https://transformativememory.ubc.ca/.

62 Diettes, interview with author, May 2022. In addition to the images that she has made with relatives in Colombia and Argentina, Diettes also plans to include images from elsewhere, including Uganda, where she has visited with the Transformative Memory project. On the story of the remains in Pozo de Vargas, see *La Noche del Mundo*, 69:00, available on YouTube: "La Fosa Clandestina del Pozo de Vargas | La Noche Del Mundo," posted July 4, 2023, https://www.youtube.com/watch?v=ENNGAormH2E. Erika Diettes speaks about her trip in my interview with her published in Delgado et al., *Staging Difficult Pasts*.

63 Nancy, *Ground of the Image*, 10.

64 Nancy, *Ground of the Image*, 10.

65 Nancy, *Ground of the Image*, 11.

66 Nancy, *Ground of the Image*, 10.

67 Diettes, interview with author, July 2021.

68 Diettes, interview with author, October 2021.

69 Nancy, *Ground of the Image*, 11.

70 Diettes, interview with author, July 2021.

71 Nancy, *Ground of the Image*, 24.

72 The term "intra-action" evokes the work of Barad, *Meeting the Universe Halfway*. Huyssen writes also about the impermanence of installation art, and in particular William Kentridge's use of stenciled images that will fade in "Triumphs and Laments: Project for the City of Rome" (2016). See Huyssen, *Memory Art*, 67–70.

73 Foster, "An Archival Impulse."

74 Diettes, interview with author, July 2021.

75 Nancy, *Evidence of Film*, 42.

76 Nancy, *Evidence of Film*, 74. In his discussion of Kiarostami's films, Nancy argues that art does not make evidence visible but precisely—because it is not life, but film—makes visible that *there is* evidence. Since there is no resurrection possible through art, it can only sustain the evidence of existences. An existence is more than life, and can continue beyond life, which ends. Art offers images to and for that existence; however, this is not about creating a truthful image but something like the glimpse of "the truth of life offering images to itself." Nancy, *Evidence of Film*, 76.

77 Nancy, *Evidence of Film*, 16–18.

78 Nancy, *Evidence of Film*, 24, 25. My translation.

Epigraph: Stengers, "Challenge of Ontological Politics," 96.

This chapter draws upon the argument of a previous article published in *Social and Legal Studies*.

1 Stengers, "William James," 12.
2 Stengers, "Cosmopolitical Proposal."
3 Motamedi-Fraser makes the point nicely, in relation to the task of writing of sociology; there is a crucial difference between something being "made up" and something having the potential to "make believe." See Motamedi-Fraser, "Once Upon a Problem."
4 Stengers is referencing the work of François Jullien here. Jullien, *Propensity of Things*.
5 Stengers, "Cosmopolitical Proposal," 1000–1001.
6 Stengers, *Invention*, 89.
7 Felman, *Juridical Unconscious*. Carlos Nino wrote: "The drama of a trial, with the victims and perpetrators under the public light, with accusations and defences, with witnesses from all social sectors, and with the terrifying prospect of punishment, inevitably attracts great public attention and may even provoke 'dummy' trials in the streets or around the dinner tables." Nino, *Radical Evil*, 131. Extending Nino's work, Mark Osiel noted that it is imperative that the architects of perpetrator trials remain sensitive to the communicable mimesis that accompanies such public dramas, since it helps to animate the sense that justice must be done. According to Osiel, the choreography of the court is key: "There is nothing necessarily illiberal in the efforts of courts and prosecutors to give a little thought to props and décor, mise-en-scène and pacing of action, character development and narrative framing, stage and audience." Osiel, *Mass Atrocity*, 92. Osiel relates this drama to the public impulse for justice, which "cannot be presumed to arise spontaneously, [it] must be consciously cultivated through strategic decisions about how the public spectacle might be most compellingly staged." Osiel, *Mass Atrocity*, 239.
8 This latter point is, of course, crucial; if audiences lose interest, are frightened and turn away, or are more concerned about other objects, their role in witnessing, attesting, and sustaining the truths is lost. They must gather and engage in the art of "testing" propositions that are presented before them.
9 Stengers, "Challenge of Ontological Politics," 90.
10 Stengers, "Cosmopolitical Proposal," 1003.
11 Christodoulidis, "Objection That Cannot Be Heard," 193.
12 See Bell, *Art of Post-Dictatorship*, chapter 4.
13 Quoted in Wilson, *Writing History*, 2. That said, these trials have seen individuals put on trial many times over, for different crimes. This has been one of the criticisms of the trials, that spend time and money prosecuting individuals who are already recipients of life sentences (interview with Lorena Balardini, November 2015).
14 See Collins, *Post-Transitional Justice*.

15 In December 2013 sentences were handed down to thirty-four individuals, ex-police and ex-army members, in Tucumán's largest *megacausa* for crimes against humanity committed during 1976 and 1977. The *megacausa* centered around the use of the ex–Arsenal Miguel de Azcuénaga as a detention, torture, and extermination center, as well as some other sites, which showed the systematic nature of the use of disappearance in the region. Further large trials were in preparation at the time of the interview.

16 Pablo Camuña, interview, November 2015. This interview was conducted together with Mario di Paolantonio.

17 Camuña, interview, November 2015.

18 Douglas, *Perpetrator*; Arendt, *Between Past and Future*.

19 Camuña, interview, November 2015.

20 "When you read a statement you cannot get angry, indignant, or emotional or put yourself in the place of the person who made the statement. . . . You will never get the same impact . . . nor the richness of the live witness." Interview with Camuña, November 2015. That said, the witness's evidence is not guaranteed to be dramatic. Borges himself complained at the time of the famous trials of the Junta in 1985, that the witnesses may also speak about their experiences "with simplicity . . . almost indifference . . . [with] no hate in her voice." Borges, "Lunes, 22 de Julio de 1985."

21 Keenan, "Getting the Dead," 52.

22 Tucumán Federal Court No 1, "Arsenal Miguel de Azcuénaga CCD s/Secuestros y Desapariciones" (Expte. 400443/84).

23 Camuña, interview, November 2015.

24 This is not to assume that their evidence is understood by all parties as neutral. As Rosenblatt has explained, some of the Madres de Plaza de Mayo found the exhumation of remains not only apolitical but also depoliticizing, insofar as achieving certainty about the whereabouts of one's loved ones potentially turned "*Madres*, members of an activist organization, back into merely *madres*, mothers in a conventional sense." Rosenblatt, *Digging for the Disappeared*, 99.

25 Snow has described the procedure adopted by the team and employed across the world: At the site of a suspected mass grave, techniques from archaeology are used, to skim off surface vegetation and plot out the area as a grid to make sample digs or "shafts" within some of the squares marked by the grid lines. Once the edges of the grave are located, a trench is dug all around so rainwater can drain off and the bodies are left on higher ground. Then, when the bones are discovered, archaeologists delicately expose the skeletons in situ without disturbing their positions. The scene in its totality is of interest to the scientists, and photography is important at this point. The skeletons are photographed repeatedly as they are uncovered, as well as everything around them. In the laboratory, the bones are examined, X-rayed, and recorded in an inventory. Beyond issues of measurement to establish gender, stature and so on, the fact that bones are malleable means they are responsive to life events, nutrition, habits, and so on. Weizman, "Osteobiography," 69.

26 Edwards, "Photography and the Performance."

27 The photographs of the EAAF (Equipo Argentino de Antropologia Forense) have an important role in the scientific investigative forum of their laboratories, and

then are asked to inflect the forum of the law court. The photographs smuggled out of the ESMA, the clandestine detention center in Buenos Aires, somewhat similarly, were taken as part of a process of incrimination of the kidnapped and disappeared, but have emerged within other forums, including the law courts of the 1985 junta trials and the more recent trials including the 2011 ESMA trial. See Bell, *Art of Post-Dictatorship*.

28 As Marco Somigliana, member of the EAAF, explains, there were more mass graves in Córdoba and Tucumán where the repression did not use the death flights that were more common in the Buenos Aires metropolitan area. Somigliana, "El Trabajo del EAAF," 195.

29 Luis Fondebrider, interview, November 2015; Weizman et al., *Forensis*.

30 Somogliana, "El Trabajo del EAAF," 197. Snow comments that bones are "wonderful witnesses. They don't forget, they don't lie." In Weizman, "Osteobiography," 72.

31 In a law court, to be clear, the role of the forensic expert is not the same as the role she has within the scientific forum, the site at which the bodies are uncovered or the laboratory where they are studied. As Somigliana explains it, the forensic anthropologists set themselves the puzzle of what has occurred, an investigation into the identity of the skeletons and how a group of people came to end their lives together at this site, a puzzle into which enter many forms of evidence beyond the bones alone (and of which many aspects may remain unsolved). Somigliana discusses many other aspects such as the material objects found with the bodies (such as personal possessions, the rope that tied hands and feet, as found at the grave in Tucumán), as well as the family reports or official records of who disappeared—information from the archives, in other words—from the same place or at the same time, as contributing to solving the puzzles the graves pose for the team. Somigliana, "El Trabajo del EAAF."

32 In Weizman, "Osteobiography," 72.

33 Snow reports that special permission was needed for him to present his evidence at the 1985 trial of the juntas in person rather than by report as would have been—and remains today—more usual for expert evidence. In Weizman, "Osteobiography."

34 In Weizman, "Osteobiography," 72.

35 In Weizman, "Osteobiography," 72.

36 Camuña, interview, November 2015.

37 Maria del Pilar Gómez Sánchez, interview, November 2015.

38 Conte discusses the audiovisual judicial records in more detail in his article, "A Topography of Memory," 88–89.

39 Gonzalo Conte, interview, November 2015.

40 Keenan, "Getting the Dead," 45.

41 Laura Sobredo, interview, November 2015.

42 Sobredo, interview, November 2015. "Certainly, I don't think the court is the place to talk about everything," she suggests.

43 Sobredo says: "It is very easy for a witness to become an object in the trial . . . and this is terrible for a survivor of torture because . . . the situation of torture is also

to be an object, in the care of no one, with no voice. So if they have the possibility of making space for the personal details and experience [this is a positive thing]." Interview, November 2015.

44 Sobredo, interview, November 2015.

45 As I argued previously, the judges do indeed seem to recall these intense moments after the *megacausas*. See Bell, "On Fernando's Photograph."

46 This is not equivalent to saying it has no relation to legal process, of course. There is relation in terms of the modes of engagement that these spaces allow in terms of the discussions, reflections, alignments, and disagreements possible within them, that are enfolded within and constitute activities of the *nomos*. See Bell and Di Paolantonio, "Haunted Nomos." And also, insofar as the materials of the legal process feed the creativity of these spheres.

47 Rancière, "Assemblies in Art," 30.

48 Huyssen, *Memory Art*, 18. I do not mean to suggest therefore, that art is an unchanging forum with set rules; on the contrary, this use of art spaces has its own history such that contemporary artists of the late twentieth and twenty-first centuries addressing violence have the legacy of modernism and contemporary avant-garde to provide the context and license for their exploratory work. I credit my conversation with Shannon Jackson for nuancing this point.

49 Rancière, "Assemblies in Art," 39.

50 Blejmar, *Playful Memories*, 69.

51 Stengers, "Challenge of Ontological Politics," 92.

52 Diana Taylor wrote about the "staging of social memory," where she wondered, among many other issues, about how theatrical performances might enable a posing of complex questions, including how to remember those violent events for which there are no remaining witnesses, and how to consider the future remembrance of events that have left their traces only within embodied knowledge and performance that are unlikely or unable to be recorded and deposited in traditional archives. Taylor, *Colour of Theatre*, 53.

53 Groys, "Politics of Installation," n.p.

54 Williams, "Memorial Museums," 233.

55 Marstine, "Contingent Nature," 7.

56 Museo de la Memoria is unique in the country in being a museum as opposed to a Space of Memory or memorial site.

57 Simon, "Afterword," 208.

58 Viviana Nardoni, interview, November 2015.

59 Nardoni, interview, November 2015.

60 See Andermann, "Show-Casing Dictatorship," 84.

61 Nardoni, interview, November 2015.

62 Bell, *Art of Post-Dictatorship*, 117.

63 Nardoni, interview, November 2015. These decisions are subject to debate, of course, and some have argued that the generalized "history of human violations" is one that, for example, eclipses the political ambitions of those targeted by the dictatorship and the historical geopolitical context in which they struggle. See Andermann, "Show-Casing Dictatorship." My point here is not to take sides

on this debate, but to point out that the museum fuels such debate precisely because it generates a sense of itself as a forum bound by its rules of relevance.

64 Celina Flores, interview, 2019; Verónica Torras, interview, 2019.

65 Roger Simon asks what "'supplemental' value audiovisual testimonies might . . . contribute to the substance of our historical consciousness?" Answering himself, he argued that video testimony amplifies and complicates our sense of past wrongs and our present desire for justice "through the video presence of 'survivors' conveying to us the details of their lives and evoking the memory of individuals, families, and communities that have been lost." Simon, *Touch of the Past*, 157–58.

66 Claudia Bacci, interview, November 2015.

67 Alejandra Oberti, interview, 2019.

68 Bacci, interview, November 2015.

69 Bacci, interview, November 2015.

70 Oberti, interview, 2019. Oberti said that this is true for all but a few cases, where the people working at the archive felt obliged to make ethical decisions based on the need to protect the privacy of the interviewees or people being named in the testimonies. For example, in one case, when an activist spoke about a number of military actions—including kidnappings—conducted by his organization, he named a lot of people involved. In this case, it was decided to erase the names.

71 Bacci, interview, November 2015.

72 Bacci, interview, November 2015.

73 Conte speaks of sense of a hole opening up as "the core, the deepest part" of one's very self, briefly emerges within a survivor's communicative attempts. Interview, November 2015.

74 Oberti, interview, 2019.

75 The book the team published is called *Y nadie quería saber* (And Nobody Wanted to Know). It can be downloaded free from Memoria Abierta's website, https://www.memoriaabierta.org.ar/wp/en/and-nobody-wanted-to-know/.

6. RISKING IMAGES, AFTER ALL

Epigraph: Pollock, *After-Affects/After-Images*, 4.

Part of this chapter was foreshadowed in a chapter published in Gómez, *Performing Human Rights*.

1 ESMA is the commonly used acronym for the Escuela Superior de Mecánica de la Armada.

2 The "death flights" were dramatically described and confirmed in the mid-1990s by the confessions of Adolfo Scilingo. See Verbitsky, *The Flight*.

3 On that first trip the only obviously installed images on the whole site were those tied temporarily to the railings outside. These were silhouettes that sought both to remind passersby of the history of these buildings, as well as forms of protest that intended to keep up the pressure for the trials of those responsible for these crimes, which at that time had not yet begun.

4 Lyotard, *Heidegger*.

5 Lyotard, *Heidegger*, 17.

6 Lyotard, *Heidegger*, 26.

7 CONADEP was the Comisión Nacional sobre la Desaparición de Personas (National Commission on the Disappearance of Persons) that investigated the practice of disappearance used by the military junta. It was set up by then President Alfonsín when he came to power at the restitution of democracy in 1983.

8 Guerin, *Image and the Witness*, 8–9. Jens Andermann has raised the concern, as did commentators at that time, that by this seeming reversal of attitude, the ex-ESMA was in danger of being caught up in a global trend, or "rush" as Paul Williams termed it, to commemorate atrocities, a rush that followed a contemporary curatorial fashion for a certain "postmemorial aesthetics of mourning." Andermann, "Returning to the Site of Horror," 82. See also Brodsky, *Memoria en construcción*.

9 Pollock, *After-Affects/After-Images*.

10 Seamus Deane, cited in Kelly, *Thinking Long*.

11 Lyotard, *Heidegger*, 32.

12 Lyotard, *Heidegger*, 32.

13 Lyotard, *Heidegger*, 32.

14 Lyotard, *Heidegger*, 47.

15 Lyotard, *Heidegger*, 47.

16 Butler, *Precarious Life*, 144.

17 Longoni, "Photographs and Silhouettes," 5; Nelly Richard, quoted in Longoni, "Photographs and Silhouettes," 7.

18 A related if somewhat different strategy of presentation has also been used on the noticeboards that line a central path through the estate, where a collage of images gives a scrapbook effect to the presentation of stories of the disappeared. Unlike the portrait photography, there is also text working together with the images, informing the visitor of the facts of the disappeared. For example, one presents the couple Verónica ("Vicky") Freier (b. 1955) and Sergio Kacs (b. 1953), who were kidnapped in June 1978 and remain disappeared. They were both seen by other detainees held in the ESMA. The facts convey the ordinariness of these young people, their past-times, accompanied by texts that in this case for example, give snippets of lives—how the couple met, as well as their participation in various political groups including the Movimiento Revolucionario 17 de Octubre, where they met one another. In other words these stories center on the loss of young lives, and the pain of those left only with these photographs and their memories. We imagine the vitality of the lives these young people once led—the pleasures of childhood, of young love, the conviction of political belief, and so on. They may even request that the viewers find analogies or parallels, and therefore modes of empathy, within their own life and loves, an argument made by Kaja Silverman in her beautiful *Flesh of My Flesh*.

19 Nancy, *Ground of the Image*, 21.

20 Nancy, *Ground of the Image*, 24.

21 Didi-Huberman, *Images in Spite of All*.

22 Including their "*escraches*," by which they interrupted everyday life to remind people of the perpetrators who, especially during years of impunity, were still

living in their midst. Placing mock street signs that signaled that a *represor* was living only meters away, throwing paint to mark out the homes of those targeted, and making noise in protest on the streets, the group indicated to the community that punishment had still not been meted out and, to the target of the *escraches*, that society had not forgotten, still less forgiven, their actions.

23 Julio López was a key witness in the 2006 trial of Miguel Etchecolatz who had been the Director of Investigations of the Buenos Aires Provincial Police in the 1970s, during some of the most violent years of repression. His disappearance was shocking, widely understood as a warning to those testifying against authorities.

24 For an interesting related discussion of the GAC images in the ex-ESMA space, understood as a space of embodied experiences of militancy, including the use of the image of Santiago Maldonado, see Teichert, "Reciclaje."

25 Silverman, *Threshold of the Visible World*.

26 The trial to which I refer here is the ESMA *megacausa*, which began in December 2009 and ended in October 2011, with guilty verdicts for sixteen of the eighteen defendants, among them Jorge "Tigre" Acosta, chief of intelligence, and Alfredo Astiz, infamous for his infiltration of the Madres de Plaza de Mayo. More than two hundred witnesses, eighty of them survivors of the ESMA, testified.

27 See Bell, *Art of Post-Dictatorship*, 63.

28 For discussion of his story and the photographs he smuggled out, see Bell, *Art of Post-Dictatorship*. See also Feld, "¿Hacer Visible la Desaparición?"

29 On the concept of material witness, see Schuppli, *Material Witness*.

30 Celeste Orozco, private communication.

31 As discussed in chapter 5.

32 These films work rather differently in this sense from the display on the ground floor of the building, where the portrait photographs and details of those indicted for crimes committed at the ESMA are shown, accompanied by a dramatic sound-piece that "stamps" the resulting verdict across their images. These latter appear more straightforwardly as "information" and triumphant than the witness-survivor testimonies in the *Capucha*.

33 For a relevant argument, see Simon, "Shock to Thought."

34 The curators were explicitly attempting, according to Celeste Orozco, to draw upon the philosophy of Marshall Meyer: "One of the ideas that guided the project was the concept that Marshall Meyer articulated in relation to the synagogue and that the curators took for the Site of Memory: to be 'a place where the comfortable feel uncomfortable and the uncomforted feel comfort.' That is to say: that those who feel indifference or *consustanciado* with the theme of human rights are shaken [*sacudido*] by the place and the exhibition. And that whoever is involved [*comprometido*], whether they be a relative or survivor, finds here a place of solace [*reparo*]." Private communication.

35 One of the things that witnesses find difficult in the trials is that they come face to face with the defendants. In the artwork or installation, that I-you relationship is removed. Instead there is a relationship between the spectator (who may or may not have a relation to the stories being recounted) and the "it" of the work (Georges Didi-Huberman has made this argument, at his lecture at Haus der Kunst in June 2012, available on YouTube). In the trials the witnesses have

to endure the experience, but in an art world, one's decision to tarry with the work—or not—is (usually) left to oneself. As discussed in chapter 5, the art space is "freer" in this sense.

36 Bell and Di Paolantonio, "The Haunted Nomos."

37 The photographers were Daniel García (b. 1953), Eduardo Longoni (b. 1959), Mónica Hasenberg (b. 1954), Lucila Quieto (b. 1977), Camilo del Cerro (b. 1974), Inés Ulanovsky (b. 1977), Gabriel Diaz (b. 1965), Juan Travnik (b. 1950), Paula Luttringer (b. 1955), Helen Zout (b. 1957), Marcelo Brodsky (b. 1954), and Fernando Gutiérrez (b. 1968).

38 These images were also reproduced by Marcelo Brodsky in the book that accompanied his exhibition of the same name. See Brodsky, *Buena memoria*, 66, 83.

39 The loop also shows a quotation from Travnik in which he directs our attention to the possibility of an image's power to evoke historical events: "The registration of the print, of the presence, often metaphorical, of the traces of violence. Either notorious and explicit, or more diffuse and subtle, these images appear as scars and evoke, keeping . . . in memory, a period marked by horror."

40 Pollock, *After-Affects/After-Images*, 26–27.

41 See The Aftermath Project, https://www.theaftermathproject.org/project/el -lamento-de-los-muros. For more on Paula Luttringer's photography, see Blejmar, "Mineral Memories."

42 Here I am recalling Rancière's argument in *Emancipated Spectator*, 80.

43 Sosa, "On Crying Perpetrators."

44 Under the auspices of the international research project called "Staging Difficult Pasts," https://www.stagingdifficultpasts.org/.

45 Sosa, "On Crying Perpetrators."

46 Naftal's introduction can be viewed at "Pasados conflictivos en escena," Staging Difficult Pasts, last updated 2022, https://www.stagingdifficultpasts.org/pasados -conflictivos-en-escena.

47 The girl was Andrea Krichmar, who recounted her visit to her friend Berenice Chamorro to CONADEP and in 1985, providing vital evidence. For more details see Goldman, "La Nena."

48 "Pasados conflictivos en escena," from the post-performance discussion.

49 Wojtek Ziemilski, interview with author, 2021.

50 This was the way Ziemilski put it at the time of the performance. See "Pasados conflictivos en escena."

51 They may even know that the actor's own sister was disappeared during the dictatorship. Szuchmacher is older than Chamorro would have been at the time of his command of the ESMA, and the trial. One of the audience members reportedly commented that he did not share the typical profile of a repressor in Argentina, being Jewish, with a Polish father and openly gay. See Sosa, "On Crying Perpetrators." Szuchmacher revealed that it was his Polish heritage that made him intrigued by what Ziemilski was to do at the ex-ESMA, and that persuaded him to take part, even though he had never wanted to enter the building before this event.

52 *An Impossible Scene*, at 5:00.

53 *An Impossible Scene*, at 5:26.

54 See Bell, *Art of Post-Dictatorship*; Payne, *Unsettling Accounts*. The process of bringing Astiz to trial had been long. Initially he escaped prosecution and was released from custody due to the impunity laws. He was sentenced to life in absentia in France in 1990 for the kidnapping and torture of two French Catholic nuns, Léonie Duquet and Alice Domon. Argentina did not extradite him to Spain when Judge Baltazar Garzón requested his extradition in 1997. After the Amnesty laws were declared void in 2003 by the Supreme Court, in the Simón case, it was possible to prosecute Astiz in Argentina. This took several years, however, during which time a court in Italy found him guilty of illegal detention, torture, and forced disappearance. Only in 2011 was he finally found guilty by the Federal court in Buenos Aires as part of the ESMA *megacausa*. He was sentenced to life imprisonment on thirteen counts of murder aggravated by premeditation, eighteen counts of torture aggravated by the political persecution of the victim, eighteen counts of aggravated unlawful deprivation of liberty, and aggravated robbery. See "Alfredo Ignacio Astiz," International Crimes Database, accessed October 18, 2025, https://www.internationalcrimesdatabase.org/Case/1080/Astiz/.

55 See Verbitsky, *The Flight*. See also Payne, *Unsettling Accounts*.

56 He made this remark in an interview with Marguerite Feitlowitz, quoted in Feitlowitz, *Lexicon of Terror*, 246–47.

57 Scilingo fled to Spain after being abducted and attacked in Argentina in 1997. He took part in the 2007 judicial investigation of Spanish victims of the Argentine military instigated by Garzón there, but expressed surprise when he was himself prosecuted. He was found guilty of thirty assassinations and imprisoned for Spain's maximum sentence of twenty-five years. Robben, *Argentina Betrayed*, 121–23. Robben also recalls the promised confession of Héctor Febres, who had been stationed at the ESMA, who at first denied all knowledge of the charges brought against him when brought to account in 2007 (after the Amnesty laws were repealed), and even denied being at the ESMA. When his conviction looked likely, he then told his doctor, among others, that he intended to confess at his sentencing, implicating others. Before he could do so, he was found dead in the prison apartment where he had been held in Tigre. Robben, *Argentina Betrayed*, 124.

58 Sosa, "On Crying Perpetrators." For more on the Historias Desobedientes group, see the interview with them, Díaz-Ridgeway, "Two Years of *Historias Desobedientes*."

59 Ziemilski, *An Impossible Scene*, at 11:25.

60 Ziemilski, *An Impossible Scene*, from 11:52.

61 Ziemilski, *An Impossible Scene*, at 14:09.

62 Ziemilski, *An Impossible Scene*, at 14:26.

63 Ziemilski, *An Impossible Scene*, at 16:00.

64 Ziemilski, *An Impossible Scene*, at 17:09.

65 Ziemilski, interview with author, 2021. Ziemilski was from elsewhere, and his previous work had addressed issues of the Holocaust, a comparison that has caused much debate in Argentina. The specificity of what happened in Argentina is important for the relatives and analysts alike, who do not want their experience to be regarded and understood only through that lens. Ziemilski's use of the term

perpetrator was also considered controversial in this regard; see Sosa, "On Crying Perpetrators." Yet he wanted to continue using the term, not least because it gave the piece the sense of an anachronism that was interesting, bringing with it the issue of how histories connect and refract when placed together.

66 Ziemilski, interview with author, 2021.

67 Ziemilski, interview with author, 2021. It is a thought process that approaches the dangers of the Complete Memory movement's casting of everyone as a victim. See Salvi, "We're All Victims Now."

68 Ziemilski, interview with author, 2021.

69 Ziemilski mentioned Brecht in our conversation, and clearly the central dynamic between the actor on the film and the narrator-critic is indebted to Brecht's ideas and techniques, which allowed a commentary on the characters as the play proceeds to disrupt the "manipulation" of theater's request for empathetic identification. For an interesting exploration of the interrupting stranger in Brecht, its analysis by and its resonance with Walter Benjamin, see Rokem, "Suddenly, a Stranger Appears."

70 Ziemilski has also a personal experience relevant to this, as he explained in our interview. His grandfather, to whom he was exceptionally close, was named as a former collaborator with the Communist secret police by the Institute of National Remembrance in Poland. This was a shock to Ziemilski, whose grandfather was still alive when this was revealed. He made a piece of performance about this revelation, which "questioned my heritage, which was now ambiguous. Because I was taught how to read and write by my grandfather and I was also taught how to distinguish right from wrong [by him]." Interview with author, 2021.

71 Taylor, *Disappearing Acts.*

72 The truth commission CONADEP received witnesses' statements to produce its report, but it did not call upon *represores* to testify in return for amnesty. Instead, after the famous 1985 trial of the junta, the so-called Amnesty laws were enacted by the government—the 1986 Ley de Punto Final and the 1987 Ley de Obediencia Debida—until they were declared unconstitutional and the trials began. The parallels between Argentina and South Africa have been explored at the ex-ESMA Site of Memory through an exhibition in 2022, which followed reciprocal visits between museum workers from there and from Robben Island. Interestingly, in a clear instance of the importance of investigating connections, of "multidirectional memory," Argentina sent its officers to South Africa, to the South Africa Defense Force in the 1970s in order to learn about their tactics in quelling "subversion." Both Chamorro and Astiz spent time there. On multidirectional memory, see Rothberg, *Multi-Directional Memory.*

73 As noted, these questions are intentionally unconstrained by the piece itself, but Ziemilski suggested in our conversations about the piece that he was cognizant of the debate around Karl Jaspers's writings on questions of collective guilt in the context of the "denazification program" carried out in Germany in 1945, including with Hannah Arendt. While in Argentina the more recently used term "civic-military (*cívico-militar*) dictatorship" rather than simply military dictatorship attempts to enfold issues of widespread complicity into the

historical period, the focus has been mainly on corporations' complicity, not on a widespread "collective responsibility" as was the case in Germany. On the debate between Jaspers and Arendt, see Schapp, "Guilty Subjects and Political Responsibility."

74 Pollock, *After-Affects/After-Images*, xxi.
75 Pollock, *After-Affects/After-Images*, xxiii.
76 Pollock, *After-Affects/After-Images*, xxvi.

CONCLUSION

1 Viebach, "Transitional Archives"; Rangelov, "Justice Archive."
2 Viebach et al., "Beyond Evidence."
3 Elander and Hughes, "Pressing Evidence."
4 I have written elsewhere about how I understand the relationship of these "cultural" spaces to law and legal codification, drawing on the thought of Robert Cover. See Bell, "Haunted Nomos"; see also Bell, *Art of Post-Dictatorship*.
5 Salvi, "'We're All Victims.'"
6 The notes accompanying the inclusion of the building on the UNESCO website state the importance of maintaining the building and "presenting what happened during the dictatorship in all its complex precedents and consequences and guaranteeing that the property continues to be the inheritance of all Argentinians so as to become that of the world." "ESMA Museum and Site of Memory—Former Clandestine Centre of Detention, Torture and Extermination," UNESCO, accessed October 18, 2025, https://whc.unesco.org/en/list/1681/.
7 As quoted in national newspaper *Pagina 12* in February 2024: Luciana Bertoia, "Con la venia de Villarruel, un militar retirado desembarca en el Museo de Malvinas," https://www.pagina12.com.ar/716633-con-la-venia-de-villarruel-un-militar-retirado-desembarca-en.
8 See the Amnesty International report "Eyes on Chile: Police Violence and Command Responsibility During the Period of Social Unrest," October 2020, https://www.amnesty.org/en/documents/amr22/3133/2020/en/. In January 2024, three senior police officers were served with an indictment for their role in the situation. The indictment was brought by the North Central Regional Prosecutor's Office against the current director general of the *Carabineros*, Ricardo Yáñez, who served as director of order and security during the 2019 protests; Mario Rozas, former director general of the institution; and Diego Olate, a retired general and former deputy director.
9 Campos, "Ciudad, estallido social y disputa gráfica." See also Aedo, "Against the Day," for discussion of how the memories of the dictatorship period become enfolded into contemporary political subjectivities as exemplified through reflections on the social uprising.
10 Amnesty International has called for Chile to address the disproportionate violence. See "Chile: Four Years on from the Social Unrest, Impunity and a Lack of Comprehensive Reparations Persist," Amnesty International, October 17, 2023, https://www.amnesty.org/en/latest/news/2023/10/chile-four-years-social-unrest-impunity/.

11   The Institute of Development and Peace Studies (INDEPAZ) reported that murders declined from 12,665 in 2012 to 1,238 in 2016. Quoted in United Nations report in July 2022, "Colombia: Urgent Government Action Needed as Rising Violence in Rural Areas Gravely Impacts Human Rights—UN Report," July 26, 2022, https://www.ohchr.org/en/press-releases/2022/07/colombia-urgent-government -action-needed-rising-violence-rural-areas-gravely.

12   The Colombian Ombudsman's Office reported that 181 social leaders and human rights defenders were murdered in 2023. In 2022 the number had been 2,015. "Durante el 2023, en Colombia fueron asesinados 181 líderes sociales y defensores de derechos humanos," Defensoría del Pueblo, March 9, 2024, https://www .defensoria.gov.co/web/guest. More than four hundred ex-combatants have been murdered since the 2016 Agreement was signed.

13   "ONU Mujeres condena asesinato de la lideresa indígena Carmelina Yule Paví en Toribío, Cauca," United Nations Colombia, March 19, 2024, https://colombia.un .org/es/263764-onu-mujeres-condena-asesinato-de-la-lideresa-ind%C3%ADgena -carmelina-yule-pav%C3%AD-en-torib%C3%ADo-cauca. Yule Paví was murdered on March 16, 2024.

14   The JEP's first "recognition of responsibility" event took place in Ocana, Norte de Santander, in April 2022, where ten members of the army, including a general and four colonels, recognized their responsibility for extrajudicial killings and forced disappearances and apologized to the victims' families. At a further event in July, twelve members of the Artillery Battalion Number Two who were charged with 127 extrajudicial killings in Cesar and La Guajira, accepted their responsibility and made apologies to the families and indigenous leaders of the targeted communities. "Colombia 2022 Human Rights Report: Executive Summary," 2023, https:// www.state.gov/wp-content/uploads/2023/02/415610_COLOMBIA-2022-HUMAN -RIGHTS-REPORT.pdf.

Accatino, Daniela, and Cath Collins. "Truth, Evidence, Truth: The Deployment of Testimony, Archives and Technical Data in Domestic Human Rights Trials." *Journal of Human Rights Practice* 8, no. 1 (2016): 81–100.

Acosta López, María del Rosario. "Las fragilidades de la memoria: Duelo y Resistencia al olvido en el arte colombiano (Muñoz, Salcedo, Echavarría)." In *Resistencias al olvido: Memoria y arte en Colombia*. Bogotá: Ediciones Uniandes, 2016.

Aedo, Ángel, Oriana Bernasconi, Damián Omar Martínez, Alicia Olivari, Fernando Pairican, and Juan Porma. "Against the Day: Multitude and Memory in the Chilean Social Uprising." *South Atlantic Quarterly* 123, no. 1 (2024): 192–202.

Agamben, Giorgio. *Homo Sacer: Sovereign Power and Bare Life.* Translated by Daniel Heller-Roazen. Stanford, CA: Stanford University Press, 1998. First published in Italian in 1995.

Alcalá, Pilar Riaño, with Christina Lleras, Lorena Luengas, Luis Carlos Manjarrés, and Martha Nubia Bello. *Guion conceptual: Museo de Memoria Histórica de Colombia.* Bogotá: CNMH, n.d., ca. 2018. https://www.museolamemoria.co.

Alcalá, Pilar Riaño, and María Victoria Uribe. "Constructing Memory Amidst War: The Historical Memory Group of Colombia." *International Journal of Transitional Justice* 10, no. 1 (2016): 6–24.

Andermann, Jens. "Returning to the Site of Horror: On the Reclaiming of Clandestine Concentration Camps in Argentina." *Theory, Culture and Society* 29 (2012): 76–98.

Andermann, Jens. "Show-Casing Dictatorship: Memory and the Museum in Argentina and Chile." *Journal of Educational Media, Memory and Society* 4, no. 2 (2012): 69–93.

Appadurai, Arjun. "The Archive and Aspiration." In *Information Is Alive*, edited by Joke Brower and Arjen Molder, 14–25. Rotterdam: V2 Publications, 2003.

Aranguren, J. P. "Inmunización y militarización del cuerpo social en Colombia: El Estado en emergencia permanente." *Athenea Digital* 15, no. 4 (2015): 305–27.

Arendt, Hannah. *Between Past and Future: Six Exercises in Political Thought.* Cleveland, OH: Meridian, 1963.

Arendt, Hannah. *The Human Condition.* Chicago: University of Chicago Press, 1998. First published in 1958.

Arnold-de Simine, Silke. "Memory Museum and Museum Text: Intermediality in Daniel Libeskind's Jewish Museum and W. G. Sebald's *Austerlitz*." *Theory, Culture and Society* 29, no. 1 (2012): 14–35.

Atuahene, Bernadette. "From Reparation to Restoration: Moving Beyond Restoring Property Rights to Restoring Political and Economic Visibility." *SMU Law Review* 60, no. 4 (2007): 1420–70.

Azoulay, Ariella. *The Civic Contract of Photography*. New York: Zone Books, 2008.

Azoulay, Ariella. *Potential History: Unlearning the Archive*. London: Verso, 2019.

Bal, Mieke. *Double Exposures: The Subject of Cultural Analysis*. London: Routledge, 1996.

Bal, Mieke. *Louise Bourgeois' Spider*. Chicago: University of Chicago Press, 2001.

Barad, Karen. *Meeting the Universe Halfway: Quantum Physics and the Entanglement of Matter and Meaning*. Durham, NC: Duke University Press, 2007.

Barrill, Claudia, and Sebastián Moreno, dirs. *Habeas Corpus*. Peliculas del Pez, Chile, 2015. 83 minutes.

Barthes, Roland. *Camera Lucida: Reflections on Photography*. London: Vintage, 2000. First published in French in 1980.

Batchen, Geoffrey, Mick Gidley, Nancy K. Miller, and Jay Prosser, eds. *Picturing Atrocity: Photography in Crisis*. London: Reaktion, 2012.

Becker, Howard S. *Telling About Society*. Chicago: University of Chicago Press, 2007.

Bell, Vikki. *The Art of Post-Dictatorship: Ethics and Aesthetics in Transitional Argentina*. London: Routledge, 2014.

Bell, Vikki. "Between Documentality and Imagination: Five Theses on Curating the Violent Past." *Memory Studies* 11, no. 2 (2018): 137–55.

Bell, Vikki. *Culture and Performance: The Challenge of Ethics, Politics and Feminist Theory*. Oxford: Berg, 2007.

Bell, Vikki. "Documenting Dictatorship: Writing and Resistance in Chile's *Vicaría de la Solidaridad*." *Theory, Culture and Society* 38, no. 1 (2021): 53–78.

Bell, Vikki. "On Fernando's Photograph: The Biopolitics of Aparición in Contemporary Argentina." *Theory, Culture and Society* 27, no. 4 (2010): 69–89.

Bell, Vikki. "On Isabelle Stengers' 'Cosmopolitics': A Speculative Adventure." In *Speculative Research: The Lure of Possible Futures*, edited by Alex Wilkie, Martin Savransky, and Marsha Rosengarten. London: Routledge, 2016.

Bell, Vikki, Oriana Bernasconi, Jaime Hernandez-García, and Cecilia Sosa. *Archives of Violence: Case Studies from South America*. London: Goldsmiths, 2021.

Bell, Vikki, and Mario Di Paolantonio. "The Haunted Nomos: Activist-Artists and the Impossible Politics of Memory in Transitional Argentina." *Cultural Politics* 5, no. 2 (2009): 149–78.

Benjamin, Walter. *The Origin of German Tragic Drama*. Translated by John Osborne. London: Verso, 1998. First published in German in 1963.

Benjamin, Walter. "The Storyteller: Reflections on the Work of Nikolai Leskov." In Walter Benjamin, *Illuminations*, edited by Hannah Arendt, translated by Harry Zorn. London: Pimlico, 1999. First published in German in 1955.

Benjamin, Walter. "Theses on the Philosophy of History." In Walter Benjamin, *Illuminations*, edited by Hannah Arendt, translated by Harry Zohn. London: Fontana Press, 1992. First published in German in 1955.

Berger, John. *And Our Faces, My Heart, Brief as Photos*. London: Bloomsbury, 2005. First published in 1984.

Bergson, Henri. *Key Writings*. Edited by Keith Ansell-Pearson and John Mullarkey. Continuum: London, 2002.

Berlant, Lauren. *Cruel Optimism*. Durham, NC: Duke University Press, 2011.

Bernasconi, Oriana, ed. *Resistance to Political Violence in Latin America: Documenting Atrocity*. London: Palgrave Macmillan, 2019.

Bhabha, Homi, ed. *Nation and Narration*. London: Routledge, 1990.

Blejmar, Jordana. "Mineral Memories: Photography and Disappearance in Argentina." *MAI* 9 (2022). https://maifeminism.com/mineral-memories-photography -disappearance-in-argentina/.

Blejmar, Jordana. *Playful Memories: The Autofictional Turn in Post-Dictatorship Argentina*. London: Palgrave Macmillan, 2016.

Borges, Jorge Luis. "Lunes, 22 de Julio de 1985." In *Borges: Textos Recobrados 1956–1986*, edited by Sara Luisa del Carril and Mercedes Rubio de Socchi. Buenos Aires: Emecé Editores, 2003.

Briones-M, Luis. "The Geoglyphs of the North Chilean Desert: An Archaeological and Artistic Perspective." *Antiquity* 80 (2006): 9–24.

Brodsky, Marcelo. *Buena memoria: Un racconto fotografico di Marcelo Brodsky/Un ensayo fotográfico de Marcelo Brodsky*. Buenos Aires: La Marca Editora, 1997.

Brodsky, Marcelo. *Memoria en construcción: El debate sobre la ESMA/Memory under Construction: The Debates Around ESMA*. Buenos Aires: La Marca Editora, 2005.

Butler, Judith. *Precarious Life: The Powers of Mourning and Violence*. New York: Verso, 2004.

Butler, Judith. *Parting Ways: Jewishness and the Critique of Zionism*. New York: Columbia University Press, 2012.

Campos Medina, Luis, and Oriana Bernasconi. "Ciudad, estallido social y disputa gráfica." *Atenea* 524 (2021): 111–28.

Campt, Tina. *Image Matters: Archive, Photography, and the African Diaspora in Europe*. Durham, NC: Duke University Press, 2012.

Cavarero, Adriana. "Narrative Against Destruction." *New Literary History* 46, no. 1 (2015): 1–16.

Cavarero, Adriana. *Relating Narratives: Storytelling and Selfhood*. London: Routledge, 2000.

Centro Nacional de Memoria Histórica (CNMH). *¡Basta Ya! Colombia: Memories of War and Dignity*. Bogotá: CNMH, 2016. First published in Spanish in 2013.

Centro Nacional de Memoria Histórica (CNMH). *No Hubo Tiempo para la Tristeza* (film). Dir. Jorge Mario Betancur, 2013.

Centro Nacional de Memoria Histórica (CNMH). *Trujillo: Una tragedia que no cesa*. Bogota: CNMH, 2008.

Christodoulidis, Emilios. "The Objection That Cannot Be Heard: Communication and Legitimacy in the Courtroom." In *The Trial on Trial*, vol. 1, *Truth and Due Process*, edited by Antony Duff, Lindsay Farmer, Sandra Marshall, and Victor Tadros. Oxford: Hart, 2004.

Collins, Cath. *Post-Transitional Justice: Human Rights Trials in El Salvador and Chile*. Philadelphia: Pennsylvania State University Press, 2010.

Conte, Gonzalo. "A Topography of Memory: Reconstructing the Architectures of Terror in the Argentine Dictatorship." *Memory Studies* 8, no. 1 (2015): 86–101.

de Baecque, Antoine, and Thierry Jousse. "Cinema and Its Ghosts: An Interview with Jacques Derrida." Translated by Peggy Kamuf. *Discourse* 37, no. 1–2 (2015): 22–39.

Originally published in French as Antoine de Baecque and Thierry Jousse, "Le Cinéma et ses fantômes," *Cahiers du cinéma* 556 (2001): 74–85.

De Duve, Thierry. "Art in the Face of Radical Evil." *October* 125 (Summer 2008): 3–23.

Delgado, Maria, Michal Kobialka, and Bryce Lease, eds. *Staging Difficult Pasts: Transnational Memory, Theatres, and Museums*. London: Routledge, 2024.

Derrida, Jacques. *Archive Fever: A Freudian Impression*. Translated by Eric Prenowitz. Chicago: Chicago University Press, 1996.

Derrida, Jacques. *The Beast and the Sovereign*. Vol. 2, *Seminar of 2002–2003*. Translated by Geoffrey Bennington. Chicago: University of Chicago Press, 2011. First published in French in 2009.

Derrida, Jacques. "Force of Law: The 'Mystical Foundation of Authority.'" In *Jacques Derrida: Acts of Religion*, edited by Gil Anidjar. New York: Routledge, 2002.

Derrida, Jacques. *Rogues: Two Essays on Reason*. Translated by Pascale-Anne Brault and Michael Naas. Stanford, CA: Stanford University Press, 2005.

Despret, Vinciane. "Talking Before the Dead." Seminar at Goldsmiths, University of London, January 2017.

Díaz-Ridgeway, Gwendolyn. "Two Years of *Historias Desobedientes*: Daughters and Sons of Genocide Perpetrators of the Military Dictatorship in Argentina." *Wasafiri* 35, no. 4 (2020): 80–85.

Didi-Huberman, Georges. *Images in Spite of All: Four Photographs from Auschwitz*. Translated by Shane B. Lillis. Chicago: University of Chicago Press, 2008.

Diéguez, Ileana. "Erika Diettes: Imágenes en Duelo." In *Memento Mori: Testament to Life*, by Erika Diettes. Staunton, VA: George F. Thompson, 2015.

Diettes, Erika. *Memento Mori: Testament to Life*. Staunton, VA: George F. Thompson, 2015.

Diettes, Erika. "Stories Told from the Threshold." Talk given at Saint Louis University, 2016. https://www.slu.edu/mocra/voices-podcast/erika-diettes-stories-told-from -the-threshold.

Diettes, Erika, and Anne Wilkes Tucker. "Conversation Between Erika Diettes and Anne Wilkes Tucker (February 2013)." In *Memento Mori: Testament to Life*, by Erika Diettes. Staunton, VA: George F. Thompson, 2015.

Douglas, Lawrence. "Perpetrator Proceedings and Didactic Trials." In *The Trial on Trial*, vol. 2, *Judgment and Calling to Account*, edited by Antony Duff, Lindsay Farmer, Sandra Marshall, and Victor Tadros. Oxford: Hart, 2006.

Edwards, Elizabeth. "Photography and the Performance of History." *Kronos* 27 (2001): 15–29.

Elander, Maria, and Rachel Hughes. "Pressing Evidence: Activating Khmer Rouge Archives." *Social and Legal Studies* 33, no. 6 (2024): 1–24.

Esposito, Robert. *Immunitas*. Translated by Zakiya Hanafi. Cambridge: Polity, 2011.

Facultad de Ciencias Humanas y Económias. *Exposición sobre el Fondo Documental Fabiola Lalinde*. 2018. https://www.youtube.com/watch?v=FkkdzRAj3Tg.

Feitlowitz, Marguerite. *A Lexicon of Terror: Argentina and the Legacies of Torture*. Oxford: Oxford University Press, 2011.

Feld, Claudia. "¿Hacer Visible la Desaparición? La fotografías de detenidos-desaparecidos de la ESMA en el testimonio de Victor Basterra." *Clepsidra: Revista Interdisciplinaria de Estudios Sobre Memoria* 1 (March 2014): 28–51.

Feld, Claudia, and Jessica Stites Mor, eds. *El pasado que miramos: Memoria e imagen ante la historia reciente*. Buenos Aires: Paídos, 2009.

Felman, Shoshana. *The Juridical Unconscious: Trials and Traumas in the Twentieth Century*. Cambridge, MA: Harvard University Press, 2002.

Ferraris, Maurizio. *Documentality: Why It Is Necessary to Leave Traces*. Translated by Richard Davis. New York: Fordham University Press, 2012.

Foster, Hal. "An Archival Impulse." *October* 110 (Autumn 2004): 3–22.

Foucault, Michel. "Lecture of 17th March 1976." In *Society Must Be Defended: Lectures at the College de France, 1975–1976*, translated by Graham Burchell. London: Palgrave Macmillan, 1979.

Foucault, Michel. "On the Lives of Infamous Men." In *Michel Foucault: Power (Essential Works of Foucault 1954–1984*, vol. 3), edited by James D. Faubion. New York: New Press, 2000.

Fritsch, Matthias. "Taking Turns: Democracy to Come and Intergenerational Justice." *Derrida Today* 4, no. 2 (2011): 148–72.

Gamboa, Alberto. *Vida de perros*. Vol. 3 of *Un viaje por el infierno*. Santiago de Chile: Empresa Editora Araucaria, 1984.

Garcia-Godos, Jemima, and Knut Andreas O. Lid. "Transitional Justice and Victims' Rights Before the End of Conflict: The Unusual Case of Colombia." *Journal of Latin American Studies* 42, no. 3 (2010): 487–516.

Giunta, Andrea. *The Political Body: Stories on Art, Feminism, and Emancipation in Latin America*. Translated by Jane Brodie. Berkeley: University of California Press, 2023.

Goldman, Tali. "La Nena Que Jugaba en la ESMA." *Anfibia*, May 11, 2016. https://www.revistaanfibia.com/la-nena-jugaba-la-esma/.

Gómez, Liliana, ed. *Performing Human Rights: Contested Amnesia and Aesthetics Practices in the Global South*. Chicago: Diaphanes/University of Chicago Press, 2021.

Gómez-Barris, Macarena. *Where Memory Dwells: Culture and State Violence in Chile*. Berkeley: University of California Press, 2009.

González-Ayala, Sofía N., and Alejandro Camargo. "Voices of Water and Violence: Exhibition Making and the Blue Humanities for Transitional Justice." *Curator: The Museum Journal* 64, no. 1 (2021): 183–204.

Gordillo, Gastón. *Rubble: The Afterlife of Destruction*. Durham, NC: Duke University Press, 2014.

Groys, Boris. "The Politics of Installation." *e-flux* 2 (2009). https://www.e-flux.com/journal/02/68504/politics-of-installation.

Guerin, Frances, and Roger Hallas, eds. *The Image and the Witness: Trauma, Memory and Visual Culture*. London: Wallflower, 2007.

Guzmán, Patricio, dir. *The Battle of Chile*. Three-part documentary film, Equipe Tercer Ano, 1975–79. 263 minutes.

Guzmán, Patricio, dir. *Chile, Obstinate Memory*. Documentary film, Les Films d'Ici / National Film Board of Canada / La Sept-Arte, 1997. 59 minutes.

Hansen, Mark B. N. *New Philosophy for New Media*. Cambridge, MA: MIT Press, 2006.

Haraway, Donna. *Staying with the Trouble: Making Kin in the Chthulucene*. Durham, NC: Duke University Press, 2016.

Hartman, Saidiya. "Venus in Two Acts." *Small Axe* 12, no. 2 (Number 26) (2008): 1–14.

Hartman, Saidiya. *Wayward Lives, Beautiful Experiments: Intimate Histories of Riotous Black Girls, Troublesome Women, and Queer Radicals*. New York: W. W. Norton, 2019.

Hau, Boris, Francesca Lessa, and Hugo Rojas. "Registration and Documentation of State Violence as Judicial Evidence in Human Rights Trials." In *Resistance to Political Violence in Latin America: Documenting Atrocity*, edited by Oriana Bernasconi, 197–228. London: Palgrave Macmillan, 2019.

Heynowski, Walter, and Gerhard Scheumann, dir. *Yo He Sido, Yo Soy, Yo Seré [I Have Been, I Am, I Will Be]*. Documentary film, Estudios H and S, 1974.

Hirst, K. Kris. "The Geoglyphic Art of Chile's Atacama Desert." *ThoughtCo*, 2018. https://www.thoughtco.com/geoglyphic-art-of-chiles-atacama-desert-169877.

Hochberg, Gil. *Becoming Palestine: Toward an Archival Imagination of the Future*. Durham, NC: Duke University Press, 2021.

Human Rights Watch. "Argentina: Events of 2023." *World Report 2024*. https://www.hrw .org/world-report/2024/country-chapters/argentina.

Huyssen, Andreas. *Memory Art in the Contemporary World: Confronting Violence in the Global South*. London: Lund Humphries, 2022.

James, William. *A Pluralistic Universe*. Ebook, Project Gutenberg, 2004. First published 1909.

Jamison, Gayla, dir. *Retazos de Vida* [Scraps of Life]. Twenty-eight-minute documentary, Lightfoot Films, 1991. Based on book by Marjorie Agosin. Available via the Museo de la Memoria y Derechos Humanos. https://conectadosconlamemoria.cl /series-y-peliculas/retazos-de-vida/.

Jaramillo, Úrsula, Jimena Cortés-Duque, and Carlos Flórez-Ayala, eds. *Colombia anfibia: Un país de humedales*. Vol. 1. Bogotá: Instituto de Investigación de Recursos Biológicos Alexander von Humboldt, 2015.

Jaramillo Marín, Jefferson. *Pasados y presentes de la violencia en Colombia: Estudio sobre las comisiones de investigación (1958–2011)*. Bogotá: Editorial Pontificia Universidad Javeriana, 2014.

Jelin, Elizabeth, and Ana Longoni. *Escrituras, imágenes y escenarios ante la repression*. Madrid: Siglo XXI, 2005.

Jullien, François. *The Propensity of Things: Towards a History of Efficacy in China*. Translated by Janet Lloyd. New York: Zone Books, 1999.

Kantorowicz, Ernst. *The King's Two Bodies: Study in Medieval Political Theology*. Princeton, NJ: Princeton University Press, 2016. First published 1957.

Keenan, Thomas. "Getting the Dead to Tell Me What Happened: Justice, Prosopopoeia, and Forensic Afterlives." In *Forensis: The Architecture of Public Truth*, edited by Eyal Weizman. Berlin: Sternberg, 2014.

Kelly, Liam. *Thinking Long: Contemporary Art in the North of Ireland*. Cork, Ireland: Gandon Editions, 1996.

Kottman, Paul A. "Translator's Introduction." In *Relating Narratives: Storytelling and Selfhood*, by Adriana Cavarero. London: Routledge, 2000.

Krause, Franz, and Veronica Strang. "Living Water: Introduction to Special Issue." *Worldviews* 17 (2013): 95–102.

Latour, Bruno. "Why Has Critique Run Out of Steam? From Matters of Fact to Matters of Concern." *Critical Inquiry* 30 (Winter 2004): 225–48.

Lazzara, Michael. "Militancy Then and Now: A Conversation with Carmen Castillo." *Journal of Latin American Cultural Studies* 21, no. 1 (2012): 1–14.

Lerner, Ben. "Postscript: John Berger 1926–2017." *New Yorker*, January 6, 2017.

Levi, Primo. *If This Is a Man.* Translated by Stuart Woolf. London: Abacus, 1987. First published in Italian in 1947.

Levinas, Emmanuel. "Useless Suffering." In *Entre Nous: Thinking of the Other*, translated by Michael Smith and Barbara Harshav. New York: Columbia University Press, 1998.

Lleras, Cristina, Sofia Gonzalez-Ayala, Botero-Mejía, and Claudia Marcela Velandia. "Curatorship for Meaning Making: Contributions Towards Symbolic Reparation at the Museum of Memory of Colombia." *Museum Management and Curatorship* 34, no. 6 (2019): 544–61.

Longoni, Ana. "Fotos reaparecidas." In *Reapariciones: La fotografía en deuda con su pasado*, edited by Carles Guerra, 84–119. Madrid: Fundación Mapfre, 2022.

Longoni, Ana. "Photographs and Silhouettes: Visual Politics in the Human Rights Movement of Argentina." *Afterall* 25 (Autumn 2010): 5–17.

Longoni, Ana. *Traiciones: La figura del traidor en los relatos acerca de los sobrevivientes de la represión.* Buenos Aires: Norma Editorial, 2007.

Löwy, Michael. *Fire Alarm: Reading Walter Benjamin's "On the Concept of History."* Translated by Chris Turner. London: Verso, 2016.

Luxemburg, Rosa. "Order Prevails in Berlin." January 14, 1919. Rosa Luxemburg Internet Archive. https://www.marxists.org/archive/luxemburg/1919/01/14.htm.

Lyotard, Jean-Francois. *Heidegger and "the Jews."* Translated by Andreas Michel and Mark S. Robert. Minneapolis: University of Minnesota Press, 1990. Originally published in French in 1988.

Marks, Laura U. *Touch: Sensuous Theory and Multisensory Media.* Minneapolis: University of Minnesota Press, 2002.

Martin-Jones, David. "Archival Landscapes and a Non-Anthropocentric Universal Memory." *Third Text* 27, no. 6 (2013): 707–22.

Marstine, Janet. "The Contingent Nature of the New Museum Ethics." In *The Routledge Companion to Museum Ethics: Redefining Ethics for the Twenty-First-Century Museum*, edited by Janet Marstine, 3–25. Abingdon, UK: Routledge, 2011.

Memoria Abierta. *Y nadie quería saber* [And nobody wanted to know]. Accessed September 29, 2025. http://www.memoriaabierta.org.ar/wp/en/and-nobody-wanted -to-know/.

Mihai, Mihaela. *Political Memory and the Aesthetics of Care: The Art of Complicity and Resistance.* Stanford, CA: Stanford University Press, 2022.

Mitchell, W. J. T. "What Do Pictures Really Want?" *October* 77 (Summer 1996): 71–82.

Motamedi-Fraser, Mariam. "Once Upon a Problem." *Sociological Review* 60, no. S1 (2012): 84–107.

Moten, Fred. *In the Break: The Aesthetics of the Black Radical Tradition.* Minneapolis: University of Minnesota Press, 2003.

Müller-Doohm, Stefan. *Adorno: An Intellectual Biography.* Translated by Rodney Livingstone. Cambridge: Polity, 2008.

Naas, Michael. *The End of the World and Other Teachable Moments: Jacques Derrida's Final Seminar.* New York: Fordham University Press, 2015.

Nancy, Jean-Luc. *The Evidence of Film/L'Évidence de film: Abbas Kiarostami*. Brussels: Yves Gevaert, 2001.

Nancy, Jean-Luc. *The Fall of Sleep*. Translated by Charlotte Mandell. New York: Fordham University Press, 2009.

Nancy, Jean-Luc. *The Ground of the Image*. Translated by Jeff Fort. New York: Fordham University Press, 2005.

Nino, Carlos S. *Radical Evil on Trial*. New Haven, CT: Yale University Press, 1996.

Osiel, Mark. *Mass Atrocity, Collective Memory, and the Law*. New Brunswick, NJ: Transaction, 1997.

Payne, Leigh. *Unsettling Accounts: Neither Truth nor Reconciliation in Confessions of State Violence*. Durham, NC: Duke University Press, 2008.

Pécaut, Daniel. "Considerations of Space, Time and Subjectivity in a Context of Terror: The Colombian Example." *International Journal of Politics, Culture and Society* 14, no. 1 (2000): 129–50.

Pécaut, Daniel. *La experiencia de la violencia: Los desafíos del relato y la memoria*. Medellín: La Carreta Editores E.E., 2013.

Perelman, Pablo, dir. *A La Sombra del Sol*. 1974.

Perrin, Colin. "Breath from Nowhere: The Silent 'Foundation' of Human Rights." *Social and Legal Studies* 13, no. 1 (2004): 133–51.

Phu, Thy, Andrea Noble, and Erina Duganne, eds. *Cold War Camera*. Durham, NC: Duke University Press, 2023.

Pollock, Griselda. *After-Affects/After-Images: Trauma and Aesthetic Transformation in the Virtual Feminist Museum*. Manchester: Manchester University Press, 2013.

Potter, Sally. "Afterword." In *A Jar of Wild Flowers: Essays in Celebration of John Berger*, edited by Yasmin Gunaratnam with Amarjit Chandan. London: Zed, 2016.

Ramírez, Mari Carmen, with Marcelo E. Pacheco and Andrea Giunta. *Cantos paralelos: La parodia plástica en el arte argentino contemporáneo/Visual Parody in Contemporary Argentinean Art*. Austin: University of Texas Press, 1999.

Rancière, Jacques. *The Emancipated Spectator*. Translated by Gregory Elliott. London: Verso, 2009. First published in French 2008.

Rancière, Jacques, with Nikos Papastergiadis and Charles Esche. "Assemblies in Art and Politics: An Interview with Jacques Rancière." *Theory, Culture and Society* 31, no. 7–8 (2014): 27–41.

Rangelov, Iavor, and Ruti Teitel. "The Justice Archive: Transitional Justice and Digital Memory." *London Review of International Law* 11, no. 1 (2023): 83–109.

Rappaport, Joanne. *Cowards Don't Make History: Orlando Fals Borda and the Origins of Participatory Action Research*. Durham, NC: Duke University Press, 2020.

Richard, Nelly. *Fracturas de la memoria: Arte y pensamiento crítico*. Buenos Aires: Siglo XXI.

Robben, Antonius. *Argentina Betrayed: Memory, Mourning, and Accountability*. Philadelphia: University of Pennsylvania Press, 2018.

Rokem, Freddie. "'Suddenly, a Stranger Appears': Walter Benjamin's Readings of Bertolt Brecht's Epic Theatre." *Nordic Theatre Studies* 31, no. 1 (2019): 8–21.

Rosenblatt, Adam. *Digging for the Disappeared: Forensic Science After Atrocity*. Stanford, CA: Stanford University Press, 2015.

Rothberg, Michael. *The Implicated Subject: Beyond Victims and Perpetrators*. Stanford, CA: Stanford University Press, 2019.

Rothberg, Michael. *Multi-Directional Memory: Remembering the Holocaust in the Age of Decolonization*. Stanford, CA: Stanford University Press, 2009.

Ruiz, Lucía Sepúlveda. *119 de nosotros*. Santiago: LOM ediciones, 2005.

Ruiz, Marcela, and Oriana Bernasconi. "Reports on Categorization and Classification of Human Rights Violations in Chile (1974–1978)." *Discourse and Society* 30, no. 1 (2019): 44–63.

Russell, Lynette. "Affect in the Archive: Trauma, Grief, Delight and Texts." *Archives and Manuscripts* 46 (2018): 200–207.

Saadawi, Ahmed. *Frankenstein in Baghdad*. Translated by Jonathan Wright. London: Penguin, 2018.

Salvi, Valentina. "'We're All Victims Now': Changes in the Narrative of 'National Reconciliation' in Argentina." *Latin American Perspectives* 42, no. 3, Issue 202 (2015): 39–51.

Santner, Eric. *On Creaturely Life: Rilke, Benjamin, Sebald*. Chicago: University of Chicago Press, 2006.

Santner, Eric. *The Royal Remains: The People's Two Bodies and the Endgames of Sovereignty*. Chicago: University of Chicago Press, 2011.

Schapp, Andrew. "Guilty Subjects and Political Responsibility: Arendt, Jaspers and the Resonance of the 'German Question' in Politics of Reconciliation." *Political Studies* 49 (2001): 749–66.

Schuppli, Susan. *Material Witness: Media, Forensics, Evidence*. Cambridge, MA: MIT Press, 2020.

Sharpe, Christina. *In the Wake: On Blackness and Being*. Durham, NC: Duke University Press, 2016.

Silva da Catela, Ludmila. "Photography and Disappearance in Argentina: Sacredness and Rituals in the Face of Death." In *Familiar Faces: Photography, Memory and Argentina's Disappeared*, edited by Piotr Cieplak. London: Goldsmiths University Press, 2024.

Silverman, Kaja. *Flesh of My Flesh*. Stanford, CA: Stanford University Press, 2009.

Silverman, Kaja. *Threshold of the Visible World*. London: Routledge, 1996.

Simon, Roger I. "Afterword: The Turn to Pedagogy: A Needed Conversation on the Practice of Curating Difficult Knowledge." In *Curating Difficult Knowledge: Violent Pasts in Public Places*, edited by Erica Lehrer, Cynthia E. Milton, and Monica Eileen Patterson. Basingstoke, UK: Palgrave Macmillan, 2011.

Simon, Roger I. "A Shock to Thought: Curatorial Judgment and the Public Exhibition of 'Difficult Knowledge.'" *Memory Studies* 4, no. 4 (2011): 432–49.

Simon, Roger I. *The Touch of the Past: Remembrance, Learning, and Ethics*. New York: Palgrave Macmillan, 2005.

Somogliana, Marco. "El Trabajo del EAAF: Datos concretos frente a la incerteza de la desaparición." *Clepsidra: Revista Interdisciplinaria de Estudios sobre Memoria* 1 (March 2014): 192–207.

Sosa, Cecilia. "On Crying Perpetrators and Subversive Laughter: Trans-Affiliative Encounters Inside ESMA Memory Museum." In *Staging Difficult Pasts: Transnational*

Memory, Theatres, and Museums, edited by Maria Delgado, Michal Kobialka, and Bryce Lease. London: Routledge, 2024.

Stengers, Isabelle. "The Challenge of Ontological Politics." In *A World of Many Worlds*, edited by Marisol de la Cadena and Mario Blaser. Durham, NC: Duke University Press, 2018.

Stengers, Isabelle. "The Cosmopolitical Proposal." In *Making Things Public: Atmospheres of Democracy*, edited by Bruno Latour and Peter Weibel. Boston: MIT Press, 2004.

Stengers, Isabelle. "Introductory Notes on an Ecology of Practices." *Cultural Studies Review* 11, no. 5 (2005): 183–96.

Stengers, Isabelle. *The Invention of Modern Science*. Minneapolis: University of Minnesota Press, 2000.

Stengers, Isabelle. "Speculative Philosophy and the Art of Dramatization." In *The Allure of Things: Process and Object in Contemporary Philosophy*, edited by Roland Faber and Andrew Goffey. London: Bloomsbury, 2014.

Stengers, Isabelle. "William James: An Ethics of Thought?" *Radical Philosophy* 157 (2009): 9–19.

Stern, Steve. "The Artist's Truth: The Post-Auschwitz Predicament After Latin America's Age of Dirty Wars." In *Art from a Fractured Past: Memory in Post–Shining Path Peru*, edited by Cynthia Milton. Durham, NC: Duke University Press, 2013.

Stoler, Ann Laura. *Along the Archival Grain: Epistemic Anxieties and Colonial Common Sense*. Princeton, NJ: Princeton University Press, 2010.

Stoler, Ann Laura. "On Archiving as Dissensus." *Comparative Studies of South Asia, Africa and the Middle East* 38, no. 1 (2018): 43–56.

Stone, Nathan. "The Battle of Chile." *Not Even Past*, 2017. https://notevenpast.org/the-battle-of-chile/.

Taylor, Diana. *The Archive and the Repertoire: Performing Cultural Memory in the Americas*. Durham, NC: Duke University Press, 2003.

Taylor, Diana. *Disappearing Acts: Spectacles of Gender and Nationalism in Argentina's "Dirty War."* Durham, NC: Duke University Press, 1997.

Taylor, Diana. *¡Presente! The Politics of Presence*. Durham, NC: Duke University Press, 2020.

Taylor, Diana. "Staging Social Memory: Yuyachkani." In *The Color of Theater: Race, Culture and Contemporary Performance*, edited by Roberta Uno and Lucy Mae San Pablo Burns. New York: Continuum, 2002.

Teichert, Erika. "Reciclaje: Materializaciones de militancia en la ExESMA." *Teatro XXI* 36 (2020): 75–90.

Thomas, Nicholas. "The Museum as Method." *Museum Anthropology* 33, no. 1 (2010): 6–10.

Uribe, María Victoria. "Dismembering and Expelling Semantics of Political Terror in Colombia." *Political Culture* 16, no. 1 (2004): 79–95.

Uribe, María Victoria. "Violence as a Symptom: The Case of Colombia." *Violence: An International Journal* 1, no. 1 (2020): 8–20.

Verbitsky, Horacio. *The Flight: Confessions of an Argentine Dirty Warrior*. Translated by Esther Allen. New York: New Press, 1996.

Viebach, Julia. "Transitional Archives: Towards a Conceptualisation of Archives in Transitional Justice." *International Journal of Human Rights* 25, no. 3 (2021): 403–39.

Viebach, Julia, Dagmar Hovestädt, and Ulrike Lühe. "Beyond Evidence: The Use of Archives in Transitional Justice." *International Journal of Human Rights* 25, no. 3 (2021): 381–402.

Weizman, Eyal. "Osteobiography: An Interview with Clyde Snow." *Cabinet* 43 (2011): 68–74.

Weld, Kirsten. *Paper Cadavers: The Archives of Dictatorship in Guatemala*. Durham, NC: Duke University Press, 2014.

Williams, Paul. "Memorial Museums and the Objectification of Suffering." In *The Routledge Companion to Museum Ethics: Redefining Ethics for the Twenty-First-Century Museum,* edited by Janet Marstine, 220–36. Abingdon, UK: Routledge, 2011.

Wilson, Richard. *Writing History in International Criminal Trials*. Cambridge: Cambridge University Press, 2011.

Index